Economic Cooperation and Regional Integration in Africa

Economic Cooperation and Regional Integration in Africa

First Experiences and Prospects

Edited by
Naceur Bourenane, Serah W. Mwanycky, Iba Kone
and Ne Ngangu Massamba

Proceedings of the Symposium on
Economic Cooperation and Regional Integration in Africa.
Organized by the African Academy of Sciences
in Algiers, Algeria 3–6 June 1992

Citation: Economic Cooperation and Regional Integration in Africa.
Ed. Naceur Bourenane *et al*. Proceedings of the Symposium on Economic
Cooperation and Regional Integration, Algiers, Algeria, 1992.

ISBN: 9966-831-31-2

Published by Academy Science Publishers
African Academy of Sciences, P.O. Box 14798, Nairobi, Kenya
Telephone 254-02-884620/884401-5; Fax 254-02-884406; E-mail aas@arcc.permanet.org
Miotoni Lane, Karen, off Miotoni Road, off Ngong Road

Table of Contents

Annexes

Glossary of Key Terms and Abbreviations

AAF-SAP	African Alternative Framework to Structural Adjustment Programs for Socio-economic Recovery and Transformation
AAS	African Academy of Sciences
ABCA	L'Association des Banques Centrales Africaines
ACBI	African Capacity Building Initiative
ACP	Africa, the Caribbean and the Pacific
ADB	African Development Bank
AEA	African Environmental Agenda
AEC	African Economic Community
APD	L'Aide publique au développement
ASEAN	Association of Southeast Asian Nations
BCEAC	Banque Centrale des Etats de l'Afrique Centrale
BEAC	Banque des Etats de l'Afrique Centrale
BENELUX	Belgium, the Netherlands and Luxembourg
BLS	Botswana, Lesotho and Swaziland
CACM	Central American Common Market
CAEM	Le Centre Africain d'Etudes Monétaires
CAP	Common Agricultural Policy
CARICOM	Caribbean Common Market
CCA	Conseil de Coopération Arabe
CCAO	Chambre de Compensation de l'Afrique de l'Ouest
CCG	Le Conseil de Coopération du Golfe
CCM	Conseil Consultatif Maghrébin
CEA	Commission Economique des Nations Unies pour l'Afrique
CEAO	Communauté Economique de l'Afrique de l'Ouest
CEE	Communauté Economique Européene
CEPGL	Economic Community of the Countries of the Great Lakes
CILSS	Comité Inter-Etats de Lutte contre la Sécheresse au Sahel
CIM	Coordination and implementation committee
CMA	Common Monetary Area of Southern Africa
CMEA	Council for Mutual Economic Assistance
CONSAS	Constellation of Southern African States
CP	Le Conseil Présidentiel
DICT	Division International Capitaliste du Travail

DIT	Division Internationale du Travail
EAC	East African Community
EADB	East African Development Bank
EAEC	European Atomic Energy Community
EC	European Community
ECCAS	Economic Community of Central African States
ECOWAS	Economic Community of West African States
ECSC	European Coal and Steel Community
ECU	European Currency Unit
EEA	European Economic Area
EEC	European Economic Community
EEMU	European Economic and Monetary Union
EFTA	European Free Trade Association
EIADC	Economic Integration Among Developing Countries
EMS	European Monetary System
EMU	European Monetary Union
EPU	European Payments Union
ERU	Exchange rate union
FTA	Free Trade Area
GATS	General Agreement Trade in Services
GATT	General Agreement on Tariffs and Trade
GCA	Global Coalition for Africa
GSP	Generalized scheme of preferences
IFD	Institutions Financières de Développement
IGOs	Intergovernmental organizations
LAFTA	Latin American Free Trade Association
LPA	Lagos Plan of Action
MC	Le Marché Commun
MRU	Mano River Union
MTO	Multilateral Trade Organization
NIE	Newly Industrializing Economies
NPI	Nouveaux pays industrialisés
OAU	Organization of African Unity
OECD	Organization for Economic Cooperation and Development
OECS	Organization of the Small Eastern Caribbean States
OEEC	Organization for European Economic Cooperation
OUA	Organisation de l'Unité Africaine
PAC	Politique Agricole Commune
PAS	Programmes d'ajustement structurel

PMI	Petites et moyennes entreprises
PSC	Permanent Steering Committee
PTA	Preferential Trade Area for Eastern and Southern African States
RECs	Regional economic communities
SACU	Southern African Customs Union
SADCC	Southern African Development Coordination Conference
SAPEM	Southern Africa Political and Economic Monthly
SAPES	Southern African Political Economy Series
SAPs	Structural Adjustment Programmes
TDC	Tarif Douanier Commun
TNC	Trade Negotiating Committee
TRIMs	Trade-related investment measures
TRIPs	Trade-related aspects of intellectual property
TTEC	Tarif Extérieur Commun
UD	Union Douanière
UMA	L'Union du Maghreb Arabe
UMOA	L'Union Monétaire Ouest Africaine en Afrique de l'Ouest
UNDEAC	L'Union Douanière et Economique de l'Afrique Centrale
UNTACDA	UN Transport and Communications Decade for A´ica
VERs	Voluntary export restraints
WACH	West African Clearing House
WAMU	West African Monetary Union
ZIPA	Zimbabwe People's Army
ZLE	Zone de Libre Echange
ZPF	Zimbabwe Patriotic Front

Introduction

Naceur Bourenane

Le thème de l'intégration économique est l'un de ceux qui aura retenu le plus l'attention ces dernières années, tant au niveau international qu'à l'échelon du continent africain.

Au plan international, cet intérêt pour l'intégration reflète une série de processus technologiques et scientifiques, économiques, socio-politiques et culturels. Ces derniers induisent une désintégration des espaces géo-économiques traditionnels et l'apparition d'une triade aux éléments fortement solidaires, bien que conflictuels. Elle se compose des USA, du Japon et de l'Union Européenne. Par conséquent les intérêts des pays du tiers monde investent dans les stratégies des grandes puissances de la guerre froide s'en trouvent durablement affectés. On observe un déplacement des centres d'intérêt, des régions jusque-là considérées comme sensibles.

Ces processus entraînent une redéfinition des rapports économiques et politiques internationaux, notamment des règles du commerce international. Au système traditionnel, des barrières douanières et tarifaires se substituent progressivement un autre fondé sur la mise en place de normes de qualité et de nouveaux standards pour les biens et services échangés. Ils induisent également une révision des accords servant de cadre à la coopération multilatérale, voire bilatérale avec les pays en développement, notamment africains. Pour ces derniers, tant la Convention de Lomé que les protocoles d'accord liant l'Europe Communautaire aux pays tiers méditerranéens ne pourront qu'être continuellement revus, dans une direction moins favorable. Une réduction drastique des systèmes de subvention et d'assistance dont ont pu bénéficier par le passé ces pays est inévitable. En même temps elle sera de moins en moins multilatérale et de plus en plus bilatérale. Même l'assistance qui arrivera par le canal multilatéral sera davantage liée au pays dont elle émane. Cette tendance déjà observable sera d'autant plus forte qu'il y a de moins en moins de justification économique (avec la montée de nouveaux producteurs beaucoup plus compétitifs que les pays africains pour certains produits traditionnels) et géo-stratégique au maintien des flux d'aide. Bilatérale ou multilatérale, l'aide tend à être "**sécuritaire**". Sa finalité première est de fixer les populations dans leurs pays d'origine et d'éviter des migrations susceptibles de remettre en cause les équilibres d'ensemble.

1

De fait, l'intérêt économique, ainsi que la proximité géographique et culturelle des anciens pays d'Europe de l'Est et des pays européens de l'ex-URSS pour les pays de l'Union Européenne, ceux d'Amérique Latine et du Sud pour les USA, de l'Extrême Orient et du Pacifique pour les USA et le Japon ne peuvent que militer en faveur d'une aggravation de la tendance à la marginalisation internationale des pays africains. Il peut exister toutefois quelques exceptions liées à la proximité géographique, à la présence d'une forte population de souche européenne, au niveau des investissements déjà réalisés par l'Etat ou opérés par les multinationales, à la nature de leurs ressources naturelles ou à la dimension du marché et du niveau de revenu national. C'est le cas pour l'Egypte, pour l'Afrique du Sud et pour les pays du Maghreb (Algérie, Maroc et Tunisie).

Une telle évolution viendra accroître les tensions internes des pays africains. Elle pourra pousser de nombreux Etats à un isolationnisme forcené vis-à-vis de leurs voisins immédiats, en cherchant à leur faire endosser la responsabilité de l'instabilité interne et en les considérant comme une source permanente de tensions supplémentaires, voire à l'origine de la situation difficile à laquelle ils font face.

Si elle se confirmait, cette évolution serait désastreuse pour les pays et les populations du continent africain. Elle intervient en effet dans le seul continent à avoir enregistré une régression significative de son pouvoir d'achat pendant les trente dernières années. En Afrique plus que dans le reste du tiers-monde, l'instabilité socio-politique est croissante. Elle est l'expression d'un mouvement revendicatif multiforme et non structuré, par intermittence, violent dans ses manifestations. Ni les appareils répressifs au service des Etats, ni les partis politiques d'opposition, ni les structures d'autorité traditionnelle n'arrivent à le contenir ou à le prévenir.

Cette évolution a également des conséquences négatives sur l'équilibre international dans son ensemble. L'instabilité structurelle au niveau du continent impliquera inévitablement des mouvements de population en direction d'autres régions du monde. Elle est également synonyme de pertes de marchés, certes au poids limité, mais, malgré tout, fort utiles pour la stabilité sociale de certains des pays européens, tels que la France, la Grande Bretagne et l'Italie. Dans ce cas, la seule façon de contenir les effets négatifs ci-dessus mentionnés est une intervention militaire externe, au titre du maintien de la paix. Cependant elle ne peut être envisagée durablement, que si les pertes humaines qui l'accompagnent concernent des Africains. Dans ce cas de figure, ces pays devront aider à lever les armées et à assurer, de façon durable, leur entretien.

Du coup, la question de la stabilité économique et politique et de la prise en charge des effets de la croissance démographique deviennent importantes, pas seulement pour les pays du continent, mais également pour leurs partenaires traditionnels. Dans l'intérêt même des pays développés, la relance de la croissance et la stabilité politique du continent s'avéreront rapidement moins coûteuses et plus bénéfiques que la politique sécuritaire et de "containement".

Outre une plus grande démocratisation et une transparence de la gestion des affaires publiques, la stabilité économique et politique des pays du continent implique une relance durable de la croissance. Celle-ci ne peut se faire dans le cadre étroit des économies nationales, par trop segmentées. Elle suppose la promotion de la coopération et l'intégration entre les secteurs d'activité économique des pays voisins, voire des pays n'ayant pas de frontières en commun.

Ce processus d'unification d'espaces nationaux contigüs est déjà en oeuvre. Il est en partie la résultante d'une volonté d'agents économiques locaux, d'assurer leur propre survie et leur enrichissement. Ces derniers sont aujourdhui suffisament nombreux et puissants pour maintenir la tendance à l'intégration. La solidité et le dynamisme des circuits parallèles de circulation des marchandises entre les pays en témoignent. Pour le moment, ces agents tirent leurs profits des avantages comparatifs induits par le système de parité monétaire ou par les lourdeurs bureaucratiques des administrations des douanes. Les programmes d'ajustement structurel, à travers les règles de gestion et d'administration qu'ils ont introduites contribuent également à ces processus. En unifiant les modes de gestion des économies et en imposant à tous la libéralisation des échanges extérieurs, on facilite la réunion des conditions d'intégration et la levée des obstacles réglementaires à sa réalisation. Ces programmes ont également contribué à renforcer le pouvoir économique de certains acteurs sociaux ayant acquis une assise et une vocation supra-nationale. En même temps, ils ont agi dans le sens de l'homogénéisation des modèles de consommation de larges catégories sociales affectées négativement, telles que certaines couches urbaines. **Les besoins des partenaires extérieurs au continent de simplifier les procédures d'import et d'export entre des pays voisins, afin de réduire leurs coûts est un autre élément à prendre en fin de compte.**

En fait, l'intégration est déjà en marche. Elle se fera avec ou sans le consentement des dirigeants politiques et des Etats. La première question est de savoir selon quelles modalités, à quels coûts, au profit et au détriment de quelles catégories d'agents économiques, et dans quel horizon temporel. La seconde question porte sur l'identification des modalités les plus efficaces, en termes de coûts-avantages pour les pays et les populations.

Les Etats africains semblent avoir pris ces dernières années la mesure des enjeux pour l'avenir de leurs pays et pour leur propre survie. En 1990, les chefs d'Etats réunis à

Abuja (Nigéria) ont adopté un Traité qui définit et oriente les processus d'intégration économique des pays du continent en 34 années, sur une base progressive, allant du renforcement et de l'homogénéisation des principes régissant les communautés économiques régionales existantes, jusqu'à la constitution d'une entité panafricaine. S'inscrivant dans cette perspective, les principales institutions existant au niveau panafricain, la BAD, la CEA et l'OUA ont décidé de la mise en place d'un Secrétariat conjoint, en vue de participer activement à cet effort et de mobiliser un maximum de ressources à cet effet. Trois ans après son adoption le nombre de pays ayant ratifié le Traité a conféré à ce dernier un caractère obligatoire pour l'ensemble des membres de l'OUA.

Cependant, malgré cet engagement apparent, les Etats, tout comme le Secrétariat conjoint font montre d'un faible empressement à assurer la mise en oeuvre du Traité d'Abuja et des traités ayant institué les communautés régionales.

Une telle attitude a pu être interprétée ici et là comme l'expression de la faible volonté politique des dirigeants africains à coopérer. Cette explication des écarts entre les engagements politiques et leur concrétisation sur le terrain nous paraît quelque peu hâtive. Il y aurait plutôt lieu d'y voir l'expression d'une difficulté à passer aux actes, du fait de l'ampleur des contraintes et des obstacles qui hypothèquent durablement tout processus de construction communautaire en Afrique, de la faiblesse des moyens dont disposent les Etats et du fait de l'absence de perspective claire sur le moyen et le long terme, voire sur le court terme dans bon nombre de pays. Il n'y a donc pas lieu d'interpréter systématiquement ces écarts, comme la preuve irréfutable d'une **mauvaise volonté politique des responsables d'Etats**. Les discours volontaristes peuvent aussi se lire comme une réponse concertée, mais irréaliste à des difficultés nées en partie de l'évolution de la situation internationale et de ses répercussions internes, et sur lesquelles les Etats n'ont qu'une faible prise. N'ayant pas de prise directe sur les processus en cours pris individuellement, les responsables pensent pouvoir en avoir collectivement; d'où les résolutions et les déclarations faites à l'adresse des partenaires de l'Afrique à chaque sommet régional ou continental. Si on admet une telle explication, l'adoption du Traité, tout comme les discours périodiques des chefs d'Etats exprimant leur souci de poursuivre le processus de renforcement des communautés économiques régionales existantes peuvent être analysés comme une volonté de prise en charge collective de problèmes communs, imputés à des facteurs externes.

Mais au delà des déclarations et des pétitions de principe des responsables africains, les projets d'intégration régionale, particulièrement la création d'une communauté économique africaine, paraîssent illusoires face aux quatres contraintes majeures auxquelles font face les pays du continent, à savoir la tendance structurelle à la baisse de leur pouvoir d'achat, l'instabilité socio-politique croissante, le caractère non structuré d'un mouvement social revendicatif, multiforme et volatile (que n'arrivent plus à contenir, ni à canaliser les appareils d'Etat, eux-mêmes directement affectés par ce type d'évolution), la "bazarisation" des économies nationales dont des pans entiers sombrent dans l'informel non productif et spéculatif.[1]

Ainsi se trouve-t-on face à un paradoxe, l'urgence de la démarche communautaire pour sortir de la crise et l'impossibilité d'une telle démarche à cause des effets de cette crise.

Du fait du caractère multiforme, irréductible et handicapant de la crise actuelle, le débat sur les modalités et le contenu de l'intégration apparaît important. De par les solutions qu'il permettra de mettre au point, ce débat contribuera à identifier les sentiers les plus sûrs d'une reprise durable de la croissance et partant, à retrouver une certaine stabilité politique aujourdhui largement entamée. Ce débat pourrait s'articuler autour des questionnements suivants:

(1)   Quelles relations existe-t-il entre construction communautaire, développement national et environnement économique international?

(2)   A quels types de problèmes se heurte la mise en place des communautés économiques régionales?

(3)   Quelles stratégies industrielles adopter dans un cadre régional?

(4)   Comment faire de la coopération monétaire un instrument au service de l'intégration régionale?

(5)   Quels sont les pré-requis à une coopération régionale dynamique et irréversible?

(6)   Quels sont les enseignements que l'on peut tirer des expériences d'autres régions telle que l'Europe?

(7)   Quelles sont les conditions générales de réussite d'un programme réaliste d'intégration?

Les contributions contenues dans le présent ouvrage et qui ont été préparées à l'occasion du symposium panafricain organisé à Alger en Juin 1992, à l'initiative de l'Académie Africaine des Sciences (AAS), avec l'appui du Ministère Algérien de l'Enseignement Supérieur participent de ce débat et de la volonté d'identifier les conditions optimales à une bonne conduite des processus d'intégration. Bien qu'écrites avant que des bouleversements importants n'interviennent sur la scène africaine et internationale, notamment la disparition constitutionnelle du régime de l'apartheid, les présentations faites lors de la réunion d'Alger conservent toute leur pertinence. Leurs auteurs se sont attachés à l'analyse des contraintes structurelles et de leurs effets sur les pays africains. Ils ont également avancé des propositions concrètes. Celles-ci conservent toute leur pertinence. Elles sont susceptibles de contribuer à mieux cadrer les actions à mener.

Structuration de l'ouvrage

Les articles que contient cet ouvrage s'articulent autour de trois axes essentiels: la construction communautaire, son intérêt, ses contraintes et ses conditions; le rôle de la monnaie et des politiques financières dans l'intégration économique; et les stratégies industrielles de construction communautaire.

Le choix des questions abordées dans cet ouvrage répond au souci des auteurs d'offrir au lecteur et surtout aux décideurs africains des éléments de réponse à certaines de leurs interrogations. On y passe notamment en revue l'approche traditionnelle de l'intégration, ses fondements et ses limites, l'expérience de l'Union Européenne, les perspectives d'une construction communautaire dans un système économique et politique régional non démocratique. L'ouvrage s'intéresse également aux chances de réussite de la construction communautaire dans certaines régions du continent. Il tente de définir le type de politiques monétaires et le type de coopération industrielle susceptibles de faciliter l'intégration.

Van Brabant entreprend une analyse des fondements de l'approche traditionnelle de l'intégration. Il voit dans la construction européenne un modèle d'intégration au service des pays en développement en général et de l'Afrique en particulier. Il montre en effet que la réussite de l'expérience communautaire européenne se fonde sur plusieurs conditions: l'existence préalable d'un niveau d'échanges élevé entre les pays concernés, des écarts de niveau de revenu per capita et de niveau de développement industriel faibles (ce qui rend possible une certaine spécialisation industrielle), un consensus politique acquis à la faveur de la seconde guerre mondiale et du Plan Marshall, une volonté et une capacité financière à mettre en place un système de compensation telle que la Politique Agricole Commune. Sur la base de son analyse, l'auteur tire plusieurs conclusions importantes, notamment la nécessité pour les pays de disposer d'une stratégie de développement cohérente et de dépasser l'évaluation strictement économique de l'intégration et des pertes qu'elle peut générer sur le court terme. Il introduit à cette occasion un concept important, celui de la sécurité économique collective, comme pierre angulaire de toute problématique de l'intégration. Il énonce trois principes: le nécessaire renoncement, au moins partiel à la souveraineté économique; l'abandon des démarches mimétiques à l'égard de modèles du type de celui de l'Union Européenne; et un pragmatisme dans le choix des mesures à mettre en oeuvre. Dans ce cadre, il rappelle que l'union douanière peut être source de surcoûts au regard des possibilités offertes par ailleurs et que des économies de structures similaires tirent des avantages de leur union, par la compétition qu'elle induit entre les partenaires. Il souligne enfin qu'il est illusoire de penser promouvoir les échanges et intensifier l'action entre les espaces et les agents économiques sans avoir réglé le problème des transferts monétaires entre les pays.

Van Hoek, dans sa contribution, tire les leçons de l'expérience de la coopération régionale et de l'intégration européenne. Après en avoir examiné les fondements historiques, les étapes, les conditions de réussite et les effets induits par le Marché Unique, l'auteur montre que certains principes et certains enseignements peuvent en être tirés, notamment la nécessité d'une action prudente, fondée sur ce qu'il est possible de faire et non pas sur ce qu'il est souhaitable de réaliser. Une autre leçon concerne l'adéquation des institutions et des organismes régionaux aux objectifs recherchés et leur dotation de pouvoirs réels. Le troisième principe autour duquel devrait s'articuler l'intégration est l'association constante des acteurs économiques, syndicats, patronat, etc. dans les activités de la Communauté. Dans le cas européen, outre l'existence d'un conseil économique et social européen, la Communauté rend compte, de façon périodique, au Parlement Européen.

A partir d'une analyse de l'expérience historique du Burkina Faso, B. Guissou montre combien la construction économique nationale demeure illusoire dans le contexte présent et pourquoi on ne peut envisager de reproduire l'expérience des pays d'Asie du Sud-Est en Afrique. Il rappelle à cette occasion que la création d'ensembles économiques coloniaux poursuivait un objectif unique, la mise en place, par la contrainte de zones de mise en valeur. Si celles-ci n'ont pas survécu au lendemain des indépendances, c'est parce qu'elles ont été constituées d'entités sociologiquement et culturellement non viables. L'auteur conclut sur le fait que seule la promotion de la coopération économique en vue de l'intégration est susceptible de permettre aux pays de retrouver les sentiers de la croissance. Mais celà devra se faire en conformité avec les points de vue des Institutions de Bretton Woods, sans l'accord desquels l'accès aux ressources financières internationales est quasi-impossible.

I. Mandaza aborde la question de la construction communautaire en Afrique Australe et en Afrique du Sud. Il se fonde, pour ce faire, sur un rappel des conditions historiques régionales. Son analyse (du reste menée avant même l'abolition officielle du régime d'apartheid) montre que la construction communautaire au profit des Etats de la région restera illusoire tant que le système sud-africain demeure en place, c'est-à-dire tant que le fonctionnement satellitaire des Etats de la région par rapport à l'Afrique du Sud n'est pas profondément modifié, et tant que la question de la démocratisation économique n'est pas réglée dans ce pays.

Cette analyse amène à se demander si on peut envisager une intégration économique ayant pour objectif un accroissement des richesses et leur meilleure répartition sociale, tant que les fondements des systèmes coloniaux demeurent en place, tel que c'est le cas dans un grand nombre de pays africains, tout particulièrement en Afrique Australe. Le recouvrement de l'indépendance politique et la substitution d'un pouvoir indigène à celui qui lui pré-existait suffisent-ils à assurer le succès des expériences d'intégration. Ceci amène une autre question. Comment construire une communauté trans-nationale articulée autour de l'échange équilibré entre les régions et les pays et de la participation active de tous les partenaires, à partir de systèmes quasi-partimoniaux, fondés sur l'exclusive, l'ostracisme et l'exclusion?

M. Benallègue et J. Senghor rappellent dans leur introduction respective les expériences des pays du Maghreb et d'Afrique de l'Ouest et les caractéristiques de la dynamique de construction communautaire.

Benallègue souligne la confusion constante qui s'établit dans la démarche maghrébine entre la coopération multilatérale et la construction communautaire. Il appelle une approche innovative et non mimétique. Celle-ci ne se limiterait pas au seul développement des échanges commerciaux. Elle chercherait à accroître le pouvoir de négociation des pays de l'UMA avec leurs partenaires. J. Senghor met en exergue le caractère restrictif du Traité instituant la CEDEAO, tant du point de vue des objectifs que de celui du type d'institutions et des prérogatives qui leur sont dévolues.

Ces deux contributions mettent en relief les limites de traités et d'accords ne tenant pas compte des contraintes objectives qui pèsent sur les pays.

P. Gakunu entreprend une analyse du contexte international et de l'impact de ses nouveaux développements sur les pays ACP en général et sur les pays africains en particulier, ceux directement concernés par le devenir de la Convention de Lomé. De fait, les mesures prises dans le cadre de l'Uruguay Round ont rendu caducs, plusieurs des dispositions favorables aux pays ACP, avant même la conclusion des négociations. D'où des pertes estimées à plus de 180 millions de dollars Etats-Unis dès 1988. Depuis, la situation ne s'est guère améliorée, particulièrement avec l'ouverture progressive de la Communauté Européenne en direction d'autres pays d'Asie et d'Amérique. Cette évolution a des conséquences directes sur la coopération entre les pays ACP et l'Union Européenne dans le cadre de la Convention de Lomé dont la révision a été rendue inévitable avant même son achèvement. Ces éléments imposent à leur tour, la coopération régionale entre pays africains. Elle constitue la voie la moins onéreuse dans la réduction des effets négatifs de l'évolution du contexte international.

Selon H.M. Onitiri, la création de la Communauté Economique Africaine, telle qu'elle est définie par le Traité d'Abuja constitue la réponse globale aux problèmes du continent. Viendrait s'y insérer les diverses actions et programmes sectoriels visant l'intégration. Leur mise en oeuvre suppose en effet la création d'un environnement politique, socio-économique et scientifique favorable. Le Traité d'Abuja devrait permettre d'y contribuer de façon essentielle, notamment parce qu'il induit une réduction des tensions et une gestion collective et participative des conflits. Mais, comme le souligne l'auteur, le passage du cadre légal du Traité à un ensemble de programmes et de projets collectifs précis suppose réglées certaines questions essentielles, tels que le financement des opérations multinationales, la répartition des gains générés par ces opérations, la libéralisation des économies africaines. Autant de problèmes qui confèrent aux Etats un rôle essentiel dans l'intégration.

Pour S. Tomori l'intégration monétaire est essentielle dans la construction communautaire. Elle se fonde sur deux éléments, le taux de change et la convertibilité. Selon l'auteur, l'intégration monétaire implique celle des marchés du travail et des capitaux. Son avantage premier est d'assurer un accroissement des chances d'une allocation optimale des ressources, une réduction des besoins en devises et une plus grande stabilité des prix.

Le document de travail élaboré par le Centre Africain des Etudes Monétaires s'intéresse aux formes d'unions monétaires et aux schémas de leur construction. Il souligne le fait que les unions qui existent en Afrique ne correspondent pas à un stade avancé d'intégration économique, comme le veut la théorie des étapes de Balassa. En conséquence, il n'y a pas lieu de poser le primat de l'intégration économique sur l'intégration monétaire. Le document insiste également sur le fait que le premier intérêt de l'union monétaire est la réduction des risques de déséquilibres macro-économiques.

Situant ses réflexions dans le prolongement de ces conclusions, Mah'moud s'intéresse plus particulièrement aux expériences de la CEDEAO, de la ZEP et de la SADC. Il constate que les méthodes de coordination monétaire et des politiques fiscales ne sont pas clairement définies dans ces communautés. Sur la base de l'examen des différentes formules possibles, Mah'moud recommande la recherche d'une coordination progressive, gagnant en intensité, avec la mise en place d'un conseil permanent des banques centrales. Ce conseil se chargerait d'étudier et d'arrêter les mesures les plus appropriées dans ce domaine.

S. Mouhoubi entreprend l'analyse des systèmes de compensation et des unions monétaires, en mettant en relief l'existence de deux approches fondamentales, celle défendue par les tenants de l'union immédiate et celle qui voit dans l'union monétaire, le résultat de la convergence des politiques économiques et des performances des divers partenaires. Au terme de son analyse, l'auteur insiste sur le fait que l'inter-convertibilité à parité fixe est une condition essentielle dans la promotion des échanges et du fonctionnement des chambres de compensation. Sur cette base, l'auteur entreprend d'examiner les dispositions prévues par le Traité d'Abuja. Il conclue à l'inadéquation du calendrier de mise en oeuvre du traité au regard des problèmes à surmonter.

P. Bitoumbou invite à une analyse réaliste des contraintes et des limites à la construction d'une union monétaire. Se fondant sur l'expérience des deux zones monétaires opérationnelles en Afrique, celle du franc CFA et celle du Rand, l'auteur conclue au fait que ce type d'unions n'a guère d'incidence positive sur l'évolution du volume des échanges. Celà amène Bitoumbou à déplacer la question de la constitution des unions monétaires à celle du financement de l'intégration: l'intégration économique a un coût dont il faut assurer le financement. Sans Institutions de financement du développement multilatéral aux ressources renouvelables de façon quasi-automatique, il est difficile d'envisager la promotion de la coopération et de l'intégration régionale. Or le problème en Afrique est la faiblesse des taux nationaux d'épargne. Pour dépasser cette contrainte, l'une des solutions les plus appropriées est de faire jouer un rôle encore plus dynamique aux institutions régionales telle que la BAD et d'encourager la création et le développement d'institutions financières spécialisées dans la promotion des échanges de marchandises et de capitaux. La Banque Africaine d'Import-Export installée au Caire devrait répondre en partie à cette attente.

La question de l'industrie comme moteur et vecteur de l'intégration est abordée dans cet ouvrage sous deux angles, d'une part globale, d'autre part pour une filière particulière, le textile. A partir d'une analyse de la filière textile.

F. Benyoucef et N. Bourenane font ressortir les tendances lourdes de son évolution, les restructurations qui s'y mettent en place et les implications pour les pays en développement qui veulent maintenir ou améliorer leur part du marché. Ils relèvent notamment la nécessité d'investissements croissants et lourds pour faire face aux transformations technologiques et aux autres changements qui affectent le marché du textile et de l'habillement. Dans le cas des pays africains, la limitation des ressources rend une réflexion sur l'intégration de la filière à l'échelle sous-régionale voire régionale, fort utile. Celle-ci peut constituer une sorte d'alternative à l'internationalisation de la filière textile.

Dans sa contribution, M. Hadjseyd met en relief les limites du développement de l'industrie textile à l'échelle d'un pays en particulier, y compris dans les pays africains où elle apparaît performante. Son développement demeure d'autant plus fragile que les segments tournés vers l'exportation fonctionnent comme des enclaves, à terme et à effet d'entraînement négatif, du fait même des investissements que leur maintien exige, dans un contexte d'ajustement structurel renforcé. De l'analyse de cette filière, il tire une conclusion importante, à savoir que la réussite d'une industrie tournée vers l'exportation suppose la construction d'un ensemble industriel complexe et articulé et ne saurait se fonder durablement sur la promotion d'un facteur en particulier, une main d'oeuvre peu coûteuse par exemple; d'où la nécessité de l'intégration économique comme moyen dans la mise en place de cet ensemble industriel. Pour rendre un tel projet réalisable, Hadjseyd en définit les conditions générales de base: harmonisation des politiques macro-économiques, mise en place de politiques de soutien indirect à l'effort de construction industrielle, notamment sous la forme d'une politique hardie de promotion de la formation et d'intégration du secteur informel. Il insiste dans ce cadre sur la nécessité de prendre en compte l'environnement économique international, paramètre capital et bien souvent sous-estimé dans la définition des politiques et des programmes sectoriels.

C'est à ce niveau que le débat que lance L. Sangaré est encore d'actualité, bien qu'il puisse paraître de prime abord dépassé. Dans sa contribution, Sangaré souligne que la dégradation inexorable des termes de l'échange et la perte de compétitivité pour les exportations traditionnelles de l'Afrique commande l'industrialisation. Celle-ci ne peut se faire qu'à l'échelle des régions. Elle implique à son tour une certaine ferméture des marchés, par l'établissement de tarifs extérieurs communs. Ces barrières seraient levées progressivement, au fur et à mesure que les entités industrielles deviennent compétitives. L'idée de l'indispensable industrialisation du continent pour sortir du marasme actuel peut paraître illusoire au regard des écarts technologiques grandissants et quasiment insurmontables qui existent entre les pays africains et le reste du monde. Il en va de même de la thèse de la protection du marché pendant les phases de montée en production des nouvelles unités industrielles. Elles poussent toutefois vers la recherche d'une approche alternative et viable. Elle ne pourra qu'être différente de celle qui fonde les démantèlements des entités productives existantes dans le cadre des PAS. C'est dans ce cadre que la proposition de l'auteur à travailler à l'émergence de systèmes productifs industriels régionaux demeure pertinente.

Pour une démarche alternative en matière de construction communautaire
On ne saurait suffisament insister sur la nature du contexte dans lequel se déroule les tentatives africaines actuelles. Il se caractérise par un triple phénomène, un essoufflement durable de la croissance économique, la "financiarisatio"n de l'économie mondiale et la perte de compétitivité pour les pays et les secteurs industriels traditionnels. Celà a pour conséquence une baisse de l'intérêt porté aux matières primaires traditionnelles.

On observe sur le long terme une dépréciation durable de leur valeur, aggravée par une organisation fortement spéculative des marchés. D'où les difficultés financières des pays africains, déjà confrontés à des problèmes structurels liés notamment à une croissance démographique non contrôlée, à une gestion non planifiée de l'environnement, à la généralisation de modèles de consommation en rupture avec les moyens propres à ces pays, à un gaspillage des ressources, tant humaines que matérielles.

Dans un tel contexte, la construction communautaire pourrait apparaître comme la voie la plus appropriée pour assurer la survie et le redéploiement d'activités économiques et de pans de la société appelés à disparaître, en cas de poursuite de programmes d'ajustement direct aux marchés internationaux. En fait l'intégration régionale peut être utilisée comme un levier dans la solution des problèmes.

Cependant, la dynamique de la construction des différentes communautés régionales apparait largement inhibée. A l'origine d'un tel phénomène, on peut distinguer entre des facteurs internes et des facteurs externes. Les premiers se réfèrent aux modes de construction des communautés et de fonctionnement des structures supposées en assurer la cohérence et la gestion. Les facteurs externes renvoient à la nature des stratégies des acteurs, intervenant à la fois aux plans régional et local, ainsi qu'à la conjoncture régionale dans laquelle ces communautés déploient leurs activités.

Au delà de ces facteurs, la réussite de l'intégration économique suppose réunies certaines conditions. Leur inexistence au niveau des espaces nationaux rend difficile tout processus de construction communautaire.

Si on admet que l'intégration est un processus qui ne peut être décrétée par une autorité centrale isolée, sa mise en oeuvre suppose que l'on se situe dans un **espace de proximité.** Ce dernier est régi par un minimum de principes, susceptibles d'en permettre le maintien et le développement. Il peut ne pas être géographique, il doit être cependant à la fois, institutionnel, économique, politique, social et culturel.[2]

Du point de vue institutionnel, ce que requiert l'intégration en termes de proximité est l'existence d'un tissu assurant l'intéraction entre les acteurs économiques, à la fois comparable entre les pays et suffisament dense. Ce tissu institutionnel recouvre notamment l'appareil administratif des Etats, les marchés et les structures de concertation sociale (telles que les chambres de commerce, d'industrie et d'agriculture et les organismes paritaires Etat-Patronat). Dans l'ensemble de ces institutions, le comportement des acteurs doit obéir à un certain nombre de principes acceptés par tous, tels que la concertation avant la prise de décision, la transparence des moyens dont disposent les acteurs pour infléchir toute décision, un mode de fonctionnement basé sur le respect des règlements, le libre accès des acteurs à l'information disponible, la soumission de tous aux décisions finales émanant des institutions.

Du point de vue économique, l'intégration suppose l'existence de ressources matérielles, humaines et financières, rapidement mobilisables, à la fois pour réaliser les projets et pour couvrir les coûts directs et indirects induits par les actions inscrites aux programmes d'intégration. Sa réussite implique également l'existence de réserves de productivité chez les différents partenaires. C'est leur libération qui rend possible le financement partiel de ces coûts, sans que celà ne se traduise par des transferts de ressources, susceptibles de remettre en cause l'équilibre économique interne, dans les secteurs d'activité économique considérés socialement comme les plus importants.

Du point de vue politique, un pouvoir légitime, disposant de pôles d'ancrage et de relais efficaces au sein de la société constitue un élément essentiel dans le dispositif, tant pour la mise en oeuvre des processus d'intégration que pour leur poursuite. L'existence d'un tel pouvoir permet de créer les conditions d'autonomie des actions engagées au plan régional, à l'égard du niveau national, et d'assurer ainsi leur irréversibilité. La gestion consensuelle des difficultés qui peuvent apparaître en dépend.

Du point de vue social, l'intégration suppose l'existence d'une masse critique d'acteurs économiques à dimension et à vocation supra-nationale, dont la croissance et le développement, voire le maintien rendent indispensable, la recherche de nouveaux espaces extra-nationaux.

Du point de vue culturel, l'adhésion à un système commun de normes et l'existence d'un modèle de conduite de référence aux comportements individuels et collectifs sont également importants.

Dans les projets d'intégration économique, la dimension culturelle constitue probablement l'un des déterminants dont on a tendance à sous-estimer le plus la portée. Sa prise en compte recouvre au moins trois aspects:

(1)   D'une part l'acceptation à titre d'alter-ego de l'autre, dans sa spécificité et avec ses particularismes. Cet élément contribue de façon essentielle à l'instauration d'un climat de confiance, "non passionnel", entre les partenaires.

(2)   D'autre part un système commun de normes et de valeurs, relatives à l'organisation sociale (les rapports inter-individuels, le type de famille à promouvoir, les statuts et les rôles des diverses catégories sociales) et

économique (rapports au travail, à l'accumulation et à la circulation des richesses).

(3)   Enfin, l'existence d'un savoir-faire, voire d'un savoir technologique et scientifique techniquement perfectible, reconnu socialement et culturellement reproductible.

Si l'on examine la situation des pays africains, il apparaît clair qu'il existe actuellement peu, voire pas de régions, ni de pays susceptibles de réunir ces conditions, qu'il s'agisse du court ou du moyen terme.

En conséquence, il y a lieu de prendre en compte les diversités et les contraintes qui pèsent sur chaque pays, et d'oeuvrer sur cette base à la création d'espaces de proximité, au lieu de considérer ces derniers comme donnés.

Dans cette approche, il est important d'intégrer une dimension dont nous n'avons tenu compte qu'indirectement, la dimension géo-stratégique. Comme il a été rappelé ci-dessus, seuls quelques pays continuent à représenter un certain intérêt pour les grandes puissances, du reste non pas tant pour leurs matières premières que pour leur proximité géographique, voire culturelle, ou simplement pour leur fonction stabilisatrice dans la région où ils se trouvent.

Les réflexions précédentes amènent à s'interroger sur le type de démarche à adopter, dans une perspective de construction communautaire. Trois principes généraux doivent présider à la construction de la démarche:

(1)   l'élaboration et l'adoption, sur la base d'une large concertation, impliquant un maximum d'acteurs économiques et sociaux, d'une vision réaliste et évolutive de la construction communautaire, prenant en compte les spécificités de chaque pays et les contraintes qui pèsent sur lui et faisant chaque fois ressortir les pré-requis "consensuels" à la progression sur le sentier de la construction communautaire;

(2)   l'abandon de toute velléité de planification impérative et de toute libéralisation intempestive et non contrôlée des mouvements des biens, des services et des personnes, au profit du pragmatisme des choix, de la prudence dans la mise en oeuvre et de l'exploitation des opportunités, au moment où elles se présentent. La priorité devrait être donnée aux projets et aux actions dont la mise en oeuvre n'induit pas des retombées négatives sur les partenaires directs ou indirects impliqués dans chacun des pays, ni n'entraine des prélèvements ou des détournements de richesses au détriment de l'un d'entre eux. C'est le cas par exemple avec la promotion des infrastructures d'échanges et de communica-

tion, la mise en place de réseaux électriques interconnectés, la création de banques de données communes sur les productions, les besoins, les importations et les exportations de chacun des partenaires, en vue d'une gestion concertée, l'élaboration et la promotion de stratégies de filières à l'échelle régionale, la coordination et la création de cartes universitaires et de formation spécialisée régionales, ainsi que le développement des zones frontalières;

(3)   la promotion de la culture de la construction communautaire, par l'adoption d'une dynamique de concessions mutuelles, fondée sur le rejet de toute précipitation dans les prises de décision (de sorte à pouvoir prendre en compte les préoccupations de l'ensemble des acteurs sociaux, y compris de ceux qui sont hostiles) et sur l'irréversibilité des mesures arrêtées, à partir de la prise en compte des intérêts et des attentes de l'ensemble des partenaires.

Celà implique de la modestie et plus de réalisme dans les projets d'intégration. Pour ce faire, les Etats devront se départir de l'une des premières caractéristiques du mode de prise des décisions collectives, qu'il s'agisse de celles qui se situent à un niveau régional ou à de celles qui concernent le continent dans son ensemble, leur nature réactionnelle. Souvent les déclarations solennelles, comme les dispositions générales qu'elles induisent apparaissent comme des sortes de réactions immédiates, provoquées par des changements externes, imposés et que l'on ne réussit pas à contrôler.

Dans ce cadre, dans une première phase, il serait plus prudent d'examiner la possibilité de limiter les actions de construction communautaire, aux domaines et aux champs qui ne risquent pas d'induire de blocage au niveau des relations avec les partenaires non régionaux de l'Afrique. En même temps, il faut chercher à fonder les programmes de construction, sur la mobilisation prioritaire de l'épargne intérieure, et non de l'épargne internationale.

Une telle approche de la construction communautaire, pragmatique, évolutive et participative implique une révision des traités, des mesures prises dans ce cadre et de leur calendrier d'exécution. Cependant une question se pose à ce niveau. Il s'agit de savoir si les Etats africains sont susceptibles, voire capables, d'entreprendre une telle révision. Une réponse affirmative paraît difficilement envisageable dans les conditions présentes. Dans ce cas, une large mobilisation de l'ensemble des partenaires concernés par les processus d'intégration est nécessaire. Pour ce faire, il y a lieu d'assurer la large diffusion et la vulgarisation du savoir existant sur l'intégration et la construction communautaire, ainsi que sur les risques et les enjeux que recouvrent les expériences en cours en Afrique. Ce travail devra concerner l'ensemble des acteurs sociaux, les cadres des organisations inter-gouvernementales et des administrations nationales en charge des échanges et de la coopération, les entrepreneurs, les collectifs de travailleurs, les universitaires, etc.

Notes

1   Il y a lieu de distinguer entre le secteur des micro-entreprises opérant dans le domaine de la production des biens et services, dit secteur informel, du secteur informel auquel nous faisons référence. Ce dernier correspond aux agents qui se sont spécialisés dans la contrebande de toutes sortes et à grande échelle, créant des réseaux de circulation de richesses fondées sur la corruption, le contournement des lois en vigueur et sur la fuite des capitaux.

2   C'est ce que montrerait l'analyse des expériences passées et celles en cours, tant en Europe (y compris celle de l'Europe de l'Est), qu'en Asie et en Amérique.

Introduction

Naceur Bourenane

The issue of economic integration has been one of the most engaging topics in recent years, both at the international level and in Africa.

At the international level, the interest in integration reflects technological, scientific, economic, socio-political and cultural changes. These have led to a disintegration of conventional geoeconomic structures and the emergence of a triad with highly interdependent albeit conflicting components. The latter comprise North America, Japan and the European Union. As a result the interests of the Third World countries vested in the superpower strategies of the cold war have been dealt a lasting blow. The traditional stake in areas hitherto considered as sensitive has shifted to other regions.

These changes have necessitated a redefinition of international economic and political relationships, notably the rules of international trade. The traditional system of customs and tariff barriers is being gradually replaced with one based on quality norms and new standards for trade. The changes are also inducing a revision of agreements serving as the framework for multilateral and even bilateral cooperation with developing countries, notably those of Africa. For the latter, this can only mean a continual erosion of the benefits of the Lome Convention and the protocol agreements linking the European Community to the Mediterranean countries. There is bound to be a drastic reduction in the subsidies and assistance enjoyed by these countries in the past. At the same time, such assistance will be decreasingly multilateral and increasingly bilateral. Even assistance offered through multilateral channels will be more than ever tied to the originating countries. This trend which is already in evidence will grow even more (with the emergence of more competitive non-African producers of certain traditional commodities) as there is less economic and geo-strategic justifications for the maintenance of aid flow.

Be it bilateral or multilateral, aid tends to be geared towards the maintenance of "law and order". Its primary purpose is to keep populations in their countries of origin and stem migration flows likely to upset global equilibriums.

Indeed, economic interest, as well as the geographic and cultural proximity of former East European and Soviet bloc countries to countries of the European Union, Latin and South America, the Far East and the Pacific to the USA and Japan can only serve to deepen the trend towards the marginalization of African countries on the international scene. However, a few exceptions may exist relating to factors such as geographic proximity, entrenchment of a strong population of European origin, levels of investments already committed by the State or multinational companies, the type of natural resources produced or the size of the market and levels of national income. This is the case of Egypt, South Africa and Maghreb countries (Algeria, Morocco and Tunisia).

The trend towards marginalization will deepen the internal tensions existing in African countries. It could push many states into adopting a frenzied isolationism against their immediate neighbours, blaming them for their own internal instability and considering them as the constant source of additional tensions, if not the originators of the difficult situation in which they find themselves.

If this trend continues, it may prove to be disastrous for the countries of the African continent. It is indeed occurring in the only continent to have recorded a significant decline in its purchasing power over the last thirty years. In Africa, more than the rest of the Third World, socio-political instability is growing. It is the expression of a multi-facetted and unstructured protest movement marked by periodic violent manifestations. Neither the state security machineries, opposition political parties nor traditional public authorities are able to contain or prevent it.

Marginalization also produces adverse effects on overall international equilibrium. Structural instability at the continental level will inevitably lead to migratory flows to other regions of the world. It is also synonymous with the loss of markets, albeit limited in size, but still useful for the social stability of some European countries such as France, Great Britain and Italy. In such a case, the only way to contain the adverse effects mentioned above is through external military intervention for the purpose of maintaining peace. However, it can only be envisaged on a long term basis if the accompanying human losses involved are Africans. In such a situation, the countries concerned must help raise armies and ensure their maintenance.

Thus, the issue of economic and political stability and responsibility for the impact of population growth become important not only for countries of the continent, but also for their traditional partners. In the interest of developed countries themselves, improved growth and political stability of the African continent will be less costly and more beneficial than policies on law and order and containment.

In addition to greater democratization and good governance, the economic and political stability of African countries, implies sustainable growth. This is not possible within the narrow confines of the fragmented national economies. It supposes the promotion of cooperation and integration between—the economic activity sectors of neighbouring countries or even countries without common borders.

This process of unification of contiguous national spaces is already under way. It is partly driven by the efforts of local economic agents to ensure their own survival and wealth. The strength and dynamism of parallel trade channels operating between countries is a testimony to this. In the meantime, these agents reap their profits from the relative benefits induced by the system of monetary parity or customs administrative bottlenecks. The management and administrative rules introduced by structural adjustment programmes also contribute to these processes. The streamlining of modes of economic management and imposition of the liberalization of external trade on all enhance the conditions for integration and removal of regulatory obstacles required for their implementation. Such programmes have also contributed to strengthening the economic power of certain social actors who have acquired a supra-national status and vocation. At the same time, the latter have worked towards homogenizing the consumer patterns of broad social classes, such as certain urban classes, that have been negatively affected. Another factor to be taken into account is the need to simplify import and export procedures among neighbouring countries for the continent's external partners in order to reduce costs.

In fact, integration is already under way. And it will continue with or without the consent of political leaders and governments. The first set of questions that this raises is what the modalities will be, at what costs, to the benefit and at the expense of which category of economic agents and within what time-frame? The second question is how can the effectiveness of the process be identified in terms of cost-benefits for countries and populations?

In recent years, African governments seem to have weighed the challenges for the future of their countries and their own survival. In 1990, African Heads of State and Government met in Abuja, Nigeria and adopted a Treaty which defines and directs the process of the economic integration of African countries in 34 years on a gradual basis ranging from the homogenization of principles governing existing regional economic communities to the establishment of a Pan-African body. In line with this, major Pan-African institutions have decided to set up a joint secretariat to actively participate in this effort and mobilize resources for it. Three years after its adoption, a large number of countries that have ratified the treaty has rendered the latter mandatory for all the OAU members. However, despite this apparent commitment, Governments, as well as the joint secretariat have been slow in ensuring the implementation of the Abuja Treaty and those establishing regional communities.

Such a behaviour has been variously interpreted as an indication of the weak political will of African leaders to cooperate. But then, this way of dismissing discrepancies between political commitments and their implementation appears to be somewhat hasty. It rather reflects the magnitude of the constraints and obstacles that hamper, on a long term basis, any community-building process in Africa, the weak resources of governments and the absence of clear medium and long-term perspectives in many countries. There is therefore no need to systematically interpret these discrepancies as the irrefutable evidence of **lack of political will by state leaders.** The voluntarist pronouncements can also be interpreted as a concerted response, albeit unrealistic, to difficulties arising from global trends and their internal repercussions over which states only have a small control. Since taken individually they have no direct control over such on-going processes, African leaders think they have some collectively. Hence, the resolutions and declarations made by Africa's partners at each regional or continental summit. If such an explanation is assumed, then the adoption of the Treaty, just like the periodic speeches of Heads of States expressing their concern for the strengthening of existing regional economic communities, can be analysed as a desire to collectively assume responsibility for common problems caused by external factors.

But over and above the declarations and petitions of principle made by African leaders, regional integration projects, especially those relating to the creation of an African economic community appear to be an illusion in view of the four major constraints facing countries of the continent: the structural decline of their purchasing power, increasing socio-political instability, the unstructured nature of a multi-facetted, volatile, social protest movement (which government machineries can no longer contain or channel since they themselves are directly affected by this type of trend), the break down of national economies with whole sectors falling into the unproductive and speculative informal sector.[1]

Thus, we are faced with a paradox, the urgency of a community approach to help resolve the crisis and the impossibility of such an approach, because of the effects of this crisis.

Because of the multi-facetted, irreducible and disabling nature of the current crisis, the debate on the modalities and content of integration appears to be important. In view of the solutions that it offers, this debate will help identify the most viable paths of a lasting growth recovery and, consequently, to regain some of the political stability which is largely eroded today. The debate could hinge on the following questions:

1. What are the relationships between community-building, national development and the international economic environment?

2. What types of problems hinder the setting up of regional economic communities?

3. What industrial strategies must be adopted within a regional framework?

4. How can monetary cooperation be a tool at the service of regional integration?

5. What are the pre-requisites for a dynamic and irreversible regional cooperation?

6. What lessons can be drawn from the experiences of other regions such as Europe?

7. What are the general conditions for ensuring the success of a realistic integration programme?

The papers contained in this book and which were prepared on the occasion of the Pan-African Symposium organized in Algiers in June 1992, at the initiative of the AAS, with the support of the Algerian Minister of Higher Education pursue this debate and attempt to identify the optimum conditions for successfully conducting an integration process. Although they were written before the major upheavals on the African and international scene, notably the constitutional demise of the regime of apartheid, the papers presented at the Algiers meeting still remain relevant. The authors have focused on analysing structural constraints and their effects on African countries. They have also made concrete proposals which have remained largely relevant. These are likely to help define the actions to be undertaken.

Organization of the book

The papers contained in this book centre on three main thrusts:

1. community-building, its interest, constraints and conditions;

2. the role of currency and financial policies in economic integration; and

3. industrial strategies of community-building.

The choice of issues addressed in the book is dictated by the desire of the authors to offer the reader and, particularly, African decision-makers answers to some of their preoccupations. Notably, it reviews the traditional approach to integration, its foundations and limitations, the experience of the European Union, the prospects for community-building in a non-democratic regional political and economic system. The book also focuses on the chances of success of community-building in certain regions of the continent. It attempts to define the type of monetary policies and the type of industrial cooperation likely to facilitate integration.

Van Brabant analyses the foundations of the traditional approach to integration. He sees in the construction of the European Union a model for developing countries in general and Africa in particular. He shows that the success of the European community experience is based on several conditions: the prior existence of a high level of trade between countries concerned, low margins between levels of income per capita and levels of industrial development (making industrialization possible), a political consensus attained as a result of the Second World War and the Marshall Plan, a will and financial capacity to put in place a system of compensation such as the Common Agricultural Policy. On the basis of his analysis, the author draws several important conclusions, notably the need for countries to have a coherent development strategy and go beyond the strictly economic evaluation of integration and the losses it may generate in the short term. Here, he introduces an important concept, that of collective economic security, as the cornerstone of integration. He outlines three principles: the need to renounce, at least partially, economic sovereignty, abandoning mimetic procedures copied on the European model and pragmatism in the choice of measures to be implemented. In this connection, he recalls that customs union can cause additional costs in comparison with alternatives existing otherwise and that economies of similar structures draw benefits from their union, through the competition which it induces between partners. He stressed lastly that it is an illusion to think of promoting trade and intensifying action between spaces and economic agents without resolving the problem of monetary transfers between countries.

In his contribution Van Hoek draws lessons from the experience of regional cooperation and European integration. After reviewing the historical foundations, stages, conditions of success and effects induced by the single market, the author demonstrates that certain principles and lessons can be drawn from the experience. First, there was the need for prudent action based on what can be done and not what is desirable. Second, the need to assess the adequacy and real power of regional institutions and organizations to achieve the desired objectives. The third principle around which integration must be centred is the constant association of economic actors, trade unions, business owners etc. in the activities of the Community. In the European case, in addition to the existence of a European economic and social council, the Community gives periodic reports to the European Parliament.

On the basis of an analysis of the historic experience of Burkina Faso, B. Guissou shows how the construction of the national economy remains illusionary in the current context and why it would not be possible to reproduce the experience of countries of South East Asia in Africa. He recalls in this regard that the creation of colonial economic groupings followed a single objective: the forcible setting up of development areas. The reason the latter did not survive after independence was that they were made up of elements that were sociologically and culturally inviable. The author concludes that only the promotion of economic cooperation geared towards integration is likely to lead countries on to the path of growth. But this will have to be done in conjunction with the Bretton Woods Institutions, without whose support access to international financial resources is almost impossible.

I. Mandaza addresses the issue of community-building in southern and South Africa and other southern states. He first reviews the regional historical conditions. His analysis (carried out before the official abolition of apartheid) shows that community-building for the countries of the region will remain a delusion as long as the South African system remains in place, i.e. as long as the satellite role of countries of the region in relation to South Africa is not profoundly changed, and as long as the question of the economic democratization is not resolved in the country.

The analysis leads one to wonder if economic integration aimed at increased wealth and its improved social distribution can be envisaged as long as the bases of the colonial systems remain in place, as is the case in a great number of African countries, particularly Southern Africa. Are the recovery of political independence and substitution of an indigenous power for the one that existed before sufficient to ensure the success of integration? This leads to another question. How can a transnational community be built around balanced trade between regions and countries and the active participation of all the partners on the basis of quasi-patrimonial systems built on exclusion principles?

In their respective introductions, M. Benallègue and J. Senghor review the experiences of countries of the Maghreb and West Africa and the dynamics of community-building.

Benallègue discusses the constant confusion between multilateral cooperation and community building that has characterized the Maghreb approach. He calls for an innovative and not imitative approach. The latter should not be limited to the mere development of trade ties. It should seek to enhance the negotiation power of the Arab Maghreb Union countries with their partners. J. Senghor highlights the restrictive nature of the ECOWAS Treaty from the point of view of both the objectives and the type of institutions as well as prerogatives that are devolved upon them. The two contributions highlight the limitations of treaties and agreements that do not take into account the objective constraints facing countries.

P. Gakunu undertakes an analysis of the international context and the impact of new developments on ACP countries in general and African countries in particular i.e., those directly concerned with the future of the Lome Convention. In fact, measures taken under the Uruguay Round have rendered ineffective a number of advantages to ACP countries, even before the conclusion of negotiations accounting for losses of over US$180 million beginning 1988. The situation has hardly improved since, particularly with the gradual opening of the European Community towards Asian and American countries. This trend has had direct consequences on cooperation between ACP and European Union countries with regard to the Lome Convention which needed revision even before its completion. This in turn has made regional cooperation among African countries a necessity. It constitutes the least expensive way of reducing the negative effects of international trends.

According to H.M. Onitiri, the creation of the African Economic Community as defined by the Abuja Treaty represents the global response to the continent's problems. The various integration actions and programmes would subsequently be embodied in it. Indeed, their implementation presupposes the creation of an enabling political, socio-economic and scientific environment. The Abuja Treaty should be able to contribute in a significant way, notably because it helps induce a reduction of tensions and fosters a collective and participatory management of conflicts. But, as the author points out, the passage from the legal framework of the Treaty to a set of specific collective pro-grammes and projects presupposes the resolution of certain essential issues, such as the financing of multilateral operations, distribution of profits generated by these opera-tions and liberalization of African economies. These are some of the issues that underscore the essential role of states in integration.

For S. Tomori monetary integration is essential to community building. It is based on two factors: exchange rates and convertibility. According to the author, monetary integration implies that of labour and capital markets as well. Its primary advantage is to ensure increased chances of the optimal allocation of resources, a reduction of foreign exchange needs and greater stability of prices.

The working document drawn up by the African Center for Monetary Studies focuses on forms of monetary unions and plans for building them. It emphasizes the fact that unions existing in Africa do not represent an advanced stage of economic integration, as required by the Balassa step-by-step theory. Consequently, there is no need to posit the primacy of economic integration over monetary integration. The document also stresses the fact that the primary interest of monetary union is the reduction of risks of macroeconomic imbalances.

Following up on these conclusions, Mah'moud focuses on the experiences of the ECOWAS, PTA and SADC. He notes that methods of monetary coordination and tax policies are not clearly defined in these communities. On the basis of the review of the various possible formulas, Mah'moud recommends the quest for gradual coordination, growing in intensity with the setting up of a permanent council of central banks. This council would be responsible for studying and deciding on the most appropriate measures in this area.

S. Mouhoubi analyses the systems of compensation and monetary unions by highlighting the existence of two fundamental approaches, one defended by the supporters of immediate monetary union and another that sees in monetary union the result of the convergence of economic policies and performance of various partners. The author ends his analysis by emphasizing the fact that fixed parity inter-convertibility is an essential condition to the promotion of trade and functioning of clearing houses. On the basis of this, the author proceeds to examine the provisions of the Abuja Treaty. He concludes by indicating the inadequacy of the implementation timetable of the treaty in view of the problems to be overcome.

P. Bitoumbou calls for a realistic analysis of constraints and limitations hindering the building of a monetary union. Drawing on the experience of the two monetary zones operating in Africa, that of the CFA and the rand, the author concludes that this type of union has hardly any positive impact on the evolution of volume of trade. This leads Bitoumbou to shift the issue of the formation of monetary unions to that of financing of integration: economic integration comes with a price that needs financing. Without multilateral development financing institutions with quasi-automatically renewable resources, it is difficult to envisage the promotion of regional cooperation and integration. But the problem in Africa is the weak national saving rates. In order to overcome this constraint, one of the most appropriate solutions is to give regional institutions, such as the ADB, a more dynamic role and encourage the creation and development of financial institutions specializing in the promotion of goods and capital flows. The African Export and Import Bank based in Cairo should partially help meet this expectation.

The question of industry as the engine and vector of integration is dealt with in the book from two angles i.e. a global view and the particular perspective of the textile sub-sector. F. Benyoucef and N. Bourenane highlight the major trends of its development, the ongoing restructuring exercises and their implications for developing countries which wish to maintain or increase their share of the market. Notably, they point out the need for increased heavy investments to cater for the technological transformations and other changes affecting the textile and clothes market. In the case of African countries, the limitation of resources makes reflection on the integration of the sub-sector on a sub-regional and even regional basis highly useful. This can be a possible alternative to the internationalization of the textile sub-sector.

In his contribution, M. Hadjseyd dwells on the limitations of the textile industry at country level, including African countries where it appears to be thriving. The development of the industry remains all the more fragile as the sectors that are export-oriented operate in the form of enclaves. This generates a long-term negative effect in view of the investments needed for maintaining them in a context of high structural adjustment. In analyzing this sub-sector, he draws an important conclusion, that the success of an export-oriented industry implies the creation of a complex and structured industrial system and that this could not be sustained on the promotion of one factor in particular, for instance cheap labour; hence the importance of economic integration as a means of establishing this industrial system. Hadjseyd defines the general basic conditions for making such a project feasible: harmonization of macro-economic policies, setting up of indirect support policies for industry building, notably by instituting a bold policy to promote the development and integration of the informal sector. He emphasizes the need to take into account the international economic environment, that major, but often underestimated parameter in the definition of sectoral policies and programmes.

It is in this respect that the debate called for by L. Sangare is still topical, although it may appear out-of-date at first sight. In his contribution, Sangare points out that the inexorable degradation of terms of trade and the loss of competitiveness of African traditional exports call for industrialization. The latter can only be possible at the regional level. In turn, this implies the closing of markets by establishing common external tariffs. Such barriers would be lifted gradually as the industrial units become more competitive. The idea of the industrialization of the continent as an indispensable way of ending the current slump may appear illusionary in the face of the widening and virtually insurmountable technological margins existing between African countries and the rest of the world. The same is true of the notion of market protection during the early production stages of new industrial plants. However, this means that an alternative and viable approach must be sought. This must be different from the one which advocates the dismantling of existing productive units under SAP. It is in this context that the proposal of the author to work towards the emergence of regional productive industrial systems remains relevant.

Towards an alternative approach in community-building

One cannot overstress the relevance of the context of current African attempts at community building. This is marked by a triple phenomenon: a protracted decline of economic growth, finance-dominated global economy and loss of competitiveness of countries and traditional industrial sectors resulting in the decline in interest for traditional commodities. There is an observable depreciation of their value over the long term, worsened by a highly speculative nature of the markets. This has led to the financial difficulties of African countries already confronted with structural problems related to uncontrolled population growth, unplanned environmental management, generalized consumer patterns which are out of step with the actual resources available to these countries and the wastage of both human and material resources.

In such a context, community building could appear as the most appropriate way to ensure the survival and redeployment of economic activities and sectors of the society that are doomed to disappear should direct adjustment programmes be pursued on the international markets. In fact, regional integration may be used as a lever in the solution of problems.

However, the dynamics of the construction of various regional communities appear to be largely inhibited. The causes may be due to internal and external factors. The former relate to modes of community building and operation of structures supposed to ensure its coherence and management. The external factors relate to the nature of the strategies of actors, intervening both at the regional and local levels as well as the regional context in which these communities undertake their activities. Apart from these factors, the success of economic integration depends on certain conditions that must be met. Their absence at national levels renders the process of community building difficult.

If integration is a process that cannot be decreed by an isolated central authority, then its implementation presupposes the existence of **an affinity area.** The latter is under-pinned by a number of minimum principles likely to facilitate its maintenance and development. It may not be geographic, but it must be at the same time institutional, economic, political, social and cultural.[2]

From an institutional point of view, integration in terms of affinity implies the existence of a network ensuring interaction between economic actors. It must be similar across countries and sufficiently solid. This institutional network comprises notably the administrative machinery of states, markets and social consultative structures (such as chambers of commerce, industry and agriculture and joint state-employers organizations). In all these institutions, the behaviour of actors must obey a number of principles accepted by all, such as consultation before decisions are taken, transparency in the change of decisions, a mode of operation based on rules, free access of actors to available information, submission by all to final decisions issued by institutions.

From an economic point of view, integration presupposes the existence of material, human and financial resources, easily mobilizable for the implementation of projects and to cover the direct and indirect costs of actions defined under integration programmes. A successful integration also depends on the existence of productivity reserves among the various partners. It is by releasing such reserves that these costs can be partially financed without translating into resource transfers likely to upset the internal economic balance of sectors considered as the most important socially.

From the political point of view, a legitimate power with stable structures and effective relays within the society is essential for both the implementation and pursuance of integration processes. The existence of such a power guarantees that the actions undertaken at the regional level are autonomous in relation to the national level and, thereby, also ensures that they are irreversible. This is important for the management by consensus of difficulties which may emerge.

From the social point of view, integration implies the existence of a significant number of supra-national economic actors who require additional national spaces for their growth, development and even maintenance.

From the cultural point of view, adherence to a common system of standards and the existence of a reference code of conduct for individual and collective patterns of behaviour are equally important.

The impact of the cultural dimension, as one of the determinants of economic integration project, is often under-estimated. It covers at least three aspects:

1. Accepting to be the alter ego of the other person with his specificities and peculiarities. This factor helps ensure a climate of a "non-passionate" confidence between partners in a significant way.

2. A common system of norms and values relating to social organization, interpersonal relationships, type of family to be promoted, status and role of various social categories and economic organisation (labour, wealth accumulation and distribution).

3. The existence of a know-how, i.e. a technically perfectible technological know-how that is socially acknowledged and culturally reproducible.

An analysis of the situation of African countries indicates that currently there is practically no region or country likely to meet these conditions, either in the short or medium term.

Consequently, the diversities and constraints that hamper each country must be taken into account and used as the basis for the creation of affinity areas, instead of considering the latter as given.

With this approach, it is essential to consider a criterion which we only indirectly considered, namely, the geo-strategic criterion. As recalled earlier, only some countries continue to be of interest to the super powers, and not for their commodities, but geographic or cultural closeness or simply, their stabilizing role in the region in which they are located.

The foregoing analyses raise the question as to what kind of approach should be adopted in community building.

Three general principles must guide the community-building process:

1. the formulation and adoption, on the basis of broad consultation involving a maximum number of economic and social actors, of a **realistic and flexible vision** of community-building, taking into account the specificities of each country and the constraints facing it and, each time, highlighting the need for consensus in the progression towards community building;

2. rejection of any tendency towards rigid planning on the one hand and uncontrolled liberalization of the movement of goods and persons on the other, in preference to **pragmatic policies and prudent implementation and exploitation of opportunities** when they arise. **Projects and actions which do not create a negative impact on partners involved in each country** or lead to the diversion or withdrawal of resources at the expense of any one of them should be given priority. Examples can be cited of the promotion of trade and communication infrastructure, inter-connecting of electrical networks, creation of common data banks on productions, needs, imports and exports of each of the partners for the common management, formulation and promotion of regional chain strategies, coordination and creation of university and specialized regional training institutions as well as the development of frontier zones;

(3) promotion of a culture of community building based on **a system of mutual concessions that eschews hasty decision-taking** (in order to take into account the concerns of all the social actors, including those with dissenting views) and irreversibility of measures decided upon, based on the interests and expectations of all the stakeholder.

This implies modesty and greater realism in integration projects. To this end, governments must shed off the reactive nature of one of the primary characteristics of collective decision-taking, be it at the regional or continental levels. Often, official declarations, just like the overall effects that they produce, appear as hasty reactions to external changes over which one has no control.

In this context, in the first phase, it will be more prudent to examine the possibility to limit the actions of community buildings, in the areas and fields which do not have risks to induce the blockage in the level of relations with no regional partners of Africa. At the same time, it is advisable to set up building programmes, on the priority mobilization of the interior savings and not of the international savings.

Such approach of community buildings, pragmatic evolutive and participatory implicates a review of treaties, of measures taken in this context and their calendar of execution. Meanwhile a question is asked at this level. It is to know if the African states are susceptible, even capable to start this review. An affirmative answer seems difficult to envisage in the actual conditions. In this case, a large mobilization of all the partners concerned by the process of integration is necessary. Because of that, it should be necessary to ensure large diffusion and popularization of the knowledge which exists on the integration and the community building, and on the risks at stake which recover the on-going experiences in Africa. This work will concern all the social actors, the managers of intergovernmental organisations and national administrations in charge of exchanges and co-operation, the entrepreneurs, the union of workers, the academicians, etc.

Notes

1   A distinction must be made between the sector comprising micro-enterprises involved in the production of goods and services referred to as the informal sector and the informal sector being referred to here. The latter corresponds to agents specializing in large-scale smuggling activities of all sorts creating networks for the distribution of goods based on corruption, breaking of existing laws and capital flight.

2   This is what the analysis of past and current experiences in Europe (including Eastern Europe), Asia and America shows.

1

Economic Integration among Developing Countries—Toward a New Paradigm

Jozef M. van Brabant

There would seem to be wide agreement in the literature (for example, Balassa, 1987; El Agraa, 1982, 1989; Gunter, 1989; Hazlewood, 1987; Krauss, 1972, Langhammar and Hiemens, 1990; Robson, 1984)[1] about the futility of any attempt by developing countries[2] to emulate the comparatively successful integration path trodden, for example, by the European Community (EC) or, to a lesser extent, the European Free Trade Association (EFTA).[3] Incidentally, the same observation applies to most other countries, namely all those that exhibit marked differences in economic policies and structures from those typical of the Western European integration partners. This applies to both the type of integration pursued and the magnitude as well as the nature of the benefits that can realistically be expected to materialize in the process.

The claim that it is useful to pursue something different from the EC type integration is right and wrong. However, it is not the wish here to emphasize whether, and in what respect, the various adherent of those opposing views are wrong or right. This would indeed require an exegesis of past thinking on Economic Integration Among Developing Countries (EIADC), which is not the aim of this study, although a few pertinent comments will be offered in the third section. Instead, this paper intends to be forward-looking in a speculative way—perhaps even a deliberately provocative fashion—with respect to the meaning of economic integration and how it could usefully be applied, after all, to the situation of developing countries.

The first section summarizes the standard argument why the integration process typical of the EC simply will not do in the case of developing countries, or most other countries for that matter. The next section argues the alternative forms of economic integration that could usefully be envisaged. Certainly, integration schemes embraced by developing countries over the last thirty years or so have shown uncomfortably poor results, and the basic reasons for this state of affairs are detailed. Thereafter, a few thoughts are introduced on how EIADC could best be conceptualized. It is acknowledged that the particularities of individual countries or country groups must be recognized when deliberating about more concrete EIADC schemes.

On the effects of economic integration

The economic results of integration endeavours, such as attained in the context of the EC, are normally depicted in terms of static and dynamic effects. It is important to bear in mind that such measurements as a rule presume that, prior to the formation of the union[4], the participating economies as well as the rest of the world were efficient, hence in long-term equilibrium. That is to say, union formation is as a rule viewed as a "shock" to the structure of a global economy that was in equilibrium prior to the decision of some participants to open up their markets on a reciprocal basis.

The static effects are normally seen as consisting of net trade creation and diversion, which can be internal or external. Trade creation in consumption and production stems from enhancing competition in markets that were previously more protected. It normally involves the displacement of some domestic production by imports; but it could conceivably be confined to welfare-enhancing consumption effects that out-weigh the disadvantages of net trade diversion (Gunter, 1989). Indeed, the taxonomy on trade diversion and trade creation has become very elaborate, now comprising the traditional Vinerian production effects, the consumption effects of substituting countries and the production and consumption effects of substituting commodities, possibly as a result of shifts in terms of trade resulting from the formation of the union (Gunter, 1989).

If the concern is with the pure effects on trade, the increment in trade (at any rate a shift in the level, the commodity composition and the geographical direction of trade) that is entailed by the formation of the customs union can benefit both partners and others, but the gains are expected to be largest for partner countries. Trade diversion means essentially the displacement of former low-cost imports from countries not joining the integration arrangement by higher-cost supplies from member countries, simply because the removal of the tariff and the compression of related trade impediments led to this further distortion. These supplies are as a rule more expensive, and the diversion takes place only because the protection regime against partner supplies has been relaxed, thus exacerbating relative discrimination against the lower-cost supplier.

The net static effect of trade creation and diversion is not known *a priori*, but it is expected to be positive for the integrating partners. This does not necessarily hold for other countries. It will pertain with respect to the world as a whole, if the integrating markets are largely competitive rather than complementary.[5] Economies with similar economic structures as a rule offer scope for reaping greater benefits through competition in each other's markets following union formation than complementary economies. The latter could entail sizeable trade diversion if complementarity is, in fact, achieved, because of the reduction or elimination of intragroup customs duties. There are other circumstances that bear on the eventual balance between net trade diversion and net trade creation. These include the number of union members, the share of the production of member countries, a low common external tariff relative to the average preunion tariff and the competitive nature of these economies (see Hazlewood, 1987, p. 143). To the extent that the "new" rationale for international trade holds, externalities, scale economies, learning by doing and other circumstances may favour integration among countries that, on the basis of the traditional economic paradigm, would be considered as second-best solutions (Stewart, 1984). The latter is determined by the degree of overlap in economic activities subject to tariff protection and the extent to which the costs of producing particular commodities differ among the various union members.

In light of the above considerations, the net static effects of forming a customs union among developing countries are expected to be negative. This *a priori* notion holds because lower-cost supplies are being heavily discriminated against, given the high trade impediments that these countries as a rule maintain against non-member countries (Edwards and Savastano, 1989). Putting it another way, the static effect of union formation will be procurement from high-cost suppliers whose products are heavily protected by tall tariff walls.

On the other hand, the dynamic effects of union formation depend very much on the kind of growth promotion that the union itself will engender and the more intricate interplay between what would have happened with trade relations if there had been no union formed. These dynamic effects should, in fact, reach well beyond those traditionally associated with the growth of incomes. "New" international economics may yield very important dynamic effects that could argue in favour of elaborating regional integration schemes. In any case, it will be necessary to trace shifting comparative advantages against a new decision-making horizon. In the case of the EC, trade creation based on trade gains, including trade with non-member countries, stemming from income expansion, are widely believed to have substantially outweighed the static trade diversion effect, notably in agriculture.

Especially in the case of the Western European integration schemes, the outcome was expected to be greater trade creation than diversion, in particular when results were appraised in a dynamic perspective. This outcome has since been validated for a number of reasons that by definition are typical of the participating countries. For one thing, the EC had an extremely high level of intraregional trade before the start-up of the European Economic Community or the Common Market in 1958. Second, the dispersion of per capita incomes and levels of development and industrialization was not too extensive. This provided considerable room for the emergence of intra-industry specialization, which has been the most dynamic force in the expansion of global commerce since the late 1950s. And, once the worst effects of the Second World War and its aftermath were galvanized under force of circumstances and indeed with considerable prodding on the part of the United States, the political leadership of the Western European countries had developed a congenial level of political consensus, if not fully harmonized equanimity, about foreign affairs. Finally, these countries were, in principle, willing and able to provide some form of compensation payments, a sort of extension of domestic "regional" programmes to the level of the Common Market as a whole.

The circumstances enumerated earlier create favourable conditions for economic integration. Even so, none of the issues mentioned was resolved very quickly or without laborious deliberations. In fact, some contentious points of joining forces are still in the process of being settled after many decades, even now, when the final design of the single European market is in the process of finally being completed.

Such difficulties are likely to be much greater for other countries. For one thing, circumstances similar to those that typified the EC and EFTA in the postwar period simply did not—and cannot—prevail in most developing-country groupings. Indeed, they have been absent for other groupings, including the members of the now defunct Council for Mutual Economic Assistance (CMEA). The latter failed to an appalling degree, because they were unable to reach a consensus on even the most elementary features of regional economic integration. In addition to the environment, growth-induced gains in the EC or EPTA are hardly likely to emerge with any vibrant momentum in economies that themselves are not really internally integrated and whose development process suffers from teething problems on the way to maturation, that are triggered by deeply rooted economic and social, let alone political, structures (El-Agraa, 1989).

In as much as many developing countries can be characterized in the above manner, it is doubtful that the typical dynamic effects of union formation will be accessible to them for as long as a coherent development strategy is not in place. Even if such could be agreed upon at the outset of the integration path, substantial doubts that develop in the process of implementing the coherent strategy will inevitably complicate further progress. Also, the various leadership involved must find ways to capitalize on dynamic externalities and scale economies, and reach *a modus vivendi* on how to divide the costs and share the benefits of formulating and implementing a joint development strategy. Very often this must be pursued with rather rudimentary monetary and fiscal policies in place.

This suggests that countries may find it more useful, from the point of view of accomplishing positive effects, to focus their attention on somewhat narrower targets than on agreeing to integrate their entire economies in a declamatory manner. The ambitious nature of many EIADC schemes in the past has been the very reason for their failure. Managing integration schemes is not simply a matter that can be achieved through high-level political agreement or by putting in place some institutional supports for the integration schemes. That is to say, economic integration should be kept separate from more politically oriented ambitions that are aiming at bolstering cooperation among developing countries. Simon Bolivar may have dreamed of integrating Spanish America economically and politically (Edwards and Savastono, 1989), but accomplishing precisely that (even after making allowance for Portuguese Brazil) requires much more than a solid dream or a political incantation. Merging different economies is a complex undertaking not only in and of itself, but also because it entails asymmetric benefits and costs in a variety of perceptions of how societies ought to function.

It would be naive to conclude from the literature on customs unions that EIADC would be futile in all instances (Hazlewood, 1987). Certainly, trade diversion is in principle detrimental and trade creation beneficial, regardless of the type of country under consideration (El-Agraa, 1989). Both measures should be applied to the situation at hand. Such may be comparative statics for mature market economies, but this frame of reference is patently inadequate in the case of most developing countries. For developing countries, the prime concern should be development, that is, to change factor endowments, incomes and patterns of consumption (Stewart, 1984); in other words, countries that stand to gain from working within a larger market, from scale economies and externalities as the development process gets under way, and from jointly developing or adapting technology to prevailing conditions could, in principle, be the subject of beneficial customs unions.

The above considerations are not the only ones to be factored into the equation. It is also necessary to go beyond the definition of successful economic integration that is implicit in the heuristic treatment of customs unions. Indeed, success with economic integration context cannot be appraised solely in terms of economic rationality. Because of the second-best nature of regional economic integration endeavours in economic theory, proposals for integration based solely on economic logic would as a rule be rather poorly designed policy. Even if fuller account is taken of the real world, economic integration cannot—and should not—be confined to its economic benefits as such. In some cases, other benefits may outweigh the economic losses that are temporarily incurred in order to place the participating countries onto a new growth path for the societies in question.

Even when placed against such a broader backdrop for judging outcomes of most, if perhaps not all, integration efforts launched by developing countries over the past three decades or so (UNCTAD, 1990b), there seems to be wide agreement that nearly all have utterly failed (Mytelka, unpublished data). In many ways, the same can be said for less formalized economic cooperation among developing countries (see UNCTAD, 1990a,c). The few forms of regional integration among developing countries that have not yet completely collapsed[6] have little to show for the enormous energy expanded on these undertakings.

Most literature suggests that developing countries should aim at something different from EC-type integration. This applied in particular to when these countries reach some *modus vivendi* on forging ahead with their intragroup economic collaboration other than direct contact among economic agents, such as fostered within the context of relatively flexible market economies. One of the latest suggestions is that they explore free-trade agreements among themselves (Etzan and Yeats, 1992), but this is not necessarily a panacea, either.

Economic integration and structural transformation

Economic integration, by its very definition, is a process designed to completely abolish discrimination between local and partner goods, services and factors over some agreed period of time. That is to say, economic integration expands the effective market horizon within which economic agents can move the resources they hope to utilize productively. In contrast, economic cooperation includes concerted actions aimed at lessening discrimination in certain areas of common interest. The two concepts, although interrelated, have been kept separate if only for heuristic reasons.

Economic cooperation is at the same time more limited and broader in scope than economic integration. It is broader because cooperation can be extended to areas that economic integration normally does not cover (such as cooperation in statistics, medical research, scientific and technical collaboration, or setting up the institutions of the market economy). Yet, it is more limited, because the cooperative arrangements that countries engage in are voluntary. For that very reason, they are also often hard to enforce and monitor. This is in some contrast to the essence of economic integration, where it is the compulsion of competition in a market-based framework for reaching economic decisions that should ultimately be the driving force for the welfare gains to emerge. In any case, the question about adequate regional governance in the case of cooperation is as a rule more complex, although at times on a smaller scale, than for more formal integration schemes.

Both cooperation and economic integration merit consideration by all countries. Because of the "scale economies" that can be expected in the unintegrated environment of developing countries, however, cooperation could profitably be pushed very far for those countries, certainly much further than in the case of countries that can credibly depend on markets to adjust with some speed to emergent opportunities. In many ways it would be a prelude to more formal, certainly more encompassing schemes of economic togetherness. Various cooperative arrangements can realistically be conceived for implementation without setting up very elaborate institutions and policies. Action at the grassroot level would certainly recommend itself.

Integration schemes, particularly those pursued in Africa, have set for themselves very ambitious targets that could not possibly be met given the limited resources available to the participants (Diejomach, 1987, p. 332). A deliberate choice of a narrower range of activities that concentrate on the essential and feasible schemes could be more useful. These still merit exploitation with some determination at this stage. This is particularly true when such efforts can be conceived within a dovetailed conceptual framework on what the book hopes to achieve and how best this can be arranged organizationally as well as financially.

There is still the question of whether developing countries can be assumed to have market economies and indeed whether the current international sentiment for spearheading the margin of the market and export-oriented development strategies are the proper targets for developing countries. If the integration process cannot really depend on market forces, can one imagine another more suitable mechanism? Its main purpose would be to bring about behaviour on the part of economic agents by the means available from within a framework that is in some conformity with the basis operation of markets. But such behaviour will first have to be generated by different means, including deliberate state policy-making and perhaps even forward-looking, target-oriented planning of some activities that will hopefully help elicit behaviour on the part of economic agents that is more consonant with the presence of fairly integrated markets.

There are at least two cogent reasons why EIADC should be rethought and placed on a different level than the one that has frequently been utilized. One stems from the structural shifts occurring in the world economy and their implications for developing countries. Of special importance are the repercussions of shifts emanating through the existing international commercial and financial mechanisms. The other is the intrinsic rationale of gains to be reaped from economic integration, regardless of what happens elsewhere in the global economic environment. The latter may actually reinforce the motivation stemming from the former. Indeed, it should increase the collective economic security of the countries participating in the integration scheme. This reference to security is not used here as a way to exonerate the richer countries from sharing to some degree their wealth with less fortunate partners in securing and sustaining global economic welfare.

Changes in the structure of the global economy

Over the past decade or so, major changes in the world economy have taken place. Others promise to become more clearly visible in the near term. In Europe, economic and political relations are being remade in consequence of three recent events: the creation of the single European market at the end of 1992, the extension of that market through the so-called European economic area (which is also scheduled for realization in 1993) and the growing together of the reborn eastern part of Europe with the mature market economies in the West. That measurable modification in the way in which the Western European markets operate, holds promises as well as threats: for the ways in which there is developing concern that the disadvantages of the single market in Europe may manifest themselves well before the corresponding benefits can realistically be accessed (Brabant and Greenaway, 1992). Concerns that the benefits will be outweighed by the disadvantages still exist and in some cases quite legitimately. Widening of the European economic area to include the EPTA countries and parts of Eastern Europe can only exacerbate those fears (Brabant, 1992).

In the Americas major changes can also be discerned, and more are in the offing. The formation of a Free Trade Area (FTA) in the Western hemisphere, especially in North America, under the lead of the United States is likely to affect market access and the competitive pressure there for countries that are not now seeking ways and means of intensifying their reciprocal economic interactions. This is independent of whether or not such an FTA is likely to be beneficial to the developing countries involved (see Etzan and Yeats, 1992). Any effective widening of the market for the Latin American developing countries holds the potential of discriminating against other countries, notably the Newly Industrializing Economies (NIEs) that have successfully penetrated the North American markets for nearly a quarter century, and hence should be warily monitored.

In eastern and south-eastern Asia major transformations have already come to the fore and more are on the horizon (Balasubramanyam, 1989; Groser and Bridges, 1990). A formalized customs union is not even on the debating table, if only because several members have staked their economic fortunes on outward-looking economic strategies that, at least so far, have been quite successful. Less ambitious forms of formal cooperation have not been all that promising to date. An attempt to intensify economic cooperation in some sense has primarily manifested itself within the context of the Association of Southeast Asian Nations (ASEAN). More recently, an impetus to strengthen this regional cooperation has also emerged for other reasons. One derives from the backdrop to the potential widening of ASEAN to include the Indochinese countries once they loosen up their economic administrations and expand their areas of policy interest. Of course the collapse of the Soviet Union and continued uncertainty about China's place in the global economy and its own economic reform intentions have contributed to this regional interest in greater political and security cooperation. It is perhaps remarkable that the latter form of regional cooperation has been pushed forward very rapidly without there being a formal infrastructure for regional economic cooperation, except the loose, largely informal and consultative format provided by the institutional underpinnings of ASEAN, under Japan's leadership.[7] It is regrettable that none of the above schemes has allocated room for intensive collaboration with the African developing countries, in particular those of the sub-Saharan region. Certainly, the EC (and by extension the European Economic Area and prospectively perhaps all-European cooperation) has various programmes that, in the context of special relations with Africa, the Caribbean, Pacific and southern Mediterranean (Gakunu, 1992; Akder, 1992), attempt to cater to the needs of these countries. Neither arrangement offers specific mechanisms that are sufficiently flexible and generous to provide a serious fillip to the efforts of these countries to transform their economies and, indeed, their societies in a lasting way based on sustainable development in the medium to long term.

African developing countries themselves have tried many EIADC schemes since the early 1960s. Some even existed prior to political independence, but those integration programmes were designed to facilitate colonial administration rather than foster effective economic integration, and for that reason will not be considered here. From among the schemes tried since independence, unfortunately, few have yielded economic results that even remotely approach the kind of benefits in terms of trade, regional infrastructure, structural cooperation or other common arrangements that had originally been anticipated from them, at least by some responsible leaders (see Bach, 1991; Diejemach, 1987; Guillaumont and Guillaumont J. 1991; Wangwe, 1987).

As developments over at least the last two decades have demonstrated, the international environment within which developing counties have had to pursue their ambitions with regard to regional economic integration has not been very congenial. Many of the domestic policies pursued by these countries, individually and in their intragroup context, have been fundamentally misguided. Participation in international economy through positive growth presupposes that economic structures be adjusted and that economic agents shift their behaviour in such a way that the full benefit from working for a larger market can be reaped. If full integration in the global context is realistically not feasible, and if it cannot be taken advantage of for lack of domestic market institutions, then policy-makers should really ponder whether there are any other plausible options that could usefully be explored.

Autonomous need for EIADC

Even if abstraction can be made of politics and the direct or indirect influence that outsiders may attempt to exert on integration schemes, developing countries are likely to have difficulties that are peculiar to their integration efforts. As a result, they require distinctive solutions that are "more flexible and better adapted to each case with respect to integration formulas they employ" (Salgado, 1987, p. 356). Differences in underlying economic structures and size of potential markets imply that the integrating partners have to be realistic in selecting their common objectives and in tracing out a desirable agenda for gradual progression in their common endeavour. They certainly should avoid blind adherence to rigid models.

Pragmatism is likely to be a better strategy for moving forward than either ideology or imitative fervor. The arguments in favour of EIADC go beyond the purely defensive. The rationale for fostering such integration rests mainly on the effects of the creation of regional markets on the structural problems of these countries. These include the desirability of widening the opportunities for profitable domestic and foreign investment; the need to mobilize unemployed labour, idle or underutilized resources; to reap the advantages of so-called efficiency; to raise the level of technical sophistication; to improve the range and depth of human capital, the terms of trade and distribution of income and other development imperatives. Clearly, some developing countries are not yet ready to engage in innovation-type integration schemes, such as through the circle of learning and technological change (Mytelka, unpublished data). To the degree that within-group cooperation can help advance the cause of development to a level where these countries might usefully engage in scientific and technical innovation, EIADC should remain a worthwhile endeavour.

In evaluating the desirability of any EIADC scheme, it is not its impact on existing production or trade that should be decisive (Robson, 1984, pp. 151ff). Instead, the prospective patterns of production and trade that are likely to emerge in the years ahead with and without the integration scheme should be given prime billing on policy deliberations. Certainly, trade and production cooperation are not necessarily the alpha-and-omega of external economic cooperation (Mytelka, unpublished data), but neither should these more traditional channels for reaping the benefits of regional economic integration be ignored as providing a potentially powerful impetus to bolstering the development process in some developing countries. There is simply no solid economic reason to eschew *a priori* potentially lucrative trade and cooperative ties with developed countries. Indeed, ties with developed countries may provide the wherewithal through the transfer of technology for bolstering cooperation among selected developing countries.[8] The reverse can be imagined too, with enhanced EIADC providing the platform from which some markets in the "north" can be creatively conquered (Stewart, 1984).

To the degree that a reasonable case can be made in favour of EIADC, basically because trade and investment diversion in the end will not outweigh trade and investment creation, an autonomous argument in favour of fostering regional integration can be built up. It would hold if the external environment turned sour, but it would not lose its persuasiveness. If the global economy were to remain congenial, EIADC could help foster trade creation to a larger extent than it does trade diversion. These effects should be looked at from the point of view of static trade creation and diversion effects resulting from lowering the customs barrier, but also as a result of terms-of-trade effects that the formation of a customs union may entail. Furthermore, and this is particularly important in the case of developing countries, the arguments referring to the benefits of reaping scale economies, learning by doing, as well as capitalizing on externalities should be upheld. Indeed economies of scale are at the very heart of the rationale for EIADC (El-Agraa, 1989; Stewart, 1984). Such externalities are available and some require an intensification of EIADC both as a reactive mechanism and as a pro-active device. It has to be forward-looking to spur on domestic growth to a pace that exceeds what can reasonably be anticipated on the strength of going it alone. As Arthur Lewis (1978, 1980) argued nearly two decades ago, if the industrial economies collectively do not provide the locomotive that can propel the development process in the southern hemisphere, developing countries should explore their intragroup possibilities much more intensively. And if the purview of such investigations cannot address all developing countries, it may still be worth to fall back upon alternative ways of enhancing regional integration.

Why past efforts failed
When agreed schemes for EIADC were implemented, they promoted trade diversion and fostered a prolonged process of regional import substitution. Many reasons could

be cited for this. It is perhaps too simple to condense them into internal shortcomings rather than external features, as the fundamental rationale underlying the failure of EIADC. The external environment since the early 1970s has been far from propitious in supporting EIADC, but the lack of conceptual clarity as well as the inappropriateness of the integration concepts should be singled out for blame as well. Even the usefulness of the schemes in the most effective mode of the 1980s and 1970s is doubted by a number of observers, including Edwards and Savastano (1989), who are ardent advocates of greater openness of developing-country economies to world markets as such, rather than regional integration schemes.

One argument (Edwards and Savastano, 1989, p. 229) is that the share of intragroup trade can be sustained on a competitive basis, that is without there being very substantial trade impediments launched to restrain intercourse with outside partners, that would remain small and decline. However, whether or not the share of intragroup trade declines or rises is not necessarily indicative of there having been any serious attempt to integrate the countries under review, that is, to streamline the processes by which resources are allocated so that greater uniformity in relative product and factor prices emerges.

Many reasons can be invoked to clarify the failure of past efforts. First, members of customs unions never granted across-the-board duty free access to one another's markets, and efforts toward trade liberalization were either limited to more or less redundant tariff barriers or were aborted early. In other words, the potential benefits of forming a customs union were quickly dissipated behind high tariff walls against third parties and in some cases even against partner countries. The latter applied in particular to various non-tariff barriers. These are notoriously difficult to track even in mature market economies. They are formidable for countries with disjointed markets. Secondly, regional investment planning was high on the agenda of the various integration schemes, but most of the envisaged projects were never carried out. Some that were realized turned out to be white elephants or did not quite live up to expectations. Perhaps the core reason was continuous disputes over financing and management; some projects quickly lost their original purpose. This applied in particular to a number of projects designed around scale economies and externalities, including those embraced by the original five members of ASEAN. If partners suddenly abandon the common approach and launch the start-up of competing units, the common edifice to serve a wider market, cannot, but simply cave in. Thirdly, the internal mechanisms of the integration schemes were not always sufficiently developed or even broadly thought out. Assumptions based on the smooth adjustment of markets to differentiate relative prices were simply invalidated in the case of economies that decided to manage their economies according to market principles. Adjustments proved to be even more difficult to enact through market-based criteria in economies in which markets were not fully developed, and, hence, other, more target-oriented approaches to integration were espoused. Joint planning can be a useful instrument, but only if the participants are willing to engage in voluntary income distribution or if fairly rigid rules of distributing costs and benefits can be agreed upon and adhered to over time.

What remains then, are chiefly intangibles, such as an improved flow of information across borders that may help improve mutual understanding, and some manag:d examples of relatively successful cooperation such as collective bargaining of ASEAN's joint effort to attract foreign aid in ECOWAS and a few common projects that are designed to solve specific bilateral and multilateral problems. These few positive pointers, when measured in terms of the initial expectations associated with any integration project, have to be rated as by-products. The main product simply failed to be delivered.

There were also weighty political reasons for the failure of earlier EIADC schemes. To the extent that the sociopolitical stability of one member of a union deteriorates to a considerable degree, its feasible role in the integration undertaking will be in doubt, as is the case of the Central American Common Market (CACM). The repercussions in foreign affairs may be such that relations among remaining members will be strained beyond the endurance of incipient cooperation schemes.

One important issue that is often not addressed in this context is the instability in policy, including an account of forced structural adjustment measures. The experience of the lost decade of the 1980s has been for countries to adopt divergent or conflicting approaches in tackling macroeconomic imbalances. When countries belonging to some regional grouping do so, it is bound to divert attention from longer-term development, the implementation of agreed integration goals and means and the innovation of appropriate responses to integration issues that crop up during implementation. There is, therefore, considerable need for economic groupings to innovate new ways and means of enhancing joint consultation and harmonization of policies affecting their partner countries (UNCTAD, 1990c).

Among the economic reasons for failure, it is important to acknowledge the deteriorating external economic environment. Indeed, since the early 1970s barriers to trade and factor mobility in the world economy have risen at an alarming secular pace. Macroeconomic policies in many countries, including the larger and more developed ones, have been arched toward purely domestic needs rather than to what would be required to foster a stable multilateral economic environment. The political economy of international policy coordination is a complex subject that has not been fully resolved. It certainly has not been fully applied. As a result, present understanding of how best to pull together major components of the world economy to the benefit of all country groups is not much more advanced than it was in the mid-1970s. There are vested interest groups, economic as well as political, that look askance at economic integration. Economic strains develop because of low visible gains reaped from economic integration for the reasons mentioned earlier.

That earlier contention of the EC's experience with regional economic integration cannot be applied to EIADC. This observation is right in the sense that developing countries should not expect to be able to institute the same kinds of arrangements as developed countries. They should not anticipate being in a position to obtain the same kinds of economic benefits from trade and other forms of economic cooperation as those that have accrued to European countries from the late 1950s.

At the same time, those commentators who contend that the EC's experience is without merit for developing countries are off the mark. They posit that the Western European example does not furnish an illustration of the types of benefits, as well as disadvantages, of economic integration and even of the type of intercountry cooperation reaching beyond pure economics that can eventually be attained. The implication would seem to be that integration in Western Europe is a *su generis* experiment that could possibly be emulated elsewhere. Insofar as the economics of integration are concerned, the question is not so much whether other countries can attain scale economies, income growth and levels of efficiency as engendered by the movement toward greater integration in Europe. Rather, the focal question is how best to capitalize on the opportunities to reap such gains in the context of the resource allocation patterns of the integrating countries and the means available to them to improve upon those potential gains.

Short of semantics, the above paradox can only be resolved by affirming positively that there are gains to be made—economically, politically, and socially—from countries bandying together in some fashion, however haphazard and *ad hoc* the available modes of cooperation may initially happen to be. At the same time, it needs to be recognized that the instruments and institutions that cater to the needs of developed countries other than those of Western Europe do not necessarily suit the aspirations of, say, developing countries. The impetus for integration in Western Europe emanated essentially from the disastrous policies of the 1930s and the traumas of the Second World War. Neither could possibly provide a solid inducement to integration among most other countries of the world. However, that is not to deny that there are many noneconomic motives that could be involved in support of pursuing economic integration, even if the short-term tangible benefits remain limited.

Perhaps the single exception to this observation was the effort made within the context of the now-defunct CMEA. It failed not because the attempt to emulate the Western European examples set by the EC and EFTA miscarried. For one thing, the CMEA was started up in early 1949, nearly a decade prior to the EC. Rather, the setback really occurred because the instruments, institutions and objectives of dovetailing economic, and possibly other policies among most of the former centrally planned economies of Asia and Europe[9] were not geared at improving resource allocation in a way that suited the aspirations of the participating countries. These countries did not have common monetary arrangements, such as that available within the context of the European Payments Union (EPU) in the 1950s or the IMF monetary arrangements since then. Without such a realistic means of comparing magnitudes, the process of economic integration cannot go very far. Each of the CMEA participants jealously guarded its own economic sovereignty to the extent the power-political situation permitted. It was indeed more coercion and hegemonic exploitation rather than innate economic interests that proved to be the rationale underlying the CMEA. Hence, that attempt failed when the balance of power among that group of countries shifted in the wake of the collapse of communism and Soviet hegemony in the East.

The lesson from this experience for developing countries, is then, that the pursuit of economic sovereignty for its own sake places severe constraints on the benefits that can realistically be anticipated to result from any EIADC scheme. This proposition holds even under the best of circumstances in terms of external environment and proclivity for adopting the "right" domestic policies. Anything short of forging greater economic openness, at least in some sectors or economic endeavours, is bound to abort the integration effort.

It is very difficult to prescribe blueprints, models or programmes for economic integration that would be suitable to any group of countries, regardless of their level of development, size, institutions, policies or diversity of aspirations. Particular circumstances have to be heeded. In this connection, it is certainly worthwhile to reiterate gain that the conventional effects of trade creation and trade diversion in attempts to integrate market economics do not necessarily apply to other countries, particularly developing countries. That is not to argue the case for basing integration schemes on some broadly perceived need to protect the economics, or major sectors thereof, in the case of developing countries. Rather, it argues for eschewing unrealistic expectations at the conceptualization of the integration scheme.

Towards a new paradigm

The experience with integration to date suggests that it is important that schemes designed to foster EIADC must pay attention to the lack of sufficiently large national markets, the desirability of fostering economic progress throughout the group of participants, the imperative to reduce and eventually eliminate market distortions and the need to correct other institutional and policy features that differentiate the economic realities of developing countries from those typical of mature market economies. Taking them into account would tend to reinforce the general rationale for the formulation of some type of economic union.

Seen in a purely economic discourse, the success of EIADC depends on the static resource reallocation effects, the terms-of-trade effects and the dynamic effects stemming from economies of scale and external economies. Regarding static resource reallocation effects, there is, in principle, no difference between those applying to mature market economies and those useful in considering integration among developing countries. Trade creation is beneficial, and trade division is generally not, regardless of whether it comes about through production, consumption, or the terms of trade, or some suitable combination thereof. In other words, trade creation has to outweigh trade diversion if the balance for fostering regional economic integration is to be sought on the basis of static economic considerations.

The terms-of-trade effects of union formation too are no different between the two groups of countries. The outcome all depends on the particular market structures that are at the roots thereof. Terms-of-trade effects in the case of developing countries are likely to be much more sharply drawn once the EIADC scheme takes hold than has been the case for comparatively mature market economies or even centrally planned economies.

Regarding scale economies and positive externalities, there should be far more scope for them in developing countries than has been the case for the Western Europe integration schemes. In as much as effective market size, which is often not identical with the national market, is an important hindrance to development, particularly in the Third World, scale effects should receive the most consideration. The same applies with respect to external economies in the two groups of countries. In fact, these motivations will be an absolute necessity for them if economic restructuring and modern development are to be achieved. That should not necessarily justify the infant-industry argument invoked for erecting formidable national or even regional protective barriers, though there are, of course, solid historical antecedents for justifying protection for infant-industry reasons. The real issue is how the process is conceived, the kind of protection afforded and the process of ensuring that the protected industry matures and hence outgrows the need for protection.

It would be misleading to suggest that the theory of economic integration as developed for mature market economies is very different from the paradigm that should be applicable to developing countries. It amounts to confusing broad theoretical generalization with their specific application to a particular group of nations whose structure is quite different from that of advanced nations. However, different structures of economies should not be confounded with different theoretical constructs (El-Agraa, 1990, p. 99). Some generalization can be attempted. One useful observation would seem to be that when developed countries, such as in the EC or EFTA context, embrace some format for economic integration, they tend to have fairly integrated markets at home and an extensive involvement in international trade based primarily on a parametric link of the home markets to the global economic framework. Though there are undoubtedly protectionist sentiments to be heeded, they tend to be of a second order of magnitude when the integration scheme is first set out. The primary purpose would seem to be to enlarge the effective markets of participating countries behind one common barrier, whose height tends to be lower than the weighted average of the national barriers prior to integration.

Both fairly integrated national markets that are shielded moderately through parametric media can be expected to succeed. That hope is certainly more justified in the cited instances than when integrating partners resort to outright interference with scarcity-related resource allocation. Including interventions against international competition. That, of course, includes inhibitions against economic interaction with the integrating partners.

It is perhaps trivial, but nonetheless essential, to observe in this connection that market links cannot be built up without there being within the group at least one truly transferable currency that economic agents can depend on for assessing their interests in catering to markets and products. The lack of such, as already noted, contributed measurably to the withering of the CMEA and its eventual demise. Without a transferable currency, it is impossible to separate the microeconomics of integration, driven by the self-interest of economic agents, from the core aspects of macroeconomic policy. This includes stances on commercial policy which would appear to be a prerequisite to acting on integration endeavours that have a chance of success.

It is important in this connection to note that when integrating countries have a convertible currency (for example, as per the IMF's article VIII), such a currency is also transferable at least for current transactions. When that is not the case, they do not in fact have a sufficiently transferable currency. Under those conditions, further action will be required before some coherent commercial policy can be agreed upon and put into place without noticeably disadvantaging some class of economic agents. Perhaps some variant of a payments union, with or without international support, might offer a useful transitory mechanism that would not unduly inhibit moving forward with the envisaged integration format.

A second general observation is that it would seem to be much easier to mesh markets via actions on the external economic frontier than to synchronize national economies and form some kind of economic union or to amalgamate countries and come to some viable political union. The latter two options would seem to be predicated on the successful completion of the first; that makes it even more urgent to enquire into the necessity of having viable markets prior to launching any far-reaching attempt at integration.

By their very nature, developing countries constitute economies that are seeking to foster rapid economic development, hence to enact major changes in their economic structures and their involvement in the world economy. These objectives can be pursued in isolation, or they can be made the object of cooperative efforts among several like-situated economies. In either case, there will have to be "training" in the broad sense. Hence, one rationale of regional integration schemes should be the sharing of the training experiment. As argued earlier, another should be defensive, namely to be prepared for any adverse change in the structure of the world economy.

In addition, EIADC should benefit from enlarging the size of the domestic market and thus achieving economies of scale, as in the case of mature market economies. The benefits of improving resource allocation and the availability of resources should be within the reach of these countries too, albeit to a quite different extent from what mature market economies expect from bandying together. At the very least, developing countries should benefit from expanding funds available for productive investment by mobilizing local private and public savings, as well as by attracting foreign risk capital. In this connection, it is instructive to bear in mind that there is little point of compensating shortcomings in domestic institutions and policies by providing all kinds of tax and tariff advantages to foreign capital. It is far more important that foreign capital be allowed to compete for domestic markets on the same terms as domestic enterprises, and that the domestic conditions for such competition be as predictable as possible. The net benefits from foreign capital are likely to be largest in the case of nearly full resource utilization. It will, hence, be most important for comparatively advanced countries that have succeeded in integrating their own domestic markets and hence generate a high degree of resource utilization.

Once the above conditions are met a cogent argument can be made for jointly engineering desirable structural changes by enhancing industrialization in the broad sense of that term. It will then prove useful to jointly produce public goods. In fact, products with a long gestation period, high capital output coefficients and decreasing marginal costs are candidates for joint production as they promise large cost savings for individual countries compared to parallel production in several protected national markets that are solely managed under national authority.

EIADC, just as regional integration schemes among mature market economics undoubtedly have noneconomic benefits, provides a certain rationale for seeking such an accommodation as a desirable policy course, even though in purely economic terms the advocacy would fall back on second-best solution. One of those benefits is the strengthening of the position of developing countries in the international economy, including improving their collective bargaining position *vis-à-vis* industrialized countries. Such a reinforced strength would be particularly valuable in case the international economy became adverse for the developing countries, as argued earlier.

Another important concomitant of economic integration is consensus building on regional political and security issues. By tying the hands of domestic policy-makers, this can provide a scapegoat for unpopular policy decisions. Pulling together calls for a degree of regional governance, at least in the economic domain, that has been elusive for nearly all tried EIADC schemes. Even in the case of mature market economics, as demonstrated most forcefully by the ups and downs of integration in the EC context, attaining a minimum consensus on desirable governance on a regional level requires some yielding of domestic economic sovereignty. Many countries are reluctant to do so. This certainly was the case for most of the CMEA members and hence was an important contributor to the demise of the organization. For developing countries that are still putting together a workable consensus on national governance, it may be particularly difficult to defer part of the coveted sovereignty to a regional authority.

When all is said and done, however, the agenda for policy action suggests that, in spite of the advocacy of EIADC in political fora, it cannot be a credible substitute for appropriate domestic economic policies. With wrong exchange rates, high barriers to trade, misleading investment activities and a high degree of government involvement in economic affairs that should be taken care of through private ownership or, at least private management operations, patterns of production and trade are distorted in such a way that regional economic integration does not offer many benefits to those gaining from the domestic economic and political regimes.

Even when domestic policies are conceived in such a way that they are in fact supportive of outward-looking policies, it must be admitted that integration in the traditional sense is not really viable for most combinations of developing countries. This observation even applies to the pursuit of intensification of economic relations with neighbouring countries. Whatever credible efforts will be made preferably need to be aimed at the structural transformation of these economies, essentially by minimizing the costs of structural adjustment and reaping the benefits of scale economies and externalities in propelling the development process.

Once these notions are acceptable, it still must be emphasized that EIADC can flourish in the sense defined only when the initiative for cooperation comes from within the countries concerned, not from without, such as one the behest of one international economic organization or another precondition for successful regional cooperation is domestic policy reform in the participating countries and the synchronization of these policies to the extent possible. Where the international environment comes in, regional cooperation should not be discouraged by the external economic or political environment that participating countries are facing. Better management of the global economy by the institutions in place and the post-war economic, financial, monetary and trade regimes deserves high priority on the policy agenda, in particular of the large developed market economies. At the same time, there is indeed room for the timely fine-tuning of these institutions and regimes so that better global economic management will become feasible to the benefit of all.

Conclusions

When the opportunities for advancing EIADC are placed in their proper perspective and carefully scrutinized, namely against the realistic backdrop of the resources presently and potentially available among participants, the outlook for advancing the cause of intragroup cooperation among developing countries is by no means as bleak as it is sometimes portrayed in the literature. That is not to say that it would be easy to engineer useful common integration projects. Potential participants must have the desire themselves and indeed be willing to make a sacrifice and earmark resources for the common good.

This is especially the case when the opportunities for developing countries are seen in the context of all those factors that help to explain trade among developed or developed-developing countries other than factor endowments. EIADC could benefit from improved trading, transportation and payment infrastructure. Trade restrictions tend to be formidable and could be relaxed. Organization links are required to enable participants to exploit the benefits of inter-industrial trade with specialization in the first instance geared to demand in developing countries to the extent that it is less formidable than demand in developed markets. Regional cooperation could be significantly enhanced by creating an effective innovative capacity for the development of more efficient products and services suitable to demand and supply conditions in the developing countries.

The many questions concerning policy formulation and effective governance in EIADC schemes, including the least ambitious ones, deserve much more attention than they have received over the past decades. They also merit more positive support from regional and international economic organizations than has been the case to date.

Notes

1. Principal Economic Affairs Officer of the Department of International Economic and Social Affairs of the United Nations Secretariat in New York. The opinions expressed here are the author's and do not necessarily reflect those that may be held by the United Nations Secretariat. The author is grateful to Richard Kozul-Wright for suggestions.

2. In much of what follows developing countries are invoked in a generic sense. The author is aware of the fact that what may be good for medium-level developing countries is likely to be quite off the mark for, say, sub-Saharan African developing countries at a low level of economic development.

3. A free trade area by definition will lead to smaller integration results than something like the economic union pursued in the EC context. Results point in the same direction, and so most of the rest of the paper limits the comparison to the EC's experiences.

4. There are, of course, important differences in the magnitude and structure of the effects of free trade areas, customs unions, common markets, economic unions and political unions. However, for the purposes at hand, these increasingly more demanding conditions on harmonization of institutions and policies can be ignored. Customs union will be used in its generic sense: taking policy decisions aimed at bringing about greater uniformity in relative product and factor prices. The latter may be achieved only in an indirect way, such as in the cases of free trade areas and customs unions.

5. This issue is frequently fudged in the literature dealing with the potential for integration among countries that are set to undergo measurable structural change. Similar economic structures are lamented as inhibiting integration (for Africa, for example, see Diejomach, 1987). For an explicit statement on why the contention does not hold for Eastern Europe, see Brabant, 1990, pp. 161-173.

6. It is a fact of life that public organizations, such as the institutions created in support to integration schemes, do not formally disappear. Rather they tend to languish for long periods of time until some major shock occurs that permits the formal abolition of replacement of the defunct organs without invoking the distinct ire of vested interest groups.

7. A more structured grouping may emerge in the wake of the collapse of the Soviet Union and indeed the strengthening of the Chinese economy. But any such formalization is more likely

to address regional security arrangements and political alliances than take the form of specific EIADC schemes (Balasubramanyan, 1989).

8. But this need not be considered an externality, as Mytelka suggests (1991, unpublished data).

9. Excluded were Albania (since late 1961), China, Laos, North Korea, and Yugoslavia (which was only an associate member).

10. The case for the payments union in the post-CMEA world has been examined at great length elsewhere (see Brabant, 1991).

References

Akder, A. Halis. 1992. The single market and commercial relations with non-member countries: views from developing countries with preferential arrangements with the EC—the Mediterranean countries. *Journal of Development Planning* , 21.

Bach, Daniel. 1991. L'intégration économique en Afrique—les flux parallèles à l'assaut de l'Etat. *Economies Prospective Internationale*, 48: 33-49.

Balassa, Bela. 1987. Economie integration. In The new Palgrave dictionary in economics, vol. 2. London: Macmillan, pp. 43-47.

Balasubramanyam, V.N. 1989. ASEAN and regional trade cooperation in Southeast Asia. In *Economic aspects of regional trading arrangements*, ed. David Greenaway, Thomas Hyclak and Robert Thornton. New York-London: Harvester Wheatleaf.

Brabant, Josef M. van. 1990. Remarking Eastern Europe—on the political economy of transition. Dordrecht-Boston-London: Kluwer Academic Publishers.

Brabant, Josef M. van. 1992. The revolutions in Eastern Europe and relations among east, south and north. *Journal of Development Planning*, 21.

Brabant, Josef M. van. and David Greenaway. 1992. The EC programme—background, motivation and implementation. *Journal of Development Planning*, 21.

Brabant, Josef M. van. and Claus Wittich. 1992. Overview of the European Single Market Act and its implications for non-member countries. *Journal of Development Planning*, 21.

Edwards, Sabastien and Miguel Savastano. 1989. Latin America's intra-regional trade: evolution and future prospects. In *Economic aspects of regional trading arrangements*, ed. David Greenaway, Thomas Hyclak and Robert Thornton. New York-London: Harvester Wheatsheaf, pp. 189-233.

El-Agraa, Ali M. ed. 1982. *International economic integration*. New York: St. Martin's Press.

El-Agraa, Ali M. 1989. *The theory and measurement of international economic integration*. Houndmille and London: Macmillan.

Etzan, Refik and Alexander Yeats. 1992. Free trade agreements with the United States—what's in it for Latin America? Washington, DC: World Bank, *Working Paper No. 827*, January.

Diejomach, V.P. 1987. The economic integration process in Africa: Experience, problems and prospects. In *Structural change, economic interdependence and world development*, vol. 4 Economic interdependence, ed. John H. Dunning and Usui Mikots. Houndmille and London: Macmillan, pp. 321-336.

Gakunu, Peter. 1992. The single market and commercial relations with non-member countries: Views from developing countries preferential arrangements with the EC-the ACP countries. *Journal of Development Planning*, 21.

Grosser, Kate and Brian Bridges. 1990. Economic interdependence in East Asia: the global context. *The pacific review*, 1:1-14.

Guillaumont, Patrick et Sylviane Guillaumont Jeannemey. 1991. La Zone franc a un tournant: vers l'intégration. *Geo Politique Africaine*. 4:11-18.

Gunter, Frank R. 1989. Customs union theory: retrospect and prospect. In *Economic aspects of regional trading arrangements*, ed. David Greenaway, Thomas Hyclak and Robert J. Thornton. New York-London: Harvester Wheatsheaf, pp. 1-30.

Hazlewood, Arthur. 1987. Customs unions. In *The new Palgrava dictionary in economics*, vol. 1. London: Macmillan, pp. 749-844.

Krauss, Molvyn B. 1972. Recent developments in customs union theory: an interpretive survey. *Journal of economic literature*, 2: 413-436

Langhammer, Rolf J. and Ulrich Hiemens. 1990. *Regional integration among developing countries—opportunities, obstacles and options*. Tubingen: J.C.B. Paul Siebeck and Denver, CO: Westview Press.

Lewis, W. Arthur. 1978. *The evolution of the international economic order*. Princeton NJ: Princeton University Press.

Lewis, W. Arthur. 1990. The slowing down of the engine of growth. *American economic review*, 4:555-84.

Robson, Peter. 1984. *The economics of international integration*. 2nd ed. London: George Allen Unwin.

Salgado, Germanico. 1987. Conclusions to part IV. In *Structural change, economic interdependence and world development*, 4 Economic interdependence, ed. John H. Dunning and Mikoto Usui. Houndmille and London: Macmillan, pp. 355-367.

Stewart, Frances. 1984. Recent theories of international trade: some implications for the south. In *Monopolistic competition and international trade*, ed. Henryk Kierzkowoki. Oxford: Clarendon Press, pp. 108.

UNCTAD. 1990a. Structural adjustment, the evolving international trading system and economic integration among developing countries: issues for the 1990a. New York: *United Nations document* TD/B/C.7/AC.3/9, December 10.

UNCTAD. 1990b. Index of economic co-operation and integration groupings of developing countries: membership and objectives. New York: *United Nations document* TD B/C.7/AC.3/ 3/Rev. 1 of December 12.

UNCTAD. 1990c. Economic integration among developing countries: trade co-operation: monetary and financial co-operation and review of recent developments in major economic co-operation groupings of developing countries. New York: *United Nations document* TD/B/ C.7/AC.3/10, December 12.

Wangwe, S.M. 1987. Economic co-operation among developing countries: status and prospects. In *Structural change, economic interdependence and world development*, vol. 4: economic interdependence, ed. John H. Dunning and Mikoto Usui. Houndmilla and London: Macmillan, pp. 337-353.

2

Regional Cooperation and Integration in Europe: Lessons to be Learned

Dr. F.J. Hoek

Historical developments

The unification of Europe has had many advocates. Throughout European history, many politicians, academics, writers and philosophers have been paying attention to this idea. Julius Caesar, Charlemagne, Dante, Erasmus, Voltaire, Rousseau, Kant, Hegel, Schiller, Cavour, Marx are examples. The main impulse, however, came after the Second World War, when Europe was in ruins and impoverished. European leaders wanted to banish the nightmare of war from Europe with close cooperation. The final objective was to achieve a democratic European Federation.

A first opportunity arose when, in 1945, the United States offered the ambitious Marshall Plan by which the United States provided economic support of $ 15 billion for the reconstruction of war-struck Europe. Three years later (in 1948), 16 European countries founded the Organization for European Economic Cooperation (OEEC) as a coordinating framework for the utilization of the resources made available under the Marshall Plan. The great merit of the Plan was that it left the responsibility of dividing the cake to the European countries who were thus forced to cooperate and arrive at a consensus. They gradually developed a common understanding and language that could have contributed to a European integration.

However, the institutions of the OEEC and the Council of Europe (founded in 1949) revealed themselves too weak to become a basis for further European integration which, in fact, was the political objective of the Marshall Plan as well as of the leading political personalities of Europe. The OEEC did not have a real executive arm, nor was there an elected Parliament. Hence, in 1961, when European reconstruction was well advanced, the OEEC was replaced by the Organization for Economic Cooperation and

Development (OECD). Membership went far beyond European boundaries. With full membership first extended to the United States and Canada, and later on to countries such as Australia, Japan and New Zealand, the reference to Europe was soon deleted. The OECD, well known for its excellency, turned into a rich men's club working on the basis of consensus but without the necessary institutional arrangements that allowed imposition of and control over implementation.

The first steps towards real economic cooperation and integration came in 1947 when Belgium, the Netherlands and Luxemburg (three small countries with intertwined histories) first started a customs union and later on integrated further towards an economic union, well known as the BENELUX. The treaty establishing BENELUX provided for free movement of persons, goods, capital and services, the coordination of economic, financial and social policies and the adoption of a common policy in respect of economic relations with third world countries. Hence BENELUX has been a model or predecessor of what later became the European Economic Community which, as a matter of fact, was largely based on a memorandum by BENELUX to its partners in the European Coal and Steel Community (ECSC). The memorandum advocated a unified Europe through the installation of common institutions, the gradual integration of national economies, the realization of a large common market and the gradual harmonization of social policies.

This was, therefore, a wider approach than that of the ECSC, which in itself was already a model of integration with the objective not only to remove customs duties, but also to undertake a common price and investment policy in the coal and steel sector of its six member states. In 1955 and 1956, an intergovernmental committee, chaired by the well-known Belgian politician, Paul-Henri Spaak, converted the BENELUX memorandum into treaty texts which culminated in the Treaties of Rome signed by the six countries on March 25, 1957. The Rome Treaties led to the foundation of the European Economic Community (EEC) and the European Atomic Energy Community (EAEC), better known as EURATOM. Together with the already existing ECSC, they constituted what is known as the European Communities (EC). The Treaty of the EEC directly or indirectly intervened in the life of its member states and their populations.

Apart from the customs union, the Treaty also provided for a number of common policies on matters such as agriculture, transport, competition, harmonization of legislation, social affairs, external trade policy and development. It also provided the necessary institutional arrangements with an executive body (the Commission), an elected parliament and a Council of Ministers.

The evolution of the European Community

In what may be called "the golden sixties", the Community achieved many of its goals. The Common Agricultural Policy came into being, the customs union was completed and the Community's institutions were strengthened. In the area of development cooperation, association agreements with the francophone countries of Africa were signed in Yaounde,Cameroon. During its first ten years of existence, the Community's struggles towards integration progressed faster than many had expected.

In contrast to the "golden sixties," the 1970s were largely characterized by crisis and stagnation. Severely hit by oil crisis and its repercussions, the six member states were tempted by a tendency towards isolation through a restrictive interpretation of the rules and regulations of the common market. Moreover, this period was marked in 1973 by the accession of three new member states (Denmark, Ireland and the United Kingdom) who, to some extent, still had to learn the rules of the game to which the original six member states were accustomed for the past 15 years. This evidently hampered further rapid progress.

With the accession of the UK, there was also the problem of future development cooperation of the enlarged EEC with at least part of the British Commonwealth developing countries, particularly those in Africa, the Caribbean and the Pacific (ACP). After many negotiations, agreement was reached between the anglophone and francophone countries, and together they established the so-called ACP group. In 1975, the EEC concluded its agreement for development cooperation with the ACP Group, embracing both aid and trade relations (the so-called Lome Conventions: Lome I in 1975, and Lome II in 1979). Furthermore the Community intensified its cooperation with the countries of the southern Mediterranean—the Magreb countries in 1976 and the Mashreg countries in 1977. In contrast to the earlier mentioned ACP/EEC Conventions, the agreements with these countries were concluded on a bilateral basis between the EEC and each of the countries concerned. Further regional cooperation will allow the conclusion of agreements between the EEC and the group of these countries.

In 1979, the European Monetary System (EMS) and the European Currency Unit (ECU) were created. The third decade of the Community saw a further geographical expansion; in 1981, Greece became the tenth member, and Spain and Portugal followed in 1986. This decade was characterized by a strong move towards the internal market, to be achieved by the end of 1992. The so-called Single European Act, signed in 1986, is designed to amend the Rome Treaties and to improve the future working of the Community, while simultaneously extending its scope. In fact, it puts a time frame on the achievement of what was the original proposal underlying the Rome Treaty signed in 1957. The route towards further progress was opened with the creation of a real single internal market in 1992, the stimulation of technological and scientific research and development, economic and social cohesion and the improvement of working conditions.

The impact of 1992 on developing countries

Notwithstanding a series of reassuring statements by the Commission and European political leaders, it is quite clear that developing countries all over the world are preoccupied with the effects the single European market may have on their economies. The European Community is their largest supplier but also their major export market, and many developing countries fear that the European Community will increasingly shield itself from competition by non-member countries. There is also a fear that the interest of the European business community in investing in developing countries will further wane as a result of the prospects offered by the single European market, as well as by the most recent evolution towards a more liberal market economy in Eastern Europe and the USSR.

In view of its historical and economic relations with many developing countries, it is clear that the European Community should carefully consider the effects that 1992 may have on developing countries and undertake detailed analyses of this potential impact and (by necessity) of the Uruguay Round. Indications are that such analyses so far seem to have been absent or weak. The usual argument that a booming European economy will have a favourable effect on developing countries assumes the so-called trickle-down effect, but experience shows that this effect does not necessarily occur and that its validity has still to be proven.[2] On the other hand, it should also be recognized that the European Community, as a regional organization, cannot be blamed for putting its act together, as long as it respects the international trading system as defined by GATT and the ongoing Uruguay Round negotiations.

In respect to GATT, it is regrettable to see that a number of developing countries, and particularly those in Africa, are absent from the Uruguay Round negotiations, as if these negotiations were of no immediate concern to them. One may ask whether there is not a role to be played by some of the regional organizations to inform their member states about the issues at stake and on progress made in these negotiations as well as to stimulate their interest and active participation.

Lessons to be learned

On the basis of European regional cooperation (OEEC and OECD) or integration (Benelux, the European Coal and Steel Community) since the Second World War, one can detect a series of elements that have played a role in this process. When talking about regional cooperation and integration in other parts of the world, and particularly amongst developing countries, these eight elements could, *ceteris paribus*, be taken into account. These elements are determination and political will, evolution, mutual interest, learning from the past, tactics, institutional dynamics, the importance of small countries, participation and accountability.

After the Second World War, there was a strong determination amongst European political leaders to carry on and consolidate various levels of cooperation and integration. This was not only rhetoric, as so often is the case. There was a real political readiness to go as far as delegating authority to regional institutions and to take into account and integrate in national policies what was agreed, by consensus or majority vote, at regional level. In order to ensure this coherence, today all member states of the European Community have, within their Cabinets, a Minister or Secretary of State in charge of European Affairs. This also goes for member states of the regional organization elsewhere.

The process of integration is a laborious and time-consuming process with only gradual evolution. Methods that have followed in Europe were the subsequent conclusion, by consensus or majority vote, of a multitude of agreements, conventions and protocols. Europe was not made all at once, nor according to a general plan. It was built from concrete and practical achievements after lengthy discussions which, however, time-consuming, helped to gradually arrive at a common language and a sense of solidarity.

The success of European integration in the past, but also with respect to the realization of the European Single Market 1992, is based on a well-balanced recognition of mutual interest. The lack of such recognition may well be one of the explanations for the failure of some past experiences in developing countries (for example, the East African Community).

Over time, the designers of the European integration have learned from the past and from the mistakes that were made. No state is prepared to easily abandon sovereignty; plans that were too direct in their attempts to compromise the sovereignty of member states (for example, the so-called Fouchet Plan of 1961 aiming a joint European foreign policy) have been avoided. The lesson that can be learned from this is: *go slowly and look for what is politically feasible rather than what is ideally desirable.*

It is not easy to overcome the distrust among member states. This can only be done with excellent preparatory work by the responsible institutions and by putting practical goals on the negotiation table. It is only through these tactics that European countries could agree to concessions on sovereignty that would have got nowhere if they had been presented only as wonderful ideals. When the approximately 300 directives for the

European Single Market 1992 were drafted, there was no question of priorities. Because of this approach, there was no fear that the interests of one member state would be favoured over those of another.

The European experiences show quite clearly that at the institutional level, a movement towards regional cooperation and integration must dispose of the necessary institutions with real power. In the case of the European Community and BENELUX, member states have to submit to the jurisdiction of their respective Courts of Justice that protect Community and BENELUX institutions. In the case of the European Community, the Treaty of Rome also specifies that the right of proposal is entrusted to the Commission: without Commission proposal, the Council of Ministers cannot move. One of the major weaknesses of many of the existing regional organizations embracing developing countries is this area of institutional dynamics. This may also find its origin in the absence of indispensable political will.

Contrary to some standard beliefs, small countries can play an important role in an integration process. BENELUX, on several occasions, has given impetus to the process of European cooperation and integration, especially in periods of crisis. BENELUX acted as a union within a larger union. The same holds for the Caribbean Common Market (CARICOM) where the Organization of the Small Eastern Caribbean States (OECS) usually speaks with one voice. This point may be taken into account by African countries when reflecting on the ways and means to put some order into the excessive multitude of different and at least geographically-overlapping regional organizations.

Finally, an important element in the unification of Europe that is not always stressed is the constant involvement, directly or indirectly, but also institutionally, of the various economic actors and their organizations. These are the trade unions or the private business community, and examples are the Economic and Social Council in the case of the European Community, and the accountability to the European Parliament and the public at large.

Notes

1. The author would like to thank Geert Laporte for his contribution to the preparation of this article, which is a somewhat elaborate version of an intervention at the Roundtable "Regional Cooperation Worldwide" held at the initiative of the University of the West Indies, Jamaica, in January 1990 and was published in Spanish by the Institute for Regional Cooperation of the Interamerican Development Bank.

2. The recent study by the European Centre for Development Policy Management on the impact of 1992 and the Uruguay Round, particularly on ACP States, will help to shed some light on a series of issues at stake, such as temperate zone agricultural products, tropical products, textiles and clothing as well as services.

3

Le Cas Ouest Africain, vu du Burkina Faso

Dr. Basile Laetare Guissou

Introduction

Les pays colonisateurs du continent africain ont toujours eu le souci de son découpage en zones de "mise en valeur", selon des critères de stricte rentabilité économique, et sans états d'âme concernant les autres aspects comme la culture, les habitudes de vie, et l'organisation socio-politique antérieures. Les colonies étaient rentables. L'Afrique Occidentale Française, en est un exemple. L'administration, les infrastructures (ports, routes, chemins de fer) et les exploitations agricoles ont toutes répondu à ce souci de l'integration et de la complémentarité de la zone économique.

Pour des raisons diverses, c'est un processus de désintégration de ces ensembles, qui a accompagné la marche des différents territoires vers l'indépendance politique en 1960.

Trente ans plus tard, le constat est clair. La conjoncture économique mondiale aggrave la crise structurelle des économies fragmentées de tous ces pays sans exception. Le problème de la nécessité inévitable de l'intégration revient aujourd'hui au premier plan de la réflexion sur le ou les futur(s) possible(s) de l'Afrique des années 2000.

Nous prendrons un pays, le Burkina Faso, comme exemple pour illustrer notre exposé sur l'intégration régionale.

Le passé: une école par la négative

L'expérience vécue par les cinquante deux pays africains, ces trente dernières années, sur les triples plans économique, social et politique, est une riche moisson pour les intellectuels et les chercheurs africains. Prises une à une, ou globalement, ces expériences sont toutes intéressantes du point de vue de la recherche scientifique. Il y a eu une accumulation extrêmement riche de situations où, l'on retrouve du meilleur et du pire. C'est dans l'utilisation qui en sera faite, que dépendra l'avenir du continent.

De notre point de vue, il sera difficile de faire pire, que ce qui a déjà été réalisé. Mais l'avenir reste intimement lié aux rapports futurs entre le savoir et le pouvoir, qui devront enfin coopérer, pour dégager des perspectives concrètes et réalistes. Au centre de tous les problèmes à résoudre en Afrique, dans les turbulences de la démocratisation actuelle des systèmes politiques en place, se trouve celui de la relance économique et de l'amélioration des conditions matérielles de vie des cinq cents millions d'Africains. Si nul ne conteste le paradoxe entre les potentialités économiques et les performances enregistrées dans la pratique de la gestion quotidienne des pays, le vide d'une critique et d'une analyse prospective qui ouvrent sur un avenir meilleur, reste à combler sous plusieurs aspects. La question de l'intégration économique est au centre du débat. La question a toujours été soulevée depuis l'accession à l'indépendance politique des pays africains. Mais elle a été pratiquement ignorée par les politiques officielles des Etats et des Gouvernements, totalement absorbés dans une dynamique nationaliste, et accrochés principalement à la défense de leurs prérogatives dites de souveraineté.

La situation de l'Afrique Occidentale Française offre un cas d'analyse en la matière: Bénin, Burkina Faso, Côte d'Ivoire, Guinée, Sénégal, Niger, Mali, Mauritanie, et Togo. Tous ces pays ont une frontière avec un ou plusieurs autres, qu'ils soient situés sur la côte atlantique ou enclavés. Leurs frontières ont souvent été redécoupées. Un territoire comme le Burkina a été supprimé, et partagé en trois parties rattachées au Mali, au Niger et à la Côte d'Ivoire, sous l'administration coloniale entre 1936 et 1947. Sur le plan économique, en conformité avec la stratégie de la mise en valeur des richesses du sol et du sous-sol, selon les cas, la complémentarité était la régle. L'objectif étant de drainer de la façon la plus rentable les productions agricoles et les richesses minières vers les marchés européens et français en particulier. Les lignes de chemins de fer, le Dakar-Niger, L'Abidjan-Niger, et le Cotonou-Niger, que la décolonisation n'a pas permis d'achever, servaient toutes en principe, la logique du "pacte colonial", pour ouvrir les territoires enclavés, sur les ports maritimes. Bien que fondamentalement extraverti, le circuit économique répondait avec cohérence à sa logique structurelle, et fonctionnait à la satisfaction de ses concepteurs. Pour développer les grandes plantations de café et de cacao dans un territoire comme la Côte d'Ivoire sous-peuplée, l'administration instaurera les travaux forcés, pour obliger les jeunes paysans du Burkina Faso à y servir d'ouvriers agricoles. Aujourd'hui ils sont au nombre approximatif des trois millions. Et la Côte d'Ivoire bâti toute son économie d'après l'indépendance sur l'agriculture, principalement l'exportation du café et du cacao, dont il est le premier producteur mondial. Le Sénégal sera spécialisé dans la culture de l'arachide pour l'exportation. Le Mali et le Burkina produiront le coton et exporteront aussi des produits de cueillette comme les noix de karité, dont le beurre sert dans la fabrication des cosmétiques.

Dans la lutte politique contre la colonisation, il s'est même constitué des partis politiques trans-territoriaux, comme le Rassemblement Démocratique Africain, qui regroupait tous les élus des territoires qui siégeaient comme députés ou sénateurs à l'assemblée nationale et au sénat français. L'unité de sort impliquait l'unité de lutte, et la dynamique unitaire était en marche.

Les élites politiques semblaient l'avoir très bien compris, au sortir de la guerre de 1939-1945, mettant à profit cette conjoncture de redistribution des forces, particulièrement favorable.

Mais, comme subitement victimes de la manipulation d'une main invisible, ces "éclaireurs de conscience", n'ont plus cessé, au fur et à mesure qu'approchait l'échéance des indépendances politiques, de s'entre-déchirer, de s'opposer, et de vouloir chacun refuser d'être "la vache à lait", du voisin de toujours. Tous les territoires indépendants vont se croire capables, de se développer chacun sans les autres, pour ne pas dire contre les autres. Aucun des domaines de la vie économique, sociale et politique n'échappera à cette volonté obstinée de diviser et de partager "l'héritage colonial", à commencer par les frontières. Le bilan est celui que nous observons tous aujourd'hui.

Tous ensemble, ou c'est l'impasse encore

Dans le contexte international actuel, marqué autant par la disparition de l'URSS, la montée, en flèche de l'hégémonisme nord américain, la marche presque forcée de l'Europe Communautaire "des douze", et le poids économique du Japon, la croissante marginalisation de l'Afrique (toujours en crise de fragmentation), ne lui laisse plus aucune marge de manoeuvre sur le marché mondial.

L'Europe accapare presque cinquante pour cent (50%) du commerce mondial, et l'Afrique doit se contenter d'un et demi pour cent (1.5%) du marché. L'Afrique est devenue à la faveur du poids de sa dette extérieure (deux cents soixante dix milliards de dollars américains), et des rigueurs "d'orthodoxie" des programmes d'ajustement structurel du Fonds Monétaire International et de la Banque Mondiale, une exportatrice nette de capitaux. Le Continent de toutes les richesses et de toutes les pauvretés partage, avec les autres pays en développement, les maigres cinquante milliards de dollars américains d'aide par an, lorsque leurs besoins réels sont chiffrés à cinq cents milliards, dans le dernier rapport du Programme des Nations Unies pour le Développement:

C'est dix fois moins qu'il n'en faut pour espérer progresser! Faut-il davantage de "preuves", pour montrer qu'à l'évidence, l'esprit du" sauve qui peut individuel", est à abandonner définitivement, pour rechercher les voies et moyens d'une tentative de développement intégré et "à comptes propres"?

C'est en ces termes que le problème de l'intégration régionale se pose aux pays africains dans leur totalité, et à l'Afrique de l'Ouest en particulier. Nous analyserons le cas spécifique d'un des plus pauvres de ces pays, le Burkina Faso, qui a osé seul, se lancer dans une aventure de développement au ras du sol, dans un environnement régional et international ouvertement hostile, de 1983 à 1991.

Bien des pays africains, dans les années 1960, dans l'euphorie des indépendances politiques, conquises souvent au prix de guerres de libération nationale, avec un million de martyrs comme en Algérie, ou négociés (grâce justement à l'expérience algérienne), comme en Afrique de l'Ouest, se sont lancés dans "l'illusion du développement en solitaire". Les recettes d'exportation du café, du pétrole, ou du cuivre, pour ne prendre que ces exemples, procuraient à l'époque, des devises suffisantes pour entretenir dans les esprits des dirigeants politiques et des planificateurs nationaux, l'idée de pouvoir construire des économies nationales fortes et indépendantes. De nombreuses et coûteuses infrastructures, unités industrielles et commerciales ont été réalisées, sur la seule base des potentialités des circuits et des marchés nationaux. Cette stratégie du développement a été celle de presque tous les pays "riches".

A côté, les pays "pauvres", éprouvaient de la peine à se contenter d'être des consommateurs de productions que le pouvoir d'achat de leurs populations ne permettait pas d'acheter. Le plus souvent, les mêmes produits, importés d'Europe ou d'Asie, revenaient moins chers sur les marchés. Ce qui posait et pose toujours un problème de coût de production, et aussi de gestion en Afrique.

Pendant les trente dernières années, le problème de l'intégration économique n'a été dans les faits qu'un slogan politique en Afrique, puisque, en pratique, chaque pays s'occupait exclusivement de ses intérêts "nationaux". Les pays développés de l'Europe de l'Ouest comme de l'Est, les Etats Unis d'Amérique et le Japon, dans la stricte logique de la défense de leurs intérêts économiques et politiques, ont trouvé dans cette situation, des conditions idéales pour renforcer leur influence et affaiblir les échanges économiques, entre pays africains. C'est en toute "souveraineté", et entre partenaires égaux, à la recherche de relations économiques et politiques "mutuellement avantageuses", que tout se négociait et se concluait.

La situation d'ensemble sur le continent était marquée par l'esprit du "sauve qui peut," chez les plus riches comme chez les plus pauvres. C'est dans ce contexte, que le Burkina Faso, à partir du 4 août 1983, avec l'arrivée au pouvoir d'une équipe militaro civile, de jeunes intellectuels de la Gauche Patriotique, va s'engager dans une voie qui mérite d'être mieux connue et comprise:

Le Burkina Faso est un pays de 274,000km², avec une population de plus de dix millions d'habitants. Il est le pays le plus peuplé du Sahel, situé en zone de savane soudano sahélienne. Les paysans burkinabès ont toujours connu des conditions difficiles dans le travail d'une terre ingrate, et insuffisamment arrosée. C'est la raison essentielle du choix de l'administration coloniale française, de supprimer purement et simplement ce territoire en 1936, pour faciliter l'exportation de son potentiel humain (une main d'oeuvre expérimentée) au service des propriétaires de grandes plantations de café et de cacao de la colonie voisine de Côte d'Ivoire. A l'époque, les colonisés n'avaient pas le droit de s'organiser, ni sur le plan syndical, ni sur plan politique. C'est donc les structures du vieil Empire du Mogho (né au Xème siècle) et les chefferies traditionnelles, qui assumeront la résistance à cette injustice, jusqu'à l'adoption de la Constitution de la Cinquième République française, reconnaissant le droit à l'existence des syndicats et des partis politiques africains dans les colonies. Le mouvement nationaliste se développe à vive allure. Pour tenter de contenir cette vague de contestation, l'administration coloniale reconstitue le territoire de la Haute-Volta en 1947, espérant s'appuyer sur le poids politique des chefferies traditionnelles, qui lui devraient cet "acte amical". Le mal était irrémédiablement fait. Et la frustration d'avoir été le parent pauvre de la colonisation, qui a vu expatrier par la force, plus de la moitié de la force de travail du pays, sans aucune compensation en investissements sociaux ou en infrastructures de développement, restera vivace jusqu'à nos jours. Encore plus de trois millions de citoyens burkinabè vivent et travaillent en Côte d'Ivoire aujourd-hui. C'est dire que le Burkina n'a jamais été programmé dans la stratégie de "mise en valeur" de l'Afrique de l'Ouest, pour être développé, mais pour servir au développement des pays côtiers jugés plus rentables. De 1960 à 1983, seule l'aide alimentaire internationale déversée par milliers de tonnes à chaque alerte de famine, servira d'écran humanitaire, pour camoufler les éfforts réels pour décourager toute volonté politique nationale d'atteindre l'auto suffisance alimentaire, et enseigner aux populations à savoir se prendre en charge. La mentalité "d'éternels assistés", commençait à pousser des racines profondes dans les eprits des paysans, qui n'avaient plus aucun intérêt à cultiver des sols ingrats, et produire des céréales, que les dons alimentaires concurrençaient de manière déloyale, sur un marché qu'on réclamait par ailleurs, devoir être "libre et incitateur de productivité plus forte". Tout le programme de développement socio-économique du régime révolutionnaire se résume dans sa volonté politique de renverser cette tendance au développement du sous-développement. Il a fallu s'organiser, dans chacun des sept mille cinq cents villages, pour réussir à créer au sein des populations, un sursaut nationaliste profond (culturel et politique) pour croire en elles-mêmes, au point d'oser chercher et trouver leurs solutions propres à leurs problèmes de développement. L'exemple a été donné dès le départ, au sein de l'Administration et surtout au niveau des dirigeants politiques. Le Président et ses ministres conservaient simplement leurs salaires d'avant l'accession au poste, sans aucune indemnité. Ils devaient payer en plus le téléphone, l'eau, l'électricité et le loyer dans les logements de fonction de l'Etat. Le parc automobile de l'Etat, qui comptait plus de six mille voitures, a été réduit de moitié. Les trois mille voitures les plus luxeuses (donc plus chers à l'entretien) ont été vendues aux enchères publiques avec interdiction aux dirigeants politiques d'en acheter. Chaque ministre a reçu comme voiture officielle une Renault Cinq, non climatisée, avec une dotation de cinquante litres d'éssence par mois. Les frais de mission hors du pays, quelque soit la destination, ont été fixés arbitrairement à trente dollars américains par jour, avec obligation de voyager uniquement en classe économique dans les avions. Tout le pays devait vivre au niveau réel de ses ressources et il a vécu ainsi pendant des années. Les salaires de tous les fonctionnaires, privés comme publics, ont été réduit de vingt à cinq pour cent, pour financer les programmes d'investissements sociaux comme les écoles, dispensaires, ambulances, médicaments, puits et forages, petits barrages et logements sociaux, dont les coûts de réalisation étaient ainsi partagés entre citadins et paysans. Le pays allait connaître ses plus forts taux de croissance économique, surtout dans l'agriculture où, en 1991 encore, il se situat en deuxième position sur tout le continent africain, juste après le Maroc, selon les chiffres de la Banque Mondiale. Le taux de scolarisation qui'était de 14 % en 1983, se trouve aujourd'hui à 30%. La quantité d'eau stockée dans tous les barrages du pays était évaluée à trois cents millions de mètres cubes en 1983. Elle est passée à deux milliards trois cents millions en 1992. Le parc téléphonique du pays est passé de sept mille à quinze mille abonnés entre 1983 et 1992. Chacun des sept mille cinq cents villages du pays possède au moins un poste de santé primaire, même s'ils ne fonctionnent pas tous correctement. Jusqu'en mars 1991, le pays a pu résister au programme d'ajustement structurel, tel que le Fonds Monétaire International et la Banque Mondiale le voulaient. Et il faut souligner que, grâce à la bonne gestion de l'economie et des finances, le Burkina reste un des rares pays de la région, qui n'a jamais cessé de payer régulièrement les salaires de ses fonctionnaires, à chaque fin de mois. Ce ne sont là que quelques exemples des résultats concrets, d'une équipe au pouvoir qui a voulu et qui a pu, mobiliser la population, et la mettre au travail en donnant l'exemple du sacrifice personnel au profit de la collectivité. Mais ce type d'expérience ne peut pas se poursuivre dans un contexte d'isolement politique sous-régional, dans l'hostilité ouverte de pays voisins avec lesquels, il est impossible de rompre les rapports économiques, et même de les réduire substantiellement. Le

Burkina est un pays enclavé, avec six frontières, et situé à mille six cents kilomètres du port maritime le plus proche. Jusqu'en 1983, il n'avait par exemple aucun barrage hydro-électrique, et tout le secteur moderne de son économie dépendait directement des hydrocarbures importés et transitant par les ports voisins. Cela lui vaut jusqu'à nos jours, d'avoir le prix du kilowatt-heure le plus élevé du monde, environ un dollar américain. Le deuxième barrage hydro-électrique du pays est en voie d'achèvement, après le tout premier qui n'a été inauguré qu'en 1987. Rien qu'à cause du coût de l'energie, aucune des unités industrielles ne pouvait être compétitive, ni dans la sous région, ni ailleurs. Le pays est membre de la zone monétaire ouest africaine, lié au franc francais, qui assure la convertibilité du franc CFA, avec une parité fixe. Si la moyenne des échanges économiques entre pays africains est évaluée à 6 %, le Burkina en est à plus de 12 %, avec ses voisins immédiats. Son appartenance à la Banque Centrale des Etats de l'Afrique de l'Ouest, dont il se doit de respecter les règles, l'oblige donc à subir les contrecoups et les difficultés économiques des autres pays membres. Le fruit des éfforts d'assainissement de son économie et de ses finances ne pouvait que se noyer dans les immenses problèmes économiques et financiers que les autres pays connaissaient. Aux "périodes fastes", de certaines économies voisines, le Burkina aussi en profitait, ne serait-ce que par ses millions d'émigrés installés chez ses voisins immédiats comme la Côte d'Ivoire. Il faut donc accepter de renvoyer l'ascenseur, bon gré mal gré!

Cette expérience d'auto-ajustement dans un seul pays, aussi intéressante et riche qu'elle ait été, a surtout permis de révéler l'impossibilité objective, dans laquelle se trouve chaque pays africain, indépendamment de ses potentialités économiques, de sa bonne ou mauvaise gestion financière et politique, de réaliser seul, une quelconque sortie du cercle infernal du sous-développement. Le sauve-qui-peut est impossible. Et même pour valoriser et tirer le maximum de profit des "acquis existants", comme les infrastructures socio-économiques, l'intégration s'impose sur le plan régional comme sur le plan continental. De 1983 à 1991, le Burkina s'est vue refuser tout décaissement de la part de la Banque Mondiale. A cause de son refus d'accepter les diktats, comme celui d'arrêter les travaux de prolongation du "chemin de fer du Sahel", pour désenclaver le Nord désertique du pays et le "point triple", de la frontière avec le Mali et le Niger. Pour les experts de la banque, cet investissement à comptes propres du Burkina n'était pas rentable. Seul le minéral de manganèse dans le Nord du pays pouvait, selon les cours mondiaux, justifier à leurs yeux cette opération. Et les cours mondiaux étaient trop bas. Le Burkina devait abandonner le chemin de fer, et s'en remettre aux bailleurs de fonds, pour lui construire une route bitumée de la capitale (Ouagadougou) à Dori, dans le Nord, comme si le chemin de fer et la route n'ont pas, de tout temps et dans tous les pays été complémentaires. Lors d'un entretien épique avec le ministre burkinabé des relations extérieures et de la coopération, la délégation de la Banque, qui exigeait une réponse claire et nette, a reçu celle ci: "s'il faut choisir entre le chemin de fer et la route, et bien! nous choisissons les deux. Pour un pays enclavé comme le mien, un aéroport et un bras de mer en plus ne nous fera pas de mal!". Ces propos ont été reçus bien sûr comme un crime de lèse-majesté, et le Burkina sera puni en retour. Même l'aide publique au développement (APD) que le pays était en droit d'attendre a été sérieusement réduit de 1983 à 1991. Parmi tous les pays membres du Comité Inter-Etats de Lutte contre la Sécheresse au Sahel (CILSS), le Burkina sera le parent pauvre parmi les pauvres. Les chiffres sont parlants: le Sénégal, a reçu 724 millions de dollars américains en 1990 (soit 99 dollars par habitant), la Mauritanie, 207 millions de dollars américains (soit 102 dollars par habitant), le Tchad, 314 millions de dollars américains (soit 55 dollars par habitant), le Mali, 462 million de dollars américains (soit 50 dollars par habitant), le Niger, 357 millions de dollars américains (soit 49 dollars par habitant), La Guinée Bisau, 118 millions de dollars américains (soit 122 dollars par habitant), et le Burkina, Seulement 305 millions de dollars (soit 34 dollars par habitant). C'est clair. La France refusera d'accorder la moindre facilité au Burkina (y compris l'aide traditionelle pour combler le déficit budgétaire, comme elle l'a toujours fait pour tous les Etats francophones) tant que l'accord de confirmation ne sera pas signé avec le Fonds Monétaire International. Pendant ce temps, tous les bailleurs de fonds multipliaient les pressions et les menaces, pour exiger le strict respect des délais de remboursements de la dette du pays. Le Burkina ne pouvait pas ne pas céder, en mars 1991, avec la signature de l'accord avec les institutions de Bretton Woods. Au moins, cette expérience devrait pouvoir servir de preuve irréfutable, qu'en dehors de l'intégration et de l'étroite coopération entre pays africains, il n'existe aucune voie de salut pour les économies africaines.

Conclusion

Le problème qui est posé aux intellectuels, aux chercheurs, et aux classes politiques dirigeantes de l'Afrique n'est plus celui de discuter de l'opportunité ou non, de la nécessité ou non de l'intégration. La vie et ses réalités quotidiennes ont déjà tranché ce débat. L'urgence se situe au seul niveau de la recherche des meilleures voies et des meilleurs moyens d'y parvenir au moindre coût. Les crises politiques et économiques actuelles seront nos meilleurs éducatrices. Sous nos yeux, les frontières dites "nationales", et les Etats figés dans la logique coloniale, incapables d'ête acceptés des citoyens comme les leurs, s'affirment comme les plus grands obstacles, et à la démocratie et au développement. Nous aurons ici l'occasion d'en débattre en profondeur, pour atteindre les racines du mal. Au moins c'est cet espoir qui m'anime. Seuls le sérieux et l'exactitude scientifique du diagnostic, nous permettront de dégager des voies et moyens réalistes et réalisables de l'intégration africaine, dans un contexte international où s'affrontent paradoxalement, la volonté d'imposer les lois d'un marché unique à tous, et le réveil des nationalistes accrochés aux guerres des frontières.

4

Southern Africa in the 1990s: Problems and Prospects of Regional Cooperation

Ibbo Mandaza

The concept of post-apartheid: an infectious ideology
The primary concern in any discussion on the future of South Africa and the rest of Southern Africa relates to the process whereby the sub-region, so characterized by inherent conflict and antagonistic contradictions, will find peace and security. Designing Southern Africa as one of the areas of *regional conflict* in the world often conceals the specificities of the problems behind a typology that is now the pre-occupation of analysts of international relations. More often than not, such perspectives are given to postulating and proposing solutions that may have little or no bearing to the fundamental questions that constitute the problem itself. Indeed, this is precisely the impression conveyed in most analyses about the current situation in South Africa and all Southern Africa; and accounts for the euphoria that has been generated ever since de Klerk's speech on 2nd February, 1990 and the subsequent release of Nelson Mandela and other political prisoners. There is good reason to celebrate such victories on the part of the National Liberation Movement of South Africa in particular and all progressive humankind in general. But there is a real danger that the euphoria thereby generated at home and abroad might confuse and even conceal the real issues about the conflict in Southern Africa. In this regard, many an African—particularly in South Africa itself—will be justified in concluding that the goal of a non-racial and democratic South Africa is a superimposition of an idealistic international liberalism that has generally been either unable or unwilling to acknowledge the nature and content of the conflict in that country; a mere slogan, nay even an ideology, designed to conceal the fundamental contradictions. Far more disturbing, however, are those analyses which convey the impression that the resolution of the South African Question is anything but the process whereby there has to be addressed the historical, economic and political factors that have together contributed towards the definition of Southern Africa as we know it

today. Such analyses emanate primarily from liberal academicians and politicians in white South Africa; but also from African nationalists in both South Africa and the sub-region, including official circles. A central feature of these analyses and/or expectations is that which is portrayed in the concept of post-apartheid: a non-racial and democratic South Africa; and therefore a new regional order based on closer economic cooperation between South Africa and the other countries of Southern Africa. Hence SADCC itself hopes that a post-apartheid South Africa will soon be a member of SADCC; and on his recent visit (April, 1991) to Europe, F.W. de Klerk wooed potential investors with the promise that the post-apartheid era was at hand, ushering peace and prosperity.

The process whereby such an apocalypse—for that is what it appears to be—will be born is never explained by the protagonist. It is merely presumed. They would not dare suggest even the parameters of such a process lest the dream dissipates in the face of a reality that is already characterized by bloody violence and with the prospects of the bitterest struggle before the apartheid state is overtaken in the emerging new dispensation.

Hence the concept of post-apartheid has become almost an infectious ideology, suggesting thereby that the resolution of the South African Question in particular might even be an overnight process, an outcome that need not take into account the complexities and intricacies that constitute the National Question in that country. There is need therefore to dispel such misconceptions of the historical process which nevertheless constitutes such an important factor as to influence the current debate, perceptions and even policy considerations about the sub-region in general and South Africa in particular. Academic analyses should seek to understand the bases of such thinking, highlighting the main elements in a sub-region so pregnant with crises, and thereby provide a more informed framework through which both the policy-maker and activist can better understand and influence positive change and development.

It is impossible to do justice to the subject in these limited pages[1], but a mere mention of the following major themes might assist in highlighting the main objectives of this brief analysis.

The colonial and national question
First, the analysis of the nature and direction of change in Southern Africa will have to begin with an account of those historical, economic and political factors that have together contributed towards the definition of South Africa and the rest of Southern Africa as we know them today. In short, it is important to remember that the sub-region

was born and has been defined in the course of a colonization process at the hands of Europeans whose main objective was variously that of creating a white dominion in Southern Africa, similar to those that were to constitute Australia, New Zealand and Canada. Such ambitions were inherent in such politico-economic formations as the Union of South Africa, the Federation of Rhodesia and Nyasaland, Portuguese East Africa and Nyasaland, Portuguese East Africa (and including the fact that Angola was treated as a province of Portugal) and British Protectorates of Bechuanaland, Basutoland and Swaziland.

It is, of course, of great political significance—and helps to highlight the major thrust of our analysis—that this colonial dream of a white Southern Africa could not be sustained and, as the current scenario illustrates, is therefore in decline against the wave of African nationalism.

This has been a process of struggle that is both complex and difficult; and given the socio-economic and political structures that arose out of this colonial situation and the capitalist economic system that sought to integrate the entire sub-region into the international capitalist system, the dream—if not the form—of a white dominion remained alive in Southern Africa. In due course, South Africa would be projected in conventional international relations as a definable political sub-system, heavily dependent on a South Africa as both its base and reference point.[2] To some extent, it is difficult to understand the history and development of Southern Africa except in terms of the central position of South Africa. This is due to the economic factors that are represented by the two inter-related broad strands in the colonization process of Southern Africa: that related to the Southern African Customs Union (SACU); and that of the Federation of Rhodesia and Nyasaland. Ironically, it has been on the bases of these two strands that the sub-region appears "integrated" and "unified" in terms of economic relations, trade and infrastructural development in transport (the railways and roads system), communications and energy (e.g. Kariba). To this day the BLS (Botswana, Lesotho and Swaziland) countries depend heavily on South Africa for both "export" of (migrant) labour and earnings from the SACU. Their economies are virtually extensions of South Africa's; and in this category should be included Namibia and Mozambique. Mozambique, a Portuguese colony, had been, from those early days, an outreach of the South African economy, with Lourenco Marques (Maputo) and Beira virtually entrepots in the Southern Africa economic configuration. And as the liberation struggle was intensified in the sub-region in the course of the 1960s and 1970s, it became increasingly the strategy for the white settlers in Southern Rhodesia and Mozambique to depend increasingly on South Africa, economically and militarily. In keeping with its own anti-guerrilla strategy, the South Africa state regarded as vital the need to develop a *cordon sanitaire,* that included not only support of Rhodesia, but also, an alliance with the Portuguese colonialists in their war against the guerrillas in Mozambique and Angola.

It should also be noted that South Africa contributed towards white settlement at the turn of this century in such countries as Namibia, Zimbabwe, Zambia and even Kenya. Just prior to World War I, most of the whites in the Kenyan highlands had come from South Africa, with the intention of creating a "white man's country" modelled on South Africa. Furthermore, South Africa provided almost half of the Europeans in Zambia during the colonial period, compared with only a quarter who came from the UK. This explains partly why the Zambian mining industry developed *pari passu* with the South African economy, largely dependent on South Africa as much for the supply of mining equipment and machinery as for skills, management and general development for most of the colonial period and even well into the post-independence period.

South African sub-imperialism?

These are the factors that have tended to reinforce the concept of South African sub-imperialism: as a regional centre for the maintenance of the economic, political and strategic interests of the imperialist centre; but also relatively independent of the imperialist centre in that its political, economic and military actions will in general coincide with and reflect those of the imperialist power. That was certainly the status and role which the South African state tended to assume throughout most of the 1970s. It was also during this period prior to the intensification of the African Nationalist Struggle that the concept of a Southern African sub-system was assigned by some, permanent and even unassailable status in international relations. To that extent, there was a strong relationship between such analyses[3] as highlighted by this concept of sub-system and those policy-makers in the international arena who believed Southern Africa to be uniquely different from the rest of the African continent. As is illustrated by this well-known sentiment that has, with but few modifications, inspired and informed US policy in Southern Africa, ever since 1969 to the present day, the dream of a white dominion had not died:

> *The whites are here to stay (in Southern Africa) and the only way that constructive change can come about is through them. There is not hope for the blacks to gain the political rights they seek through violence, which only leads to chaos and increased opportunities for the communists. We can, by selective relaxation of our stance toward the white regimes, encourage some modification of their current racial and colonial policies and through more substantial economic assistance to the black states (a total of about $5 million annually in technical assistance to the black states) help to draw the two groups together and exert some influence on both for peaceful change. Our tangible interests form a basis for our contacts in the region, and these can be maintained at an acceptable political cost.[4]*

To what extent this policy became linked subsequently to the emphasis on aid—or even a Marshall Plan—for Southern Africa is a matter for serious consideration with regard to the future of Southern Africa. But it does reflect the extent to which the US, with the assistance of the UK in particular, has become a virtual colonial power over the Southern African situation. As has been pointed out elsewhere, the UK regards itself, in the words of British Prime Minister, Margaret Thatcher, as the 'ex-colonial overlord' in Southern Africa, with a "special responsibility over the sub-region".[5] The fact that the UK (and other Commonwealth countries) have offered Mozambique and Namibia (and now also South Africa itself), the opportunity to join the Commonwealth is only another indication that the boundaries of this "ex-colonial empire" are meant to, or are perceived as, transcending the borders of the former British colonies in Southern Africa.

Essentially, however, South Africa's objective had been to try and roll back the liberation process; to forestall for all time the possibility of black majority in South Africa by intimidating the neighbouring black states, seeking to extend its influence throughout Africa through its "dialogue' policy" of the 1970s, and attempting to impose an "economic community" in the form of the Constellation of Southern African States (CONSAS). Announced in March, 1979, the CONSAS proposal sought to develop a common approach in the fields of security and political matters between South Africa, the "homelands", members of SACU and in due course, other countries in the region. This was South Africa's version of regional cooperation, a spectre that would have pre-empted SADCC were it not for changing relation and balance of forces associated with the demise of the apartheid state. This process of the decline of the apartheid state was most discernible from the time of the Portuguese coup of 1974, to the independence of Mozambique and Angola in 1975, the Soweto Uprising in 1976, Zimbabwe independence in April, 1980, and the birth of SADCC in the same year. Likewise, the political objectives—often forgotten by analysts who have tended to view destabilization as an end in itself—of South African destabilization of neighbouring states remained far from fruition as the Frontline SADCC States were now able to gain the sympathy of even those of the Western world that have been the main bulwark of the South African state. By the end of the 1980s, Mozambique began to recover from more than a decade of incessant strife and depression; and the Angolan civil war was drawing to a close, with South Africa itself thoroughly disgraced and compelled to sue for peace in an agreement that also brought Namibia's independence in 1990. Conversely, the South African state acknowledged that policies of "total onslaught" and destabilization constituted total failure, terminated the mandate of the man (Botha)—and his "hawks"—who had made this policy almost his sole mission, and, under a new leader (de Klerk) began to accept the possibility of black majority rule in South Africa.

Second, that the colonial situation constitutes the National Question. Therefore, those analysts so keen to gloss over this historical fact behind various post-apartheid scenarios, will need to be reminded, in the first instance, of what white domination in South Africa and the rest of Southern Africa has meant historically, politically, economically, socially and culturally. There is no need to elaborate these herein; and some of the more central features of the National Question will become evident in the subsequent section of this paper. But even a casual reference to South Africa should indicate that the process of change in that country is going to be a much more painful and tumultuous than the post-apartheid ideologues would have the world believe. It is an outcome likely to contradict all the predictions of a non-racial democratic society, of a benign new post-apartheid regional order. Therefore, those genuinely interested in the resolution of both national and regional questions will need to examine carefully the factors that constitute those questions. Certainly the resolution of those questions will have to mean a re-definition of both South Africa and Southern Africa. The current ideology of post-apartheid seeks only to re-interpret the very historical, political, economic and social factors that have together contributed to, and constituted, the Colonial and National Questions. We return to this theme shortly.

Resolving the national question: the role of the frontline states

Reference has already been made to the conventional US policy in Southern Africa, based as it was on the belief that Blacks could not gain political rights through violence and that only through a combination of persuading the Whites and influencing the Black states through economic aid could constructive and non-violent change be attained in Southern Africa. Related to this was the need to maintain the sub-region under the zone of influence of the US and its allies, and thereby also to keep the Soviet Union and its allies out of the area. The latter stance will have been substantially modified in the light of the recent US-Soviet detente, particularly the Soviet Union's willingness to work with the US in resolving such areas of regional conflict as Southern Africa. To what extend the US and its allies might have now acknowledged the fact that it is the struggle of the African peoples that has wrought the immense changes of the last two decades is, perhaps, evident in the extent to which the apartheid state is increasingly viewed as a pariah throughout the international community and is being compelled to face the need to change. We might speculate as to what that process of change might portend for South Africa in general. But that there is underway a process of profound change cannot be denied. The nature and direction of that change has to be assessed in the context of a struggle whose objectives are implicit if not explicit: the resolution of the National Question. We shall return to this central theme. But here it is important to outline briefly the role of the Frontline States and how, in the course of the African national struggle of which they were an integral part, they constitute an important factor in both the nature and change in Southern Africa.

A broad historical scan will show that the concept of frontline states was born out of the Organization of African Unity (OAU) and its Liberation Committee, and on the basis of Tanzanian's role as the main rear base of the liberation struggle in Southern Africa. There is no doubt that many an African had by the late 1960s become quite disillusioned at Africa's failure to deal with the white settler regimes of Southern Africa. This weakness and failure became glaringly embarrassing on the occasion of UDI, high-lighting the fact that members of the OAU—individually and collectively—could not deal with "little Rhodesia", except only if the imperialist powers themselves decided that something had to be done. As has been illustrated elsewhere, [6] this reliance on imperialism, this tendency to appeal to the conscience of the international community on issues pertaining to racism and white settler rule in Southern Africa, is one that has pervaded the foreign policy of African states, including that of the Frontline States as a vital base for the struggle in Southern Africa was a great improvement on anything that the OAU's Liberation Committee might have been able to accomplish without that grouping of Southern African States.

Tanzania and Zambia were the first two states to constitute the grouping that now stands at six, with Botswana joining in or about 1975, Mozambique and Angola at the attainment of independence in June and November 1975 respectively, and Zimbabwe at the attainment of its independence in 1980. The close liaison between Tanzania and Zambia developed out of their commitment—particularly on the part of the two leaders, Julius Nyerere and Kenneth Kaunda—to the liberation of the rest of the African continent. From the 1960s onwards, Tanzania was already becoming the rear base for those liberation movements intent on waging war against the settlers in Mozambique, Angola, Zimbabwe, Namibia and South Africa. Zambia would likewise accept the responsibility at the attainment of her independence in 1964. Zambia's independence created a glaring contrast with a Southern Africa that was not only firmly under white settler colonial rule but, as seen with reference to South Africa and Southern Rhodesia during this period, also determined to stay white for all time. Because of its leader's strong stand against both UDI in particular and white racial domination in general, Zambia earned the wrath of both Southern Rhodesia and South Africa. This is the sacrifice that Zambia had to endure as she continued to provide support and a resource base for the struggle that would intensify for two decades or more. It is understandable why Tanzania became directly involved in trying to cushion and support Zambia which was more directly in the firing line of the white settler states south of it.

Tanzania and Zambia had been members of the Conference of Heads of State and Government of East and Central Africa which, in regular meetings dating back to the first in March 1966, sought "to encourage better regional relations and to coordinate their policies, particularly with regard to Southern African question."[7] For six years hence Malawi and Zaire (then Congo Kinshasa) constituted part of what might then have been viewed as the Southern Africa delegation to a conference that consisted mostly of those of Eastern Africa and was designed to mobilize independent black Africa behind the liberation movement (See Table 1). The Conference group was designed to be smaller and less diverse than the OAU and included those states of black Southern Africa—e.g. Swaziland and Lesotho and, at least during the 1960s also Botswana—whose governments were more vulnerable to South African pressure. A major policy announcement on the part of this group during this period was the "Manifesto on Southern Africa" or the Lusaka Manifesto which was concluded by the Fifth Summit Conference of East and Central African States held in Lusaka, Zambia, 14-16 April, 1969.

Essentially, the manifesto drew a distinction between, on the one hand, the situation of Southern Rhodesia and the Portuguese colonies of Angola and Mozambique (and also Guinea Bissau), all of which necessitated armed struggle; and on the other the South African situation about which it made no reference to armed struggle, only calling for a policy of boycotting the apartheid state.[8] Many would argue that the distinction tended to suggest that South Africa was already an independent state and not a white settler state; and that, therefore, the issue about which the (non-violent) struggle had to be waged in that country was about democracy and human rights. This is a matter of controversy to this day; and will have affected to some extent both the strategy and direction of the liberation struggle in South Africa. No doubt the Lusaka Manifesto reflected Zambia's precarious position as she sought to manoeuvre in an environment of threats and intimidation from the white settler regimes south of it. Every attempt on the part of Zambia to reduce its dependence on South Africa and thereby enhance the boycott was regarded as an "act of aggression" by South Africa and Southern Rhodesia. This was further complicated by the UDI issue and the growing collusion between South Africa and Southern Rhodesia, and the South African militarization of the Caprivi Strip as a response to the growing number of South Africans (and Zimbabwe) who were undergoing military training, particularly from the mid-1960s onwards. Zambia would remain a dependent economic partner of South Africa. She would gradually loosen this legacy of dependence but only at a great cost to her economy. Following her decision to impose sanctions against Rhodesia, Zambia suffered directly as the cost of alternative sources of imports soared. The TAZARA Railway was a considerable respite for landlocked Zambia; but it reflected more her sense of political commitment to the struggle than an economically viable alternative route for exports and imports. With time, Zambia became more and more vulnerable to pressures from the white settler regimes, until even the Southern African liberation struggle as a whole became threatened and experienced several setbacks in the course of this difficult period.

Table 1: *Summit Conferences of Heads of State and Government of East and Central African States*

Date	Place	Southern Africa delegates	Chief issues
March 31– April 2, 1966	Nairobi	Pres. Nyerere, Pres. Kaunda Pres. Mobutu, Malawi's minister of Transport and Communications John Msonthi	Rhodesia, liberation of Southern Africa, refugees and border incidents
February 12–14, 1967	Kinshasa	Pres. Kaunda, Pres. Mobutu Tanzania's 2nd Vice Pres. Rashidi Kawawa, Malawi absent	Rhodesia, liberation of Southern Africa, aggression of white regimes, implementation of group decisions
December 15–16, 1967	Kampala	Pres. Kaunda, Pres. Nyerere Pres. Mobutu, Malawi absent	Mercenaries, economic and technical cooperation, security
May 13–15 1968	Dar es Salaam	Pres. Kaunda, Pres. Nyerere Malawi's Minister of State for External Affairs	Nigeria, Southern Africa, attempted coup in Congo (Brazzaville)
April 14–16 1969	Lusaka	Pres. Kaunda, Pres. Nyerere Malawi's Minister of State Nyasulu, Congo's minister	Liberation of Southern Africa (Lusaka Manifesto), Nigeria
January 26–28, 1970	Khartoum	Pres. Kaunda, Tanzania's minister, Malawi's Minister of Agriculture Richard Chidzanga	Aid to liberation movements, regional cooperation, Middle East
October 18–19 1971	Mogadishu	Pres. Nyerere, Zambia's Vice-Pres. Mark Chona a Malawi Ambassador Congolese delegation	Malawi membership Southern Africa (Mogadishu Declaration), Middle East
September 7–9, 1972	Dar es Salaam	Pres. Nyerere, Pres. Kaunda Zaire's minister, Malawi's minister	Support for armed liberation struggle, Middle East

Source : Africa Research Bulletin, Vols. III–IX (1966–72). Cited in Kenneth Grundy, Confrontation and Accommodation in Southern Africa: The Limits of Independence, 1973, p.114

The *Lusaka Manifesto* was in a sense an expression of solidarity with Zambia. But as has just been explained, these were difficult times. The white settlers regimes appeared still unassailable and, as has been illustrated with reference to US policy during this period, the international community was still of the belief that white settler rule was to be a permanent feature of Southern Africa. South Africa's policy of "dialogue" had made some inroads into the African camp, and by the end of the 1970s, Malawi in particular had moved much closer to South Africa "than had ever been thought possible between a black government and apartheid South Africa."[9] And even though conciliatory and moderate in tone, the Lusaka Manifesto was not endorsed by Malawi; and she proceeded to maintain diplomatic and economic relations with the settler regimes, including participation in the Cabora Bassa hydro-electric project in Mozambique. Subsequently, a meeting of the Conference in Mogadishu in 1971 tried in vain to have Malawi expelled from the Conference organization itself. But the same meeting succeeded in adopting the "Mogadishu Declaration" which, in rejecting the idea of dialogue and committing itself to the armed struggle against apartheid South Africa, superseded the Lusaka Manifesto. Malawi, Burundi, the Central Africa Republic and Kenya did not fully endorse this declaration.[10]

It would appear that these events helped to precipitate the development of a more well-defined grouping of states that were fully committed to the Liberation Struggle in Southern Africa. Botswana now began its "northward-looking" policy. At the UN in 1969, President Seretse Khama expressed Botswana's new stand in his endorsement of the Lusaka Manifesto and in calling for the continuation of sanctions against Rhodesia.[11] But he was even more outspoken in his opposition to apartheid and in his assertion that Botswana was an independent Africa State and not a "Bantustan", in a speech in 1970.

> Botswana is not a Tribal Homeland, based on ethnic exclusiveness and the separation of races, but a non-racial democracy which rejects all forms of apartheid and racial discrimination wherever they are applied... it would not accord with Botswana's principles or our interests to accept aid from South Africa... Doubtless the South African authorities do not relish our criticism of apartheid, but neither do we care for the arguments they advance in favour of racial separation which cast doubt on the viability of our non-racial society.[12]

The speech concluded with an attack on the Cabora Bassa project (and European support for it) which, Khama said, was "designed to perpetrate Portuguese colonialism, and threatens further to strengthen the links between South Africa on the one hand and Mozambique and Rhodesia on the other". He also supported the armed struggle "when all other paths were closed" to the people of Southern Africa; and condemned Western arms supplies to South Africa.[13] Botswana proceeded to request the US government to finance a joint Zambia-Botswana road link between the two countries.

The South African government protested that Zambia and Botswana government had no common border. The Botswana government insisted that there was a common border, although it was not defined.[14]

That link through Kazungula is now a reality; and by the mid-1970s, Botswana had established air links with Zambia. Furthermore, Botswana continued to assert her independence, "to obvious South African displeasure", by establishing diplomatic relations with the Soviet Union.[15]

By the turn of the 1970s, therefore, Botswana was overtly within that group of states that would soon become the Frontline States. Throughout the 1970s, and to this day, Botswana has played an invaluable role in its support for the liberation struggle in Southern Africa. Unobtrusively and always modest in their conduct, the Botswana people have provided refuge to thousands of refugees from Angola, South Africa, Namibia and Zimbabwe. By 1971, there were already about 4,000 such refugees in Botswana.[16] Like Zambia and other Frontline States that were variously victims of South African destabilization, Botswana has suffered overt and covert intimidation at the hands of the apartheid state. But she succeeded in proving that the historically-based dependence on South Africa does not necessarily preclude an African nation's desire to stand and be counted in the liberation process that is Southern Africa today.

In many respects therefore, Botswana's example will have been an important catalyst in drawing those countries of Southern Africa even more compromised to South Africa than herself to Black Africa. It was a significant achievement of the Frontline States, and the struggle that they have supported in the sub-region, that Botswana should have become Chairman and headquarters of SADCC. That Lesotho and Swaziland were able to join the organization is also credit to the leaders of the Frontline States. The decision to include under SADCC even those who were either so historically compromised to South Africa or found it expedient to sup with the devil, has no doubt brought more positive results than one that might have sought to exclude such countries as Malawi, Swaziland and Lesotho. For, the essence of SADCC lies particularly in the extent to which it has been a Pan Africanist force, seeking to mobilize the African states of Southern Africa into a concerted opposition to the apartheid state and thereby strengthen the forces of resistance in South Africa.

From the time that they were formally constituted in 1975, the Frontline States met almost regularly, mainly in Dar es Salaam or Lusaka, but also in Gaborone and Maputo. Because of the Angolan conflict, meetings would be held in Luanda only at a later stage; and Maputo became another regular venue as the Zimbabwe question dominated the scene for most of the late 1970s. But the main task of the Frontline States was to coordinate efforts, resources and strategy, with regard to the National Liberation Movements of Southern Africa. This also involved not only the settlement of conflicts or thorny issues within and between the movements, as the case might have been; but also providing the negotiating strategy and policy framework with which to confront the imperialist process and/or white settler regimes themselves. For example, the dominant issue in 1975 was the Angolan crisis about which the Frontline States (then of Tanzania, Zambia and Botswana and Mozambique) had to reach a decision, in late 1975, whether to back MPLA as opposed to UNITA and FNLA. The Angolan problem is one that still occupies the attention of the Frontline States to this day. But the situation could have been much worse were it left to individual members of the Frontline States to decide upon whom they might support in the conflict. At the end of the day, UNITA alliance with South Africa left little or no choice to members in deciding on whom to support.

The Frontline States were also responsible for the formation of the Zimbabwe Patriotic Front. The process began after the crisis in ZANU in 1975, when ZANU National Chairman, Herbert Chitepo, was assassinated in March 1975. It required the intervention of the Frontline States —soon to be joined later that year by Mozambique—in ensuring that the guerillas were provided with the means and policy direction with which to continue the struggle, while the leadership issue was being resolved. This led to the formation of the "Third Force" or the Zimbabwe People's Army (ZIPA), designed to be a united front of the guerrillas of ZANU and ZAPU. When that attempt at a united front failed in the course of 1976, the Frontline States prepared the ground for a joint ZANU-ZAPU line up at the Geneva Conference on Zimbabwe in late 1976. The Patriotic Front of ZANU and ZAPU was born in the course of the period beginning with that Conference. At any rate, from 1977 onwards the Patriotic Front was a reality. But it required the constant attention of the Frontline States—now consisting of Tanzania, Zambia, Botswana, Mozambique and Angola—during the last three years that saw the Patriotic Front emerge the victors in 1980.

Thereafter, Zimbabwe also joined the ranks of the Frontline States which, since 1978, had been dealing with the Namibia Question, particularly the evolution of Resolution 435 on the basis of which Namibia would be born in 1990. Currently, the Frontline States are concentrating their efforts towards the South African Question. There has been the criticism that the Frontline States appear to have lost the initiative not only with respect to South Africa but also with regard to the final stages of the Namibia Question. But the Namibia Question was tied to both the South African Question itself and to the whole issue of the balance of forces in the sub-region, centred as they were for most of the

1980s, on the conflict in Angola. To that extent, the Angolan, Namibian and South African Questions were together immeasurably more complex than any problem that the Frontline States had had to deal with hitherto. As has already been pointed out, the Frontline States did not—and could not be expected to—have a leverage entirely independent of the superpowers whose involvement in the sub-region tended to render matters even more complex. Success for the position and strategy of the Frontline States invariably relied on their ability to manoeuvre between and within the various external forces impinging on a particular problem; with the sole purpose of ensuring that the final goal—Black Majority Rule—would be achieved in those countries concerned, in the shortest possible period and with the least cost of lives and resources, particularly for both the National Liberation movements and the Frontline States themselves.

In general, the Frontline States succeeded in the difficult mission that they have almost completed. For, it is a key submission of this study that the Frontline States constitute the political basis upon which SADCC would become an African issue in 1980. As just stated in the foregoing, it was through the leadership of the Frontline States that the other states of Southern Africa—namely Lesotho, Swaziland and Malawi—were brought into the broader fraternity. This achievement alone contributed significantly to the death of the CONSAS idea and enhanced the isolation of the apartheid regime in both the sub-region and internationally. By involving the National Liberation Movements in their deliberations, the Frontline States laid a stronger foundation for the regional integration and cooperation with new nations-to-be. Not surprisingly, the birth of SADCC took place at about the same time as the attainment of national independence in Zimbabwe. Newly independent Namibia has naturally become the tenth Member State of SADCC; and all Heads of State of the Frontline and SADCC Member States acknowledge that the liberation of South Africa, and her logical accession to SADCC, will constitute a major advance towards SADCC original goal of regional cooperation and integration in Southern Africa. As we speculate elsewhere,[17] it is possible that the cumulative experience of both the Frontline and SADCC Member States might one day result in a *Federation of Southern African States or a Southern African Economic Community.* These developments represent an important phase in the process of resolving the *National Question,* even if viewed only in the context of the well-known objectives of African Nationalism and its continental of a liberated Africa. Hence the need to acknowledge the role of the OAU, its Liberation Committee and the Frontline States.[18] Even if not publicly acknowledged, (for a variety of reasons relating to legal jargon and political tactics designed to mobilize and appease anti-apartheid elements outside the main African nationalist stream), by either some members of the National Liberation Movements of South Africa or even the Frontline States themselves, the objective was to establish an independent African state in South Africa, no different in status from either Ghana, Zimbabwe or Tanzania.

The process of change in South Africa

No doubt, the future of Southern Africa still hinges heavily on what happens in South Africa. But the resolution of the South African Question has such national, regional and global dimensions that it cannot be viewed in isolation from these.

The first scenario was based on the belief that South Africa would be free, based on a negotiated settlement that would forestall violence and leave things very much as they were. Central to this process will be the inter-related issues of the protection of the white minority and safeguards for the economy. This might give rise to two other developments about which SADCC will be concerned. First, the supersession of the current SADCC efforts towards economic cooperation and integration, by the older and more tightly knit economic grouping that is the Southern African Customs Union (SACU); or, at least, a collapsing into one of both the SADCC and CONSAS idea. Conceptually, SADCC and CONSAS might not be so "mutually exclusive" or "mortal enemies" as some of the SADCC protagonists once thought.[19] But with South Africa free, there will be more reason for reconciliation than for antagonism between the SADCC concept on the one hand and the CONSAS and/or SACU concept on the other. The issue will hinge, surely, on which of the two conceptions will have developed form and content at the time that South Africa is welcomed—possibly even before formal liberation— into the community of nations. Certainly, none of the BLS (Botswana, Lesotho and Swaziland) countries—and including newly independent Namibia—has so far shown any intention of relaxing its commitment to SACU; and the other neighbouring member states appear compelled inexorably, by their own economic problems, into increased trade and economic linkages with South Africa. Indeed, there is even the tendency for many of the leaders of the SADCC member states to expect that the economic situation in their countries will improve immeasurably with the liberation of South Africa.

Viewed in this context, the oft-cited tension between SADCC and PTA might become meaningless. Southern Africa—and South Africa in particular—might well become the dominant trading partner for the East African countries of the PTA, with the central vein of the PTA/SADCC overlap constituting an important conduit within that overall economic relationship. In turn, this might complicate, or at least modify, both the conception of the OAU's Lagos Plan of Action (LPA) and the definition of the Eastern and Southern African sub-regions as we know them today. There are real possibilities for the development of a broad and loosely based economic and trading configuration of Eastern and Southern Africa, centred on South Africa and the existing SADCC, but extending as far afield as the old East African Community (Kenya, Uganda and Tanzania), and including Zaire and the islands in the Indian Ocean. Thus, the current efforts of both the SADCC and PTA might help draw together two apparently disparate but otherwise umbilically connected sub-regions, to the exclusion of those countries that have been traditionally and historically viewed as outside the British and English-speaking sphere of influence. But it will be a development that will be an outcome of the weight of the Western interest that has characterized the history of Eastern and Southern Africa; and the political solidarity and fusion that has been generated over the years between the African states in this area. Obviously, such an "economic community" of Eastern and Southern Africa will, for the foreseeable future, remain definitely a satellite of the northern hemisphere; and even smaller number of whites who will remain in Southern Africa will continue to wield disproportionate and immense economic power and influence. But not before the unfolding events in South Africa has been played out fully.

This leads us to the second scenario which is not a radical departure from the first, except that it is based on the real likelihood that a negotiated settlement in South Africa will only be the beginning of a process that will be bloody and protracted. Indeed our analysis cannot share the unbridled optimism of those analysts who see a millennium in post-apartheid Southern Africa. Ours is a bridled pessimism based on an objective analysis of the historical process in South Africa, and in the realization that much remains to be done before liberation and peace is born in that country. That process of change—towards the National Question—has begun , there can be no doubt. But the nature and pace of that process is synonymous with political struggle and the means whereby the African nationalist leaders increase and build on their capacity to outmanoeuvre the South African state. The history of white settler colonialism in Southern Africa has so far demonstrated that its defeat is not a one-day event, ending with the establishment of a black-ruled state under the Black Majority Rule, for, even the process of establishing and developing the new state is fraught with danger; the combined lobby of the white factor and an international community that is largely antithetical to the demands of both African nationalism and the resolution of the National Question, invariably compels the new state into all kinds of concessions some of which become causes for internal conflict and the gradual erosion of the legitimacy and power of the post-white settler colonial state.

These are the questions that now confront the African people of South Africa and Southern Africa:

How to rectify three centuries of colonial and racial domination without upsetting the very historical , political and economic bases upon which the Southern Africa sub-system has been built! How, on the one hand, to seek to resolve the Land Question in a country in which 87% is owned and occupied by a white minority that constitutes only 4% of the population and, on the other, still hope to leave the structure of production intact. How to address the problem of wages and improved conditions of living for the mass of the people while ensuring that the rate of capitalist exploitation and economic growth remains constant. How to pursue the democratization of the education and health systems without building a budget deficit that will in turn distort the economy and enhance unemployment and social unrest. In short, how to pursue the objectives of liberation—including that of the restoration of the dignity of the African person after centuries of white domination—to its logical conclusion without falling victim to white-mail at home and abroad.

As already stated, the resolution of all these questions involves a process of struggle. But it is one that has to be seen, by the various sections of the African constituency, to be in progress if the new state is to gain legitimacy and thereby provide the basis for national development. And as has been demonstrated in Zimbabwe, it is not a process necessarily synonymous with that towards socialism; but it does relate to those crucial questions that the history of African nationalism has brought to the fore throughout the continent. However, the fallacy of most liberal and even some radical analyses of the South African and Southern African situation has been to refuse to acknowledge that the process as one emanating out of the need to resolve a National and Colonial Question; and therefore one leading to National independence. For example, such concepts as "internal colonialism" (or "colonialism of a special type") represent the kind of attempts by some analysts to dodge the issue. Likewise, the convenient and expedient position whereby the main objective of the struggle in South Africa is viewed not as National Liberation/National Independence (because South Africa is said to have attained independence in 1910) but as "non-racial democracy". Related to this kind of reasoning is that viewpoint which, reluctant as it is to acknowledge black nationalism and the national question, posits a dichotomy between national independence and socialism.

Accordingly, the current process in South Africa is one that is likely to be most painful before that country—and the sub-region as a whole—expects to see peace and security. First, the scourge of violence will escalate to greater proportions, inevitably developing into the black-white confrontation, before it subsides. This relates to the manner in which the new dispensation might unfold in South Africa. The growing violence among the black people themselves is not incidental; it relates to the growing competition and contention as various groups bid for a piece of the cake in the new dispensation. So a major objective of the African nationalists in South Africa will be to find the best formula on the basis of which to contain and accommodate all contending factors among themselves. For, unless this is done soon, we can expect worst internecine violence and the possible development of "bandit" and "dissident" movements in South Africa. Already, elements in the apartheid regime are working hard at such a course of events, if only to ensure that the emergent African state invariably finds itself so compromised and forced to concede economic and constitutional guarantees for the white minority, as almost a precondition for attaining and sustaining state power. In the meantime, the white exodus will have gained momentum, especially on the part of those in the professional classes; those not yet in their prime of their working lives and therefore can start anew in Australia, New Zealand or Canada; and the youth whose opportunities must necessarily decline as they face greater and greater competition from their black counterparts in a free South Africa. There are no available statistics on the current rate of white emigration in South Africa; and, as in the Zimbabwe situation, these will never be reliable since prospective emigrants always hedge their bets, leaving initially as if on vacation and therefore allowing themselves the option of returning should the grass be not so greener on the other side. But the current estimates are that out of the 250 000 whites who had remained in Zimbabwe by the time of independence, there are now only 60 000. There are the obvious positive results of a situation wherein a good number of such emigrants might be die-hard racists and potential saboteurs in a new South Africa. In Zimbabwe, the flight of Rhodesian soldiers, policemen and other sections of the public and private sectors left room for the new government to manoeuvre in what were exceptionally difficult and trying times. But then Zimbabwe was in the fortunate position of having thousands of returning exiles, many of them highly skilled and, in many cases, even more qualified and experienced than the previous Rhodesian incumbents.[20] Unlike the situation in South Africa, where the Bantu education system of the last thirty years or more has been synonymous with the systematic underdevelopment and deprivation of the intellectual potential of the African people, the Zimbabwean situation was immensely less bleak and the Africans managed somewhat to overcome some of the enormous obstacles that white settler colonialism placed in the face of educational and economic development.

Therefore, it is not difficult to imagine the serious dearth of professional skills among the African people of South Africa. For example, there are only about 700 black lawyers in South Africa, in a total population of some 28 million blacks in that country.[21] By comparison, the University of Zimbabwe has produced as many lawyers—if not more—in the period since the attainment of independence. Given the industrial base of South Africa, there will be no shortage of artisan skills even though this is still concealed under a racial system which is designed to under-categorize skills among the African people. But there is real cause for concern when one considers the potential in the professional fields. The new South Africa will require that there be a reasonable correlation between Black Majority Rule and a black presence in all the sectors of the economy, particularly the state sectors. Failure to effect this will have obvious implications, as was the case, to some extent, in Zimbabwe, and more glaringly in Namibia: it lends the new government towards all kinds of compromises in the name of maintaining "high standards" and "efficiency", with the resultant continuity in white control of the economy and in the general direction of society. It is not surprising that the apartheid regime—and their allies in the international field—insist on guarantees for both the (white) minority and the economy. The two are very interrelated and in effect constitute the spectre which the post-white settler colonial situation in Southern Africa will, for the foreseeable future, find difficult to shirk. The second factor in our consideration follows closely on the foregoing. The new South African government will have to devote immensely more resources towards the social uplift of the mass of the people who have up to now been on the extreme opposite of the kind of luxury that the average white person has enjoyed. Indeed any emergent African government worth its salt will have to attend at least to these immediate demands of the people: education and human resource training; health facilities; betterment of wages and conditions of living; and so on and so forth. As in Zimbabwe, it will find this exercise relatively easier in the social developments field than in the economic sphere. But it will have serious economic repercussions all the same; and, in turn, these will have obvious social and political ramifications. To begin with, it will mean larger and larger budgetary allocations for the social development sphere; and an inevitable dent on the economy as wages will necessarily have to be raised and the profit margin reduced for local and foreign investors alike. Related to this is the possibility of a very large public service sector which, in the circumstances of newly established African States, is both inevitable and necessary: as part of the nation building exercise and therefore the need to have represented, at both the Cabinet and other structural levels, various sections of the community; as the means whereby the new state which, lacking control of the economic sphere, will have to devise the "public sector" approach and thereby extend its arena of intervention, while simultaneously creating avenues of employment for the blacks in an economy so characterized by gross inequalities and the "colour bar"; and in response to the demands of the social development sector that will obviously need more and more civil servants in the form of local government employees, teachers, health workers, etc. Obviously, all these and other demands will crease numerous other unforeseeable strains and stresses in the social and economic formation. But it does help to emphasize that South Africa is both a Third World country and just as dependent.

On the basis of these two related factors alone, the next decade is going to be a very rough one for South Africa. Contrary to predictions about a bonanza in the post-apartheid period, the road to that post-apartheid era itself will be necessarily bloody and protracted; and the cost of rectifying history and all its inequalities will necessarily be expensive and costly. It is a scenario of strife, a deepening economic crisis, and a general decline of an economy that has so far appeared to be so indispensable to the development of Southern Africa as a whole. This will be inevitable if South Africa is to become truly free and hope to rise again to be the giant that it ought to be. Of course, such a scenario might project a South Africa not so powerful and central to the region, but one which is as dependent as its neighbours and therefore more amenable in a new SADCC. Where does this leave SADCC and our dream of an economic community of Southern Africa by the year 2000?

Towards a southern African economic community?

There would appear at least three factors against which to consider this question. The first is political in that there has to be a consensus, among the member states concerned, that there is need for cooperation. The history of Southern Africa lends itself to the kind of political symbiosis that might not have been experienced in any other sub-region of the world. The quest for political unity is derived from the continental dream of African Unity; but it is reinforced by the particular historical experience that is Southern Africa. Yet, while real in its sentiment and objective, political unity can be a variable factor, depending on changing historical circumstances. Today, the political unity among the African states of the sub-region is based as much on the common historical experience of white racial domination as on the joint objective of liberating South Africa. To that extent, both the Frontline and SADCC concepts arise from the immediacy of that political objective. It is difficult to assess the extent to which this feeling of union in action will be sustained after this immediate goal has been attained.

There is talk about the possibility of a Federation of Southern Africa[22] once South Africa is liberated. But this remains still on the sentimental level, presumed rather than considered. The history and development of the so-called nation-state in Africa so far demonstrates such a high level of insecurity at the national level as would defy Federal schemes across territorial boundaries. Not until the national question is linked closely to the economic question, requiring that there be the minimum conditions that constitute a national economy which, in turn, can with confidence interact with other national economies. The current picture of a continent, marked by uneven and unequal development within and between its individual countries, is sufficient proof that real continental or sub-regional unity is still but a dream. The Organization of African Unity might stagger on as it has so far on the basis of a loosely organized assembly of nations, constituting an important lobby within the wider assembly of nations that is the United Nations. Likewise, such sub-regional organizations as SADCC, PTA or ECOWAS; even though we are likely to see the emergence of loosely based Federations in these sub-regions.

This brings us to the second factor, namely the legal and institutional arrangements that are the pre-requisite for organizational development and cohesion. It is pertinent to note that even the major actors in SADCC concede with incredible relish that the organization has survived so far—as loosely based as it is—precisely because there has been no premature attempt to weld it into a legal and structural component. There is currently talk about developing a legal framework—perhaps even a Treaty—which would render the SADCC more centralized around a Secretariat. The latter will thereby be assigned more power, with the member states having to forego absolute sovereignty within the kind of reciprocity that such a framework would require. However, the desire to establish a stronger organizational and institutional framework reflects mainly the concern, on the part of the remaining founders of SADCC, that the organization might lose the political solidarity that has so far helped it on, and flounder in the hands of subsequent generations that will have lost sight of the original objectives. For, there is so far no attempt to design a framework that will extend the interest in SADCC, beyond the forum of Heads of States; nor any serious consideration as to the mechanisms, whereby SADCC will deal with a free South Africa. All this is quite understandable given the history of regional organizations. Therefore it is unlikely any new organizational and institutional framework will in any substantive manner equate even the East African Community model. As will be recalled, the latter had the following elements which assigned it an immensely high level of cooperation and integration than SADCC:

> A Treaty which put cooperation between the partner states on a firm footing of mutual advantage, and not simply a paper over the cracks in the old structure for administering community institutions and providing measures to achieve an acceptable distribution of the benefits of cooperation between the states. The main features were: the introduction of a device known as the transfer tax to give limited protection for industries in the less-developed states against competition from those in the more-developed; the establishment of an East African Development Bank (EADB) which was to allocate its investments disproportionately in favour of Tanzania and Uganda; the relocation of the headquarters of some of the common services, including the community secretariat, so that they were not concentrated in Kenya.[23]

It is the usual argument of those who are opposed to this kind of model for SADCC to state that the EAC foundered precisely because of this "rigid" institutional framework. But such arguments are likely to be either rationalizations to conceal deep-seated "natural" interests, or a reflection of the ignorance about the issues raised herein with regard to the historical development of the so-called nation-state in Africa. The point, however, is that SADCC it is unlikely to become a cooperative and integrative agency that it purports to be until it establishes an institutional framework similar to that of the

EAC or the EEC. That it will not be able to do so for the foreseeable future has less to do with the exercise of individual choices on the part of the member states than with the historical reality wherein most of these countries have not yet resolved the national question nor developed the kind of security and confidence that is associated with a minimum of national economic, social and political development. It is, therefore, easier to understand why the South African factor might for the foreseeable future, complicate rather than facilitate, the cooperative and integrative process to which SADCC is committed.

Now, it is rather ironic that anyone should laud an organizational and institutional structure such as is SADCC's, when the objective should be how best to overcome the historical and political bases of this weakness. This would be acceptable if such boasts emanated from SADCC circles; for there is much to praise about a process that has contributed significantly towards the goal of political and economic cooperation in Southern Africa in particular and Africa in general. There is the danger of double standards on the part of observers who express one set of expectations towards (a united) Europe and another altogether towards (a divided) Africa, as the following illustrates:

> "Fortunately, we have a functioning example of how regional cooperation in Africa might work: SADCC." Thus enthused the World Bank's Regional Vice President for Africa, Edward Jaycox, in his speech to the SADCC Annual Consultative Conference in Arusha in January 1988. For the Southern African Development Coordination Conference (SADCC), this was high praise indeed, because the World Bank had been one of the doubters when SADCC was formed in 1980.[24]

More precisely, such observations miss the point, wittingly or unwittingly; project-based "regional development" is unlikely to promote coordinated and integrated cooperation, mainly because it renders the organization amorphous and porous. But this is a situation to lament rather than to laud.

> The group is explicitly not a free trade zone, nor is it a supra-national body which can impose decisions on its members. Rather, it is a kind of mutual and cooperation society, which promotes balanced development through projects which are seen to be of mutual benefit. SADCC founders argued that it would take decades of nine heterogeneous states to agree on complex treaties, and that the only way forward was to build on project by project agreement.[25]

This leads us to the consideration of the third factor in our analysis about the possible future of SADCC: economic cooperation, and the basic elements that will have to be established before this process can begin. Clearly, project-based regional development is more likely to enhance the existing vertical integration into the northern hemisphere than promote horizontal cooperation among the member states. This is mainly because the projects themselves are either northern initiated or almost entirely northern donor funded. There are, therefore, obvious attractions for many in the northern hemisphere in project-based organizations.

Conversely, any regional organization in the south that seeks to transcend the project-based approach—towards the kind of EEC model—will sooner rather than later wilt as donor funds dry up. No doubt the international cooperating partners prefer less rigid organizational structures; in general the north has difficulty with dealing with organizations in the south that seek to assert such a political and economic identity as would be interpreted as African nationalist (and therefore break with the north). This raises the question already referred earlier: namely, whether it was ever the intention on the part of even its best friends in the north, that SADCC would grow and develop into an expression of an autonomous economic community. And now that the main raison d'être—South Africa—is about to fade away, it will be expected that factors in the north will be feverishly preparing a new aid programme that might overtake SADCC.[26] At any rate, neither a free South Africa nor a SADCC that will inevitably include South Africa will in the foreseeable future begin even to chart the bases for Southern African Economic Community (that would necessarily imply a level of autonomous development and provide thereby a better basis for reciprocal relations with the north).

The current historical conjuncture would suggest that the unequal relationship between the north and the south will continue almost unabated for a long time to come. These are not conditions conducive to regional cooperation and integration in the south. Contrary to the euphoric predictions that a free South Africa will provide stronger basis for regional economic cooperation and integration in Southern Africa, the emergent dispensation in that country will place so many demands and burdens on the economy, that it will soon dispel any illusions that it is after all a Third World country. Already, the international cooperating partners are considering how South Africa might be assisted in the post-apartheid period, with aid and projects. The question is how far the existing SADCC can ensure that such programmes will operate under its auspices and thereby strengthen its base even within the current parameters of its role, or become itself marginalised and balkanized in an "aid" industry that has its own northern-based objective.

Conclusion

Accordingly, a veritable research programme in Southern Africa should, in the first, instance, highlight those historical, political, economic, social and cultural factors that have been the cause of conflict and insecurity in the sub-region. There can be no peace and security in both either South Africa or the sub-region as long as the balance of forces is still weighted heavily in favour of the South African state. The analytic framework herein sought to the fallacy of even postulating the so-called post-apartheid era. For, the danger is that in accepting such a concept, the analyst himself/herself falls victim to an ideology of deception. The focus of analysis should be the identification and projection of those factors that lend themselves to the resolution of the National Question, at both the national and regional levels; and in the context of the process of democratization as part of the dialectical relationship between the state and civil society. The resolution of the National Question in the sub-region necessarily includes the issue of human rights, democratization of the economy,[27] and the right of citizenship to the so-called migrant workers that have for decades contributed to the economic development of such countries as Zimbabwe and South Africa.[28] In addition, such a perspective will place South Africa in the proper historical and sub-regional context. For, a South Africa subjected to the demands of real change and transformation cannot forever remain so central in any consideration of the future of the entire sub-region. Besides, there are such countries as Angola and Zimbabwe both of whom might become quite formidable, at least in terms of the economic and military potential. Likewise, it should not be taken for granted that the countries of the inner periphery—i.e. Botswana, Lesotho and Swaziland—will forever remain peripheral in sub-regional developments. For instance, even "small" Lesotho might grow "larger" in political significance if and when the Sotho should rear its head in Southern Africa. This paper has sought to establish the nature and direction of that change: from an apparent sub-system which, based as it is on the colonization process in Southern Africa, appeared permanent and unassailable; to this inherent contradiction between (white settler) colonial domination and the African people, giving rise to both the National Question and the process whereby it is to be resolved. The 1990s are but only a decade in a process of change that has brought us so far; the prospects are that we shall be nearer to peace and security in Southern Africa at the end of the decade.

Notes

1   See the larger paper, "Southern Africa in the 1990s: Towards a Research Agenda", and also the first two chapters by this author in the SADCC commissioned book, Ibbo Mandaza and Arne Tostensen, SADCC: The First Ten Years: Towards a Southern African Economic Community?, Heinemann, 1991, (possibly) forthcoming.

2   See, for example, that collection of essays published at the height of white power in Southern Africa: C. P. Potholm and Richard Dale (eds.): Southern Africa in Perspective: Essays in Regional Politics, The Free Press, N.Y. and London, 1972.

3   See Note 2 above.

4   The Kissinger Study of Southern Africa (with an Introduction by Barry Cohen and Mohamed A. El-Khawas), Spokesman Books, London, 1975, p.66.

5   Speech at the occasion of her visit to Harare, Zimbabwe, 1989. Cited in Ibbo Mandaza, "Movements for National Liberation and Constitutionalism in Southern Africa," SAPEM, Vol.2. No. 9, 1989.

6   See, for example, Ibbo Mandaza, "Movements for National Liberation and Constitutionalism in Southern Africa", op. cit.

7   Kenneth Grundy, Confrontation and Accommodation in Southern Africa: The limits of Independence, University of California Press, Berkeley, 1973, p.113.

8   Sam Nolutshungu, South Africa in Africa, Manchester University Press, 1975, p.245.

9   Kenneth Grundy, op. cit.,p.113

10 Ibid.

11 Sam Nolutshungu, op. cit.,p.143.

12 Ibid. p.144.

13 Ibid.

14 Ibid.

15 Ibid.

16 Ibid. p.145.

17 See the concluding chapter in the SADCC—commissioned study: Ibbo Mandaza and Arne Tostensen, SADCC: The First Ten Years, Heinemann, forthcoming 1991.

18 For an account of the origins and development of the grouping of states that emerged as the Frontline States, see the larger paper cited in Note 1.

19 For an interesting discussion on this subject, see Balefi Tsie, "Botswana in SADCC: The Dilemma of Dependence", Paper presented to the SAPES Conference on SADCC problems and Prospects of Regional Political and Economic Cooperation, Gaborone, Botswana, Oct. 1989. (SAPES is soon to publish a book—SADCC: Problems and Prospects of Regional Political and Economic Cooperation—on the basis of both this conference and its own two-year project on the subject.)

20 See The National Manpower Survey of Zimbabwe, Harare, 1982. This author was the Director of this National Manpower Survey.

21 Discussion with colleagues of the Black Lawyers Association of South Africa, September, 1990.

22 This is a theme which has its origins in the intellectual discourse of Southern Africa, particularly within the network of the Southern African Political Economy Series (SAPES) and its publication, The Southern Africa Political and Economic Monthly (SAPEM).

23 Arthur Hazlewood, "The End of the East African Community: What are the Lessons for Regional Integration Schemes?", in R.I. Onwuka and A. Sesay (eds), The Future of Regionalism in Africa, MacMillan Publishers, London, 1985, p.174.

24 Joseph Hanlon, SADCC in the 1990s: Development on the Frontline, Special Report No.1158, The Economist Intelligence Unit, London, 1989, p.1.

25 Ibid.

26 For example, the Namibian situation: notwithstanding SADCC's efforts, the tendency of most donor countries and/or agencies has been less to provide support to an independent Namibia through a SADCC framework than on a bilateral basis.

27 For an elaboration of this theme, see Ibbo Mandaza, "The State and Democracy in Southern Africa: Towards a Conceptual Framework", in Ibbo Mandaza and Lloyd Sachikonye (eds), The One-Party State and Democracy: The Zimbabwe Debate, SAPES Books, Harare, 1991.

28 This is a novel idea raised very recently by Mapopa Chipeta (SAPES Trust) in his paper, "Some Reflections on the Status of Migrant Labour in Southern Africa", presented at the Seminar on Post-Apartheid South Africa and Its Neighbours, Maseru, April, 1991.

5

L'Union du Maghreb Arabe:
Problèmes et Perspectives

Mustapha Benallègue

Le choix du titre de cet exposé n'est pas le mien. Mais il faut dire qu'il me convient. Contrairement à la formule consacrée, la revendication de ce qui vous plaira dans ce qui va suivre sera faite par l'auteur; tout le reste sera ambigu par son extensibilité et par son exhaustivité.

On peut par exemple privilégier ceux parmi les problèmes de l'Union du Maghred Arabe (l'UMA) qui rejoignent les problèmes des autres regroupements régionaux qui se sont développés en Afrique, et en conclure que le Maghreb n'échappe pas à la règle, ni aux difficultés de la conjoncture.

On peut aussi au contraire s'appésantir sur les rares aspects ou domaines qui semblent devoir singulariser l'expérience maghrébine et s'orienter vers la conclusion inverse.

Enfin, on peut s'enferrer dans une approche "institutionnaliste", si l'on peut dire, et partir des difficultés (réelles) actuelles à réunir le Conseil Présidentiel de l'UMA, et en extrapoler l'ampleur et la gravité des divergences qui doivent certainement être à l'origine de ces reports successifs.

Ou bien encore, toujours dans cette même hypothèse, on peut déboucher sur une critique sévère de la règle diplomatique de l'unanimité et regarder d'un oeil attendri vers la supranationalité, comme solution, comme dépassement du soi-disant frein des nationalismes frileux.

On aura donc compris mon intention de mettre en relief ces deux dimensions à la fois, à travers une approche contradictoire, balancée, des réalisations de l'UMA depuis sa création, et de ses perspectives (favorables et moins favorables), pour autant que nous laisse les entrevoir une conjoncture ballottée, une conjoncture par ailleurs de plus en plus connectée, qu'on le veuille ou non, à un monde lui-même en pleine mutation. Les meilleurs prospectivistes nous disent d'ailleurs leurs difficultés à entrevoir quand on commencera seulement à en saisir les tendances lourdes, et ce n'est pas peu dire.

Je ne reviendrai pas sur l'historique de l'UMA, sur sa lente gestation pendant les années 60/70, au cours desquelles, sous l'impulsion de la Commission Economique de l'ONU pour l'Afrique, étaient tentées les premières expériences à géométrie variable (positions hésitantes libyenne et mauritanienne).

Rappelons tout de même assez brièvement les structures essentielles mises en place progressivement par les Conseils Présidentiels successifs de l'UMA:

(1)   Le Conseil Présidentiel (C.P.) lui-même, organe supreme, qui se réunit tous les six mois, avec une Présidence tournante;

(2)   Des Conseils Ministériels peuvent se réunir à n'importe quel niveau, dont deux ont été jusqu'ici privilégiés: les Premiers Ministres et les Ministres des Affaires Etrangères;

(3)   Un Comité de Suivi, composé en principe de Secrétaire d'Etat chargé, entre autres, de préparer les "Sommets";

(4)   Une Assemblée Représentative, composée de dix Deputés par pays-membre. Ce nombre porte à vingt par le Sommet de Tunis de Janvier 1990;

(5)   Une Cour de Justice, enfin, au sein de laquelle chaque pays-membre délègue deux Magistrats.

Le Premier Conseil Présidentiel (Tunis, janvier 1990), instituera notamment quatre Commissions Ministérielles Spécialisées, constituant en quelque sorte l'Exécutif réel et permanent de la Communauté. Ces Commissions ont compétence dans les domaines respectifs suivants:

•   Ressources humaines;
•   Economie et finances;
•   Sécurité alimentaire;
•   Infrastructures.

La Session décide l'institution d'un Secrétariat Général permanent et fixe, mais reporte la décision concernant sa localisation. C'est cette même Session du CP qui fixe par ailleurs la périodicité de ses convocations à six mois, et qui adopte le principe d'une Présidence tournante. Elle examine aussi des questions à caractère plus général, dont les relations futures de l'UMA avec son environnement international: Coopération, notamment avec

(1)   le Conseil de Coopération Arabe (C.C.A.)

(2)   le Conseil de Coopération du Golfe (C.C.G.), et aussi certains groupements régionaux africains,

(3)   enfin avec la CEE, dont en particulier ses membres riverains de la Méditérranée Occidentale.

Le Deuxième Conseil Présidentiel (Alger, juillet 1990), est réputé le plus économique. Il est censé avoir en effet élaboré une "Stratégie de Développement Commune". Il en fixe en tous cas le cap: le Marche Commun, et les étapes, en particulier l'Union Douanière. Des Accords Sectoriels et des branches sont appelés à concrétiser cette Union Douanière, progressivement. Ils devraient concerner essentiellement:

(1)   La libre circulation des produits agricoles;

(2)   La garantie des investissements réciproques;

(3)   La garantie contre la double imposition;

(4)   La création d'une Compagnie maghrébine de transport aérien.

Le choix du siège de l'UMA est encore une fois reporté, tandis qu'est decidée l'institution d'une Université, ainsi que d'une Académie maghrébines.

Le Troisième Conseil Présidentiel (Tripoli, janvier 1991), affine l'approche en termes d'Union Douanière, en précisant que cette dernière devra être précedée de l'instauration d'une Zone de Libre Echange, avant la fin 1992. Tandis que l'Union Douanière, toujours prevue pour fin 1995, voit son contenu se préciser quelque peu: il s'agirait notamment d'un Tarif Extérieur Commun (T.E.C.), difficile à élaborer, semble-t-il, à ce jour.

Un Marché Commun maghrébin est ciblé pour l'an 2000, tandis qu'à plus long terme, tout ceci devra déboucher sur une veritable Union Economique, fruit de l'unification préalable des politiques économiques respectives.

Le Sommet décide, parmi les instruments de réalisation de ces démarches, la généralisation des Accords bilatéraux de paiement entre les Banques Centrales, comme base d'une multilatéralisation ultérieure.

Dans ce sens, la Troisième Session des Gouverneurs des Banques Centrales, (Rabat, décembre 1991) a adopté une *Convention Bilatérale Unifiée*, appelée à se substituer à la toile d'araignée de conventions bilatérales hétérogènes existant jusqu'ici. A l'horizon du 1er avril 1992, on devra arriver à un règlement des paiements courants (du moins les soldes) en monnaie(s) nationale(s).

Cette même Session des Gouverneurs des Banques a arrêté d'autre part le principe d'une cotation quotidienne réciproque des monnaies nationales, premier pas vers une convertibilité inter-maghrébine, valable bien sur en soi, comme contribution direct à l'accélération de la circulation des biens et services, mais aussi parce qu'elle peut constituer un test d'éfficacité, avant la convertibilité internationale des monnaies maghrébines, plus ou moins inscrites à l'ordre du jour des une et des autres.

Le Quatrième Conseil Présidentiel (Casablanca, septembre 1991), s'est d'abord penché sur quelques questions institutionnelles: le Secrétaire-Général de l'UMA sera Tunisien, le Siège sera établi au Maroc, tandis qu'Alger devra arbriter le Parlement, la Tunisie la Banque, la Mauritanie la Cour de Justice, la Libye enfin les Institutions culturelles déjà créées (Université, Académie).

Il a été ensuite question des relations extérieures de l'UMA, et notamment de ses relations avec les Européens (les 4 du Sud, et les 12 de la CEE, en tant que telle). On préparait d'ailleurs un Sommet des "5+5" (voir les exposés sur ces sujets précis) pour janvier 1992, mais les développements sur la scène politique semblent avoir mis ce projet "en panne", pour ne pas dire plus.

Les résultats de ces "Sommets" peuvent paraître bien modestes, par rapport aux défis auxquels fait face la Région. En réalité, si les facteurs favorables au rapprochement sont multiples, il n'en reste pas moins qu'un certain nombre d'obstacles ne peuvent être négligés.

Il ne convient pas de sous-estimer tout particulièrement l'aggravation des difficultés qui s'est manifestée pendant la dernière période, tant au niveau de chaque pays qu'au niveau de la Région toute entière: difficultes économiques, sociales, pour tous et avec en particulier les ravages de la dette extérieure, menaces extérieures pour certains, fragilisation du processus démocratique pour d'autres.

Il faut tenir compte du fait que le problème du Sahara Occidental n'a toujours pas abouti, même si on peut considerer qu'une étape importante a été franchie sur cette voie. Nul doute qu'un règlement juste et durable de cette question constituerait une pierre supplémentaire à l'edification maghrébine.

Une autre source de "grippage" de la machine semble venir des développements déjà évoqués concernant l'Algérie, mais ces interferences sont évidemment difficiles à evaluer "à chaud", d'autant qu'elles coïncident avec celles de la nouvelle crise libyenne, crise qui remettrait en cause jusqu'à la participation elle-même de la Libye à l'UMA.

Nous considérerons donc ces problèmes comme étant en voie de règlement, jusqu'à preuve du contraire, pour approfondir les aspects strictement économiques.

Le hiatus entre la décision et l'acte concret pose un problème que l'on pourrait qualifier de sémantique. Ne serions-nous pas en quelque sorte prisonniers d'un jargon, valable assurément, en d'autres temps, et en d'autres lieux?

Le vocabulaire "officiel" de l'UMA traduit une certaine hésitation entre deux conceptions de la coopération-intégration régionale. Parfois, sans discernement, sont utilisés des concepts relevant de ces deux conceptions, et il arrive qu'on fasse carrément état de ces deux approches, sans en lever les équivoques.

Dans les textes adoptés, on parle volontiers, parfois indifféremment, de "Zone de Libre Echange", "Union Douanière", "Marché Commun", etc, le tout assorti de dates et delais plus ou moins arbitraires, mais avec référence plus ou moins explicite à la Communauté Economique Européenne, alors que dans la théorie classique dominante, qui a notamment inspiré ceux qui ont fait la CEE, ces concepts ont évidemment des contenus très précis:

(1) Dans la Zone de Libre Echange (Z.L.E.), les Etats-membres éliminent entre eux les droits de douane et les restrictions quantitatives (contingentements), mais gardent chacun ses protections douanières (tarifaires et quantitatives) vis-à-vis du reste du monde.

(2) L'Union Douanière (U.D.), c'est la Z.L.E., plus un Tarif Douanier Commun (T.D.C) vis-à-vis de l'extérieur.

(3) Le Marché Commun (M.C), c'est l'U.D, plus l'entière liberté de mouvement des hommes et des capitaux.

Mais il est vrai que dans la pratique, résultant de rapports de forces complexes et socio-économiques, les choses sont un peu plus compliquées, et chaque étape concrète (y compris pour la CEE!), est un "mixage" compliqué de ces étapes "théoriques".

Pour l'UMA, les choses sont encore un peu plus complexes, et un certain nombre d'accords relèvent quant au fond, de la Coopération "classique" entre Etats, et c'est peut-être alors leur caractère multilatéral (plusieurs Etats) qui peut prêter à confusion: on n'hésite pas alors à parler "d'integration". Mais il est clair que le caractère multilatéral de ces accords ne sauraient évidemment leur conférer une quelconque vertu "intégrationniste".

En effet, l'intégration économique régionale (ou internationale) peut être abordée soit comme un processus, soit comme le résultat de ce processus.

Elle renvoie nécessairement à la notion de Division Internationale du Travail (DIT).

Elle implique, (selon des modalités qu'il convient de redéfinir au cas par cas), la mobilité des biens et/ou des facteurs.

Elle est reliée enfin, à une action favorable, (ou défavorable) à la discrimination (ou à la non-discrimination), dans le traitement des biens et des facteurs en mouvement.

L'intégration économique est un processus tout d'abord objectif, mais en même temps réglable, dont on attend, pour l'essentiel, un gain d'efficacité provenant d'une meilleure allocation des ressources productives, ainsi que l'exploitation d'économies d'échelle de toutes sortes, par l'élargissement du marché, ainsi que par la spécialisation.

Il s'agit de mener à son terme l'indispensable intensification de la production, c'est-à-dire l'augmentation et l'extension de la production sociale de biens et services, non par une augmentation des ressources (matérielles, financières, humaines) affectées à la production, mais par une meilleure utilisation de ces ressources, fondée en particulier sur une application plus large, et plus rapide, des dernières innovations de la science et de la technique, la modification du rôle relatif des différentes catégories de travailleurs, le perfectionnement de l'organisation de la production, et du travail en général.

Les pays en voie de développement ne sont pas restés à l'écart de ce mouvement: l'Amérique Latine, l'Asie, et, plus près de nous, le Monde Arabe et l'Afrique, ont connu une série d'expériences de coopération-intégration régionale ou sous-régionale, aux contours et aux contenus pas toujours très nets, parfois sous la houlette de l'ancienne puissance colonisatrice, ou bien aujourd'hui sous le parapluie plus large de la CEE.

D'autres tentatives plus récentes montrent que la coopération économique régionale devient un facteur de plus en plus important de la vie internationale. Presque tous les pays en voie de développement participent aujourd'hui à un, ou plusieurs groupements ayant pour but de stimuler les échanges commerciaux, et au-delà, les rélations économiques, financières, monétaires, de credit, et de production. Ce mouvement obéit là aussi à la nécessité de mettre en commun les moyens, le plus souvent insuffisants à l'échelle de chaque pays pris séparément, pour faire face non seulement à une crise aux effets de plus en plus nocifs et dangereux, mais aussi pour se préparer aux grandes mutations technologiques et sociales en cours.

C'est dans ce cadre que pourrait prendre place la spécialisation, une spécialisation qui aura tout d'abord à éviter de servir de tremplin à quelque hégémonisme que ce soit. Sur de telles bases, pourraient être alors envisagées les concessions mutuelles à même de concrétiser le "développement solidaire" du Maghreb, développement solidaire dont il est possible de déterminer les grandes étapes suivantes:

(a) Développement des échanges commerciaux intra-maghrébins

Insuffisant, en soi, à mener la dynamique communautaire jusqu'à son "point de non-retour", le développement des échanges n'en constitue pas moins un élément indispensable, et prend un caractère aigü dans la conjoncture actuelle de défauts de moyens de paiement que connaissent l'ensemble des pays de la région. Un premier effort portera sur l'identification du potentiel immédiat et à venir d'échanges intra-maghrébins, ce qui ne signifie pas que les règles et précautions d'usage devront être ignorées. Ceci signifie par contre que les conditions devront (et pourront à notre avis) être progressivement créées pour des concessions mutuelles, progressivement élaborées, dans l'intérêt général bien compris. Exploiter toutes les possibilités, cela signifie évidemment tout d'abord créer le (ou les) cadre(s) adéquat(s) à un tel accroissement des échanges.

Quelle que soit la modestie des résultats à en attendre, que ce soit par rapport au degré réel de complémentarité-concurrence des appareils productifs en présence, ou que ce soit par rapport à la priorité à accorder à la mise en oeuvre d'une coopération industrielle, il n'en reste pas moins que tout devra être mis en oeuvre pour faire donner à ce facteur tout ce qu'il est susceptible de donner.

(b) Développement des interventions extérieures communes

En complément de ce qui précède, pour les mêmes raisons et sous l'effet des mêmes contraintes (financières, démographiques, technologiques,...) cette tâche est plus que jamais à l'ordre du jour, et elle consisterait notamment à développer les interventions communes, bi- et multilaterales, sur les marchés extérieurs, tant en qualité d'acheteurs que de vendeurs. Nous pouvons citer, entre autres avantages susceptibles d'en découler: économies d'échelle, amélioration du pouvoir de négociation de l'ensemble, possibilité de dynamiser les échanges internes à la zone, etc.

(c) Amélioration du pouvoir de négociation

Un cran supérieur de coopération visera ensuite la coordination progressive des relations économiques extérieures de l'ensemble des pays du Maghreb, et on ne peut ignorer, une fois de plus à ce sujet, l'importance de ses relations avec la CEE, son insertion plus ou moins poussée dans la Division Internationale Capitaliste du Travail (DICT), en liaison avec les perspectives de Coopération régionale.

Il reviendra aux structures compétentes d'élaborer une stratégie progressivement collective face à des partenaires qui seront de plus en plus constitués par des ensembles régionaux, et au sein desquels la CEE est objectivement appelée à jouer un rôle déterminant. Et si le réalisme appelle à accepter cet état de fait, il commande de même de s'y préparer avec le souci de doter progressivement et méthodiquement la région du maximum d'atouts pour affronter ces défis de la façon la moins désavantageuse possible. Ceci signifie notamment qu'il est possible, sans attendre les résultats de la coopération-intégration, d'entreprendre, dès à présent, une meilleure coordination, sinon une négociation unique, dans le cadre par exemple du renouvellement des Accords de Coopération avec la CEE.. C'est certainement ce qui se fait dans le cadre des cinq plus cinq.

Enfin, pour terminer, une étape significative pour la coopération-intégration maghrébine sera constituée par le passage à la co-production, agricole, industrielle, bi- et multilatérale, comme condition, comme garantie, finalement, d'aboutissement du processus de coopération-integration maghrébine, vers un Maghreb uni, en mesure de revendiquer, et d s'assurer, une place honorable dans une DIT en pleine mutation.

Des complémentarités existent dans ce sens. Elles demandent tout d'abord à être regardées d'un oeil nouveau, si l'on peut dire, tant on a été accoutumé à taxer de concurrentiel tout ce qui se ressemblait quelque peu.

Un regard neuf mettrait à jour des complémentarités jusque-là moins évidentes, pour des raisons déjà évoquées plus haut. Dans tous les cas, l'ampleur des problèmes, leur acuité n'autorise plus le rêve: aucun pays de la Région ne peut envisager une sortie de crise autonome, individuelle. Les nombreux défis qu'ils affrontent, ainsi que la vigoureuse réaffirmation des tendances à l'approfondissement des processus d'intégration de leur principal partenaire commun (la C.E.E.), renforcent chaque jour cette conviction.

Si l'on se réfère enfin aux débats de ces dernières années, ne sont plus à l'ordre du jour, selon nous, ni la question de l'opportunité, ni celle de la faisabilité globale (idéologiquement cohérente, serions-nous tentés d'écrire) de la construction maghrébine. Et pour paraphraser le célèbre humoriste, on pourrait écrire ou dire aujourd'hui: "la parole est aux actes".

C'est pourquoi même si la démarche pragmatique, prudente, au pas-à-pas qui continue d'être appliquée, "en haut", paraît la plus à même, aujourd'hui encore, de faire face à la difficulté et à la complexité du processus de construction d'un ensemble maghrébin cohérent, ce pragmatisme n'est pas nécessairement exclusif d'une plus grande audace des agents économiques.

La possibilité de relever un tel défi dépendra pour l'essentiel du contenu de l'Union, contenu qui dependra lui-même, en dernière instance, du rapport des forces socio-politiques qui le sous-tendent, locales, régionales, et internationales, au service d'un développement collectif relativement autonome, relativement auto-centré, c'est-à-dire basé avant tout sur la satisfaction des besoins internes, ce qui n'exclut nullement, mais sous-tend au contraire, la recherche d'un surplus exportable, un développement visant à une cohérence régionale croissante, autant d'objectifs qui peuvent trouver place dans un projet global et communautaire.

Ni incompatibilité, ni homogénéisation ne sont fatales. La tendance est aujourd'hui au développement de la coopération multi-forme entre états et régimes les plus différenciés, dans la recherche de solutions communes à des problèmes de plus en plus communs, et une telle tendance semble bien se profiler aussi au Maghreb, qui possède, assurément, les moyens d'un développement solidaire.

6

ECOWAS: Problems and Prospects: Notes for Discussion

Jeggan C. Senghor

Introduction

The Economic Community of West African States (ECOWAS) was established on 28 May 1975 primarily to further the objectives and manage the process of economic co-operation and integration in the West African sub-region. It is specifically enjoined to promote co-operation and development in the region by ensuring[1]:

(1)   elimination as between the Member States of customs duties and other charges of equivalent effect in respect of the importation and exportation of goods;

(2)   abolition of quantitative and administrative restrictions on trade among the Member States;

(3)   establishment of a common customs tariff and a common commercial policy towards third world countries;

(4)   abolition as between the Member States of the obstacles to the free movement of persons, services and capital;

(5)   harmonization of agricultural policies and the promotion of common projects in the Member States notably in the fields of marketing, research and agro-industrial enterprises;

(6)   implementation of schemes for the joint development of transport, communication, energy and other infrastructural facilities as well as the evolution of a common policy in these fields;

(7)   harmonization of the economic and industrial policies of the Member States and the elimination of disparities in the level of development of Member States;

(8)   harmonization, required for the proper functioning of the Community, of the monetary policies of the Member States;

(9)   establishment of a fund for Co-operation, Compensation and Development; and

(10)   other activities calculated to further the aims of the Community as the Member States from time to time undertake in common.

These are lofty goals which would challenge the competence and capabilities of any integration movement. More so when account is taken of the environment in which ECOWAS was born. This environment was characterized by 16 states, extremely diverse in terms of size, levels of socio-economic development, types of political systems, geographical features, boundaries, populations size, etc. Equally noteworthy, the environment was also one with historical antecedents of cooperation and centralized administrations of two major colonial powers. In a sense both sets of characteristics served to promote a commitment to cooperation in the post-colonial period, encouraged, in no small way, by the ideology of pan-Africanism and African unity which held strong sway in the continent. At the same time, centrifugal forces took the form of micronationalism which was reinforced by instability of political regimes and the overarching influence and control of the erstwhile colonial powers.

In further situating ECOWAS in its historical context it is also important to note that it was the first such sub-regional economic grouping; it had to blaze the path which the PTA, ECCAS, AMU, SADCC were to tread. As such, in its formative years it was deprived of other experiences from which to benefit, from other comrades-in-arms. In this regard, also significant is the fact that ECOWAS predated the Lagos Plan of Action and the Final Act of Lagos (1980). These two seminal statements defined the main objectives and the methodology of economic cooperation and integration and spelt out a time-table of the successive stages for establishing the all-embracing continental community. The sub-regional economic groupings were to be the building blocks of this Community. ECOWAS, as a key element, already had a head start.

The point arising from this brief discussion of the circumstances in which ECOWAS came into being is that its problems and prospects can be examined at two levels—the sub-regional and the continental. However, a more complete and realistic analysis must necessarily have as points of departure (a) the Treaty establishing ECOWAS and (b) the ECOWAS Secretariat.

Given the nature of this paper it is intended to merely highlight some of the salient issues which will serve as points for debate and discussion.

The ECOWAS Treaty

Compared to those of some of the other economic sub-groupings and the treaty establishing the African Economic Community (AEC), the ECOWAS Treaty is limited in its conception of the integration process, and hence its scope. Its approach to cooperation and integration is partial with a heavy focus on economic sectors at the expense of non-economic sectors. Clearly, the overall objective is economic cooperation and integration and not global multi-sectoral integration. Issues related to such sectors as the environment, human resources, science and technology, social affairs and culture, population, education and training are, thus, given marginal consideration or even totally excluded.

Second, there is a notable omission of a statement of fundamental sacred principles which are to guide and inspire integrative activities. Similar treaties have, for example, committed signatories to respect and protect human and peoples' rights, to promote economic justice and accountability, and to promote and sustain a democratic culture and popular participation. On their own, such principles are highly valued. For ensuring that; the proper environment exists for the realization of the goals of the Community for which they are essential prerequisites. The recently-adopted ECOWAS Declaration of Political Principles is a notable advance.

Third, the institutions responsible for organizing and managing cooperation and integration are restrictive. As provided in Article 4, they comprise the Authority of Heads of State and Government, the Council of Ministers, the Defense Council, the Executive Secretariat, the Tribunal, and the Technical and Specialized Commissions. Two other institutions that are not included, but should have an equally prominent place are a Parliament and an Economic and Social Council. For the articulation and formulation of policies and for the coordination and harmonization of programmes, in particular, these institutions are central. Similarly, for the involvement of the people and interested groups in the cooperation and integration process. After all, these are the ultimate beneficiaries.

Fourth, the type of decision-making regime adopted in any integration scheme is an important factor for the overall effectiveness of action. The ECOWAS Treaty is not explicit on a requirement for voting, and decisions tend to be on the basis of consensus or unanimity. Though this is as it should be, consensus-building sometimes calls for corridor negotiations; and give-and-take which may end up in compromises; the end-product may be confusing and diluted. This gives rise to difficulties at the stage of implementation. Where there is an option for voting and the majority required clearly defined, such possible difficulties can be avoided. Also avoided is the possibility of a minority holding the majority to ransom.

Fifth, there is little room in the Treaty for supranationality. Decisions and directives of the Authority and the Council of Ministers are binding, respectively, on the Community institutions and the subordinate institutions. They are not binding on member States.

Sixth, the method adopted for achieving integrations, as advanced in the Treaty, is market-based as opposed to the production-based approach. The interest is in promoting trade—mostly in goods not produced locally—rather than in consolidating and expanding the regional production base for a fuller exploitation of the potential capacity for integration available in key sectors such as industry, agriculture, and transport and communications. The alternative views trade expansion as occurring if production levels increase locally to respond to inter-country demand. Increased trade can stimulate expansion in production but this may not happen automatically.

The Secretariat

The Executive Secretariat is one of the six institutions of the Community, as spelt out in Chapter II, Article 4 of the Treaty. By its very definition it is the linchpin of the Community, the pivot around which all else revolves. This is demonstrated in a number of ways. First, it has been responsible for the establishment, servicing and functioning of all other institutions, from the most supreme organ, the Authority of Heads of State and Government, to task forces and similar *ad hoc* bodies set up to deal with specific issues. Second, it is responsible for taking action on and supervising implementation of protocols, decisions and resolutions of the legislative organs. Third, it initiates ideas and proposals for action by other institutions; these may relate to a vast number of subject areas bearing on the operations of the Community and the realization of its aims and objectives. Fourth, with the Executive Secretariat rests the task of ensuring that the integration process is on course and that the dynamics of the process are guided and directed towards desirable ends; in this respect it generates policies, plans and programmes and takes charge of their execution.

From the above, it is clear that without the Secretariat there would be no ECOWAS. Recent developments have served to bring out even more the crucial role of the Secretariat. The political leadership in member States, influenced by local and external factors and forces have been demonstrating renewed awareness of the need for higher levels of integration in the region. At the same time, dramatic developments in national political systems have serious implications for integrative actions at the regional level which have to be monitored and "controlled" to ensure that they do not work against Community interests.

It should also be mentioned that the political and security dimensions of cooperation and integration have now come to the fore. This complicates the tasks involved, while also throwing up additional responsibilities to the secretariat.

Finally, decision A/DEC.12/7/91 of the Authority of Heads of State and Government relating to the implementation of the rationalization of institutional arrangements governing West African integration, drastically changes the setting in which the secretariat is to function and puts it in a position very different from the past.

What all this adds up to is that the loads put on the ECOWAS secretariat have increased many fold and will continue to increase in the future. Accordingly, its capabilities and its capacities require careful assessment. Its structure, and the systems and procedures governing its functioning, require frequent appraisal. Its very role and purpose require close attention: The problems affecting its efficiency and effectiveness should therefore be of special concern.

A first problem relates to the role of the Executive Secretary vis-à-vis the institutions of the Community and the secretariat itself (Art. 8 para; 2 of the Treaty). There is limited scope for taking initiatives and action. On the contrary the fast-moving changes taking place in the sub-region, the continent and the world in general, dictate that he should have a freer hand in directing the affairs of the legislative and other bodies and in the management of resources.

Second, the procedure for the appointment of the Executive Secretary is most anachronistic. The Treaty is silent on the selection process to be followed. The practice has been, therefore, for this post, like the other statutory posts, to be allocated to a particular country which then proceeds to select a nominee. The obvious risk is one of "not having mature and competent, qualified and experienced leaders at the helm of affairs, free of any pressure that nominating countries may be tempted to exert" (FCA/ECOWAS Report, 1987 p.43). Given the increasing importance of the position and the predictable expansion in responsibilities, it is imperative that modern methods of recruitment be introduced. Here, the experience of the PTA is of relevance.

Third, for the post of Deputy Executive Secretary there are two problems. In the first place the tenure of office is not concurrent with that of the Executive Secretary. Second, the practice of rotation among member States and automatic acceptance of nominees has obvious drawbacks.

Fourth, the personnel recruitment system and procedures. Recruitment to professional posts has been based on a quota system which allocates posts to specific countries. In actually filling the post the previous practice was for only one candidate to be nominated and his suitability was rarely questioned. At present, a list of three candidates is submitted who are then subjected to an interview. Based on the order of preference recommended by the interview panel, the Executive Secretary decides. In cases of newly created posts, general criteria are first employed in determining the country of allocation; the above procedure is then applied.

Clearly, this system is untenable. The provision in Article 8 of the Treaty that in making appointments an equitable distribution of posts among citizens of member States must be respected merely requires that a global number of posts may be assigned to member States. The requirement that in recruitment paramount importance is to be attached to securing the highest standards of efficiency and technical competence (Art. 8 para. 7) places a higher premium on qualifications, suitability and ability to perform. It is against this yardstick that considerations of country of origin should be related or the quota system applied, not the reverse.

Furthermore, this calls into question the provision in Article 8 para. 6 which demands of secretariat officials loyalty entirely to the Community in the discharge of their duties as opposed to allegiance to their countries of origin. Nor does it give much credence to the Oath of Office and the Oath of Secrecy.

As in the case of top management the preferred alternative is a modern recruitment system involving open competition, based on well-defined job descriptions and post profiles, interviews etc. This need not be at the expense of equitable geographical distribution. Rather, this principle will be a consequence throughout the process and not the pre-eminent factor at the very beginning of the process.

In fairness, it should be noted that very recently the quota system has been under review and, by decision of the Council of Ministers, all professional posts are gradually becoming non-quota posts, to be filled on a competitive basis. To what extent the damage has already been done is open to debate.

Fifth, some of the key technical commissions have not functioned with the efficacy desired. A case in point is the Administration and Finance Commission which, basically, reviews the operational budgets of the Secretariat and Fund, and advises on administrative matters. The problems here are threefold: limited expertise in budgetary and administrative matters among government representatives, lack of breadth of experience required for penetrating reviews of issues before the Commission, and lack of continuity in membership and representation.

As it is likely that in the future the work of such a body will acquire increased importance within the decision-making apparatus, a preferred alternative is the creation of a semi-autonomous body, characterized by demonstrated expertise of its members in various aspects of financial management, administration and programme planning.

Issues relating ECOWAS to take sub-regional environment

Three issues dominate the sub-regional environment in which West African cooperation and integration is taking place, the relationship between member States and ECOWAS, the relationship between sub-regional intergovernmental organizations (IGOs) and ECOWAS, and ECOWAS and the maintenance of peace and security in the sub-region.

As regards member States the overriding question is the extent to which they are committed to ECOWAS, not in terms of rhetorics, but in terms of concrete acts and deeds. A first problem is that of ratification of protocols and implementation of decisions and resolutions collectively agreed upon. Until recently, most protocols were unratified by the majority of member States. The fact that the Community was not vested with the power to take decisions binding on member States, aggravated the situation. Similarly, for the absence of enforcement measures and mechanisms.

Second, and related, is the question of the extent to which member States accommodate ECOWAS interests in their thinking and actions. It is expected that this would be manifested in the following ways: inclusion of regional components in national development plans, policies and programmes; adoption of effective arrangements to ensure appropriate participation in ECOWAS meetings; promotion of public awareness of ECOWAS and its activities; provision of adequate budgetary resources to integration bodies at different levels; programmed consultations and coordination among government ministries and departments involved in integration; exchange of information; harmonization of sector programmes; creation of inter-ministerial committees operating at the level of technical committees and of concerned ministries.

These and related requirements call for policy and implementation modalities in member States. For this purpose, as long ago as 1983 the Authority had decided that member States should set up national structures and that information on the organization of each national structure should be communicated to the Executive Secretariat (see Dec. 2/5/83). Where such machineries exist they tend to be poorly resourced and poorly staffed, quantitatively and qualitatively, and often have other responsibilities besides ECOWAS affairs. The preferred option is the establishment of a full-fledged Ministry for African Integration, as has been done in Senegal.

It should be noted, on the other hand, that much is still to be done by ECOWAS to make its presence felt in the member States. The establishment of ECOWAS liaison offices at the national level or for groups of contiguous member States is a proposal worthy of attention. These offices would have responsibilities to monitor implementation of decisions and programmes and bring ECOWAS down to the national level, while at the same time bringing the realities of national life to bear on operations at the ECOWAS level.

There is, thirdly, the issue of prompt and regular payment of assessed contributions and, in general, of providing adequate resources for financing integration activities. As at September 1990 arrears of contributions stood at US$18.2 million. This perennial problem has dogged ECOWAS throughout its existence. Not only have budgetary shortfalls affected, at times, the very functioning of the secretariat and its institutions, but it has limited funding of integrative programmes and projects. The Treaty is silent on sanctions for non-payment of contributions and it has been left to the imagination of the Secretariat leadership to devise schemes for enticing/compelling member States to meet their financial obligations to ECOWAS. A preferred option would be the adoption of an independent system for the Community to generate its own resources such as a Community levy on total imports uniformly applied in all member States.

Turning next to the issue of IGOs it is a known fact that no other sub-region in the continent has as many IGO's as does the West African sub-region. It is to be regretted that given the long-standing commitment to cooperation and integration in the sub-region the proliferation of IGOs was not avoided from the outset. Nor was the issue confronted head-on at the creation of ECOWAS in 1975, and the relationship between ECOWAS and the IGOs—particularly CEAO and MRU—defined in the Treaty.

There exists two interrelated problems. First, what practical form should rationalization of the IGOs take and how will a rationalization plan be implemented. Second, what should be the institutional and other relationships between ECOWAS and the rationalized system of IGOs. Decision A/DEC.12/7/91 of the Authority designates ECOWAS as the single economic community in West Africa for the purpose of regional integration and spells out actions to be taken for implementation of the rationalization plan . The plan is to be formulated by 1993. If indeed it is resolutely implemented then the integration process in West Africa would be better streamlined and strengthened. There should then be available a framework for continuous dialogue and consultation with a view to improved harmonization of integration actions. The ECA 1984 study and the ECA/ECOWAS 1987 study contain excellent analysis on different aspects of the subject and very useful guidelines.

The final dominant issue relates to the role of ECOWAS in the resolution of conflicts—whether inter-State conflicts or internal conflicts—and the maintenance of regional peace and security. ECOWAS has, in the past, been reluctant to be involved in conflict resolution despite the Protocol on Non-Aggression of April 1978 and the Protocol on Mutual Assistance of May 1981. However, the Liberian crises, with its various implications for relations between some States and the threat it poses to peace and security in the sub-region, witnessed direct and massive action by the organization. This has brought into sharp focus the place of political factors in the integration process. It appears that from now on ECOWAS will have to pay particular attention to the problem of internal stability, given its obvious repercussions on progress towards greater economic cooperation and integration. Perhaps the most clear manifestation of this awareness is the adoption in July 1991 of the ECOWAS Declaration on Political Principles. New approaches to sub-regional peace and security will necessarily be evolved. Political cooperation aimed at promoting stability between and within States adds a new dimension to economic cooperation and integration in the sub-region as a whole.

Interactions between ECOWAS and the continental environment

The major issues involved in the relationship between ECOWAS and the continental environment are, first, interactions with the other sub-regional economic groupings, and second, with the AEC.

With the other sub-regional economic groupings, formal relations hardly exist either at the level of top management or experts. Periodic meetings, particularly those convened by ECA, UNDP or other UN system agencies, offer occasions for contacts. It is considered imperative that communications and contacts be institutionalized at all levels, given the obvious benefits to be derived therefrom.

The AEC Treaty—like the LPA and FAL before it—recognizes ECOWAS and the other economic groupings as the pillars on which the Community is to be built. It accords them multiple roles: operational arms in the implementation of Community programmes at the sub-regional level, channels of policies at the sub-regional levels for harmonization and other action at the continental level; active partners in implementing the six stages transitional to the establishment of the AEC; and representation in Community-level institutions such as the ECOSOC.

The details on the organic and functional relationships that should exist between the AEC and the economic groupings (including ECOWAS) and between the groupings themselves are the subject of a recently formulated Protocol. This also include, *inter alia*, consultative machineries, forms of reciprocal representation in decision-making organs, ways of strengthening the economic groupings, and the degree of autonomy of the groupings *vis-à-vis* the AEC. Agreement on these and related matters is a first prerequisite. There then arises the operationalization of principles agreed to and their effective functioning. This, it is anticipated, will be a drawn-out and difficult process. Yet, it must be squarely confronted.

Prospects for ECOWAS—concluding observations

This discussion paper has focused attention on some issues and problems which are not of a substantive nature, but are fundamental in the sense that they must necessarily be resolved before any meaningful content can be given to cooperation and integration in West Africa. In other words, the full realization of the tasks enumerated at the beginning of this paper is, to a great extent, conditional on the issues and problems noted above being satisfactorily tackled. Therein lies the usefulness of this paper.

It cannot be gainsaid that much has been achieved by ECOWAS. More recent concrete achievements include the adoption of a trade liberalization regime, the free movement of persons, ECOMOG, the Declaration of Political Principles, reforms aimed at strengthening the Secretariat and improving the professional and technical competence of the personnel, and the steps for rationalization of IGOs. The Committee of Eminent Persons to Review the ECOWAS Treaty, which was set up by Authority decision in May 1930, is expected to come up with wide-ranging recommendations which would, altogether, lay a solid foundation for pursuing and promoting cooperation and integration among West African States.

All this augurs well for the future of ECOWAS. More so when account is taken of the fact that there is now a renewed concern and preoccupation—at all levels within the continent and among most development partners—with regional cooperation and integration. This concern and preoccupation is due to numerous factors, not the least of which are the crisis of socioeconomic recovery and long-term transformation in the continent, the current conjuncture in African societies and politics, and recent developments in the world. These give a certain urgency to cooperation and integration in West Africa and in other sub-regions. If the challenges inherent therein are successfully handled the prospects for a better tomorrow for Africa and Africans will improve considerably.

Notes
1   Treaty of the Economic Community of West African States, para. 2.

7

ACP-EC Issues for the 1990s

Peter Gakunu

New Developments

A number of developments will influence the nature of African, Caribbean and Pacific (ACP)-European Community (EC) cooperation in the 1990s: the changes taking place in countries of Central and Eastern Europe and the former USSR; the completion of the Single European Market including the adoption of a common EC currency; the formation and enlargement of regional common markets among developed countries; the conclusion of the Uruguay Round and the establishment of a Multilateral Trade Organization; the increase in the potential for growth in South trade; demographic changes and their impact on production and trade; and the increasing concern about environmental issues.

The ACP countries, faced with a collapse of financial flows, depressed commodity prices, a decline in per capita incomes and mounting protectionist pressure and trade tensions have now to cope with these developments. Yet, long-standing problems of stagnation, poverty and marginalization, compounded by inequitable international economic relations in trade, commodities, resource flows and technology persist in most ACP countries, and in many of them, especially the least developed, they have reached crisis proportions. The problems with which these countries continue to grapple include difficulties in expanding and diversifying the production base, reducing commodity dependence, building financial and other capacities, coping with the debt burden and its consequences as well as with adverse trends in resource flows, and pursing adjustment programmes oriented to growth and development.

The very fabric of ACP-EC cooperation is under serious threat from all these developments. Uruguay Round has already rendered as irrelevant or redundant a large number of the tariff preferences granted to the ACP countries under the Lome Convention. The loss suffered by the ACP countries that would not be compelled by concessions in other markets is estimated at US$ 180 million in terms of their export values in 1988. The fate of the remaining preferences, including those in sensitive ACP products, hangs in the balance as the EC experts overhaul its generalized scheme of preferences (GSP) once the Round is concluded, perhaps to also include services. Already the EC has extended least developed country status, equivalent to the Lome treatment, to a number of countries in Central and Latin America.[3] It is most probable therefore that the remaining preferences would be rendered redundant before the end of Lome IV.

This situation has evolved because the ACP countries, preoccupied with restructuring their economies, have failed to appreciate the role that tariff preferences could play in maintaining their traditional markets in the face of a hostile and competitive international environment. They seem to have come to the conclusion that since tariff preferences have failed to enable them to increase their share of the EC market or to diversify their production base, during the past 15 years, the preferential regime under the Lome convention is irrelevant and could therefore be dispersed.

It is important to recall that developments in the field of international trade were negative during this period. Protectionist pressures mounted and trade tensions remained high throughout; there was a proliferation of trade barriers, particularly against exports of manufactured goods. Many took the form of voluntary export restraints and other bilateral arrangements, almost all of which were discriminatory. The emergence of regional trading arrangements involving major trading partners has raised uncertainties about market access and trading possibilities with the ACP countries.

The worsening of the external environment for development took place in the context of increasing unpredictability of key economic variables including exchange rates, interest rates, commodity prices and levels of production. This volatility made it difficult for the ACP countries to plan the external sectors of their economies and to manage their international debt-service obligations in a rational manner. It jeopardized the stable flow of imports of both capital and intermediate goods that these economies at a low level of diversification needed to maintain current levels of output. The formulation of rational development strategies was complicated by the lace of international market indicators that are free from wide short-term fluctuations.

The problem of depressed commodity prices and their instability was compounded by fluctuations in activity in major industrial countries and exchange rate volatility in primary commodity markets. Also, as a result of greater exchange rate instability, the costs of external trade rose, particularly since these countries did not have risk-reducing instruments. The pressure on the ACP countries to expand exports intensified despite the prospect of further terms of trade deterioration or, as regards manufacturers, of stiff protectionist reactions.

At the root of many of the structural changes that are taking place in the world economy is technological progress. The technological revolution is having a profound effect on the nature of world economic activity and international relations. It has given fresh impetus to economic integration, both global and regional, and to changes in patterns of production and exchange. Producer services—those used by enterprises as input in their own production of goods and services—have emerged as a highly dynamic sector and as a major determinant of productivity and competitiveness. International trade in services has grown rapidly, and the linkages between trade, technology, investment and services have grown more intense. It is the combination of these factors, rather than the inadequacy of tariff preferences *per se*, that was the **root** cause of the poor trade performance of the ACP countries.

The useful role of tariff preferences, while appreciated in some cases, has been seriously questioned in others whose exchange is regulated either by marketing boards or international commodity agreements; bananas *vis-à-vis* coffee, cocoa and tea. Tariff preferences can be important incentives to source imports and can assist in developing trade links because tariff preferences can be pocketed either by the importer or can be passed on to the consumers in the form of lower prices or to the producers in the form of higher prices. Either approach would benefit imports from the ACP countries and therefore work to the disadvantage of those countries not entitled to such preferences. Tariff preferences have, nevertheless, long ceased to be relevant in developing and maintaining ACP trade flows with the EC. On the other hand, other groups of countries have made full use of concessions granted to them by the EC.

The outcome of the Uruguay Round and the subsequent review of the EC's GSP which will follow the completion of the Round and the current EC actions taken in favour of some countries to globalize Lome should be viewed as the straw that breaks the camel's back to the extent that the successor to the fourth Lome convention, if ever there will be such a convention, would render the trade provisions totally irrelevant and redundant.

Even in those cases where tariff protection is now useful—bananas, pineapples, cutflowers—the EC, because of its increasing role and importance in the international economic and political scene, cannot refuse to grant trade concessions to other developing countries in Latin America and Asia. The EC, which at present operates a number of agreements which safeguard specific interests of third world countries in its market will need to globalize these arrangements with the emergence of its increased geopolitical role in international affairs. Indeed, with regard to its commitments to developing countries as a group, the EC appears to have embraced the view that these countries, including the ACP, should rely more on General Agreement on Tariffs and Trade (GATT) instead of remaining dependent on autonomous preferential regimes which lack transparency and which could therefore be withdrawn by the donor countries at any time without any prior notice. As a result, ACP market inches currently protected from external competition through tariff preferences would be whittled away.

Moreover, as the EC completes the process towards a single market and a common currency, it has started to be inward-looking so that preferential margins now enjoyed by the ACP countries are under threat. Increased intra-EC trade, in products and sectors considered to be traditional to the ACP countries, emanating from enlargement and the encouragement being afforded to the new member states towards the production of similar and substitute products, will undermine specific ACP interest areas within the EC. ACP countries which require special protection in the EC market should view the evolution of the internal market and the extension of EC frontiers with particular concern. To the extent that the completion of the single market and the enlargement of the EC grows at these specific interests, ACP-EC cooperation would be marginalized.

It is worth recalling that towards the end of the negotiations for the Lome IV convention, the ACP Group, of its own volition, decided that the trade dimension of ACP-EC cooperation was not as important as the financial one. It accordingly accepted the EC offer even though the EC had not responded in a meaningful manner to its already reduced demands. Also, the ACP Group panicked and accepted the EC offer of 12 billion ECUs in the form of aid for the period 1990–1995, because it feared that the EC would turn its attention towards the needs of these countries. After the conclusion of the negotiations Commission officials were quoted as saying that the EC had been prepared to increase its offer to the ACP countries beyond the modest amount of 15 billion ECUs demanded, and the ACP held firm to its position.

This attitude on the part of the ACP countries has encouraged the EC to make very significant concessions in the area of trade under the Uruguay Round and to make available to the countries of Central and Eastern Europe as well as the USSR substantial financial assistance, 100 times more on a *per capita* basis, than that made available to the ACP countries. Recent estimates by the World Bank indicate that these countries will require about US$ 71 billion in the near future of which US$ 8 billion had already been made available by, among others, the EC and the USA. Their continued passive attitude on these and other developments has further allowed the EC to proceed with its offer to the Andean and Central American countries and is certain to encourage it to make more significant concessions when it reviews its GSP to take account of the outcome of the Uruguay Round.

In a world in which the EC is gradually assuming the role of a major player, it would be naive and unrealistic to imagine that the ACP Group could have managed to prevent it from granting concessions to third world countries. However, their failure to support and push for compensation, a concept accepted even by GATT, has provided the EC with the excuse it needed to erode ACP preferences and consequently give less priority to ACP's legitimate concerns.

The ACP should also be concerned with the consequences of the completion of the single market and the establishment of a common currency. The developments are expected to erode the protection now afforded by firms in the respective member states. As barriers to competition are gradually lifted, intra-firm rivalry will increase as areas of specialization between them become blurred. There has been a massive increase in mergers and joint ventures, particularly new types of strategic alliances in response to the globalization of markets in response to the change, and the liberalization of competition law.

As tender procedures and competition rules within the EC are liberalized, firms from one member state will be able to compete for work contracts in other member states. It is generally believed that since individual member states, in a real single market, would be required to give national preference to firms from other member states, it would be preferable to provide financial and technical assistance within a multilateral framework rather than on a bilateral basis. Competitive national firms would therefore be in a better position to take up community preference. The traditional methods of procuring and awarding contracts would cease to apply so that bilateral assistance would gradually assume a multilateral character. Under this scenario, existing links between the metropole and its former colonies would be broken so that ACP-EC cooperation will become less relevant to the extent that EC assistance (bilateral and multilateral) to the ACP countries will fall significantly.

Following the Maastricht agreement for a common European currency, the role of the CPA as a convertible currency has been seriously questioned. Consequently, work contracts financed by France in francophone ACP countries and to be undertaken by French firms are facing certain difficulties. As the French franc disappears as a currency, this relationship is going to be strained even further.

This development will render it less attractive for individual member states to provide bilateral assistance so that they would opt for a multilateral (Community) approach to financial and technical assistance. Bilateral aid flows from the United Kingdom or France, for example, will fall as the frontiers between the member states become gradually blurred with the completion of the integration process. Increased coordination of EC assistance would give the EC a bigger role and a stronger voice in determining the way in which international aid, both bilateral and multilateral, is utilized.

The establishment of the United States of Europe will result in greater coordination of EC aid so that it would be able to influence the manner in which official financial assistance is distributed. Given its emerging political role, the EC could exercise significant influence on the way in which international financial flows are managed and allocated. However, EC financial assistance to the ACP countries would be seriously compromised so that EC financial flows to the ACP countries would no longer depend on EC policies alone.

The recent agreement with the six countries comprising the European Free Trade Association (EFTA)[3] concluded in October 1991, created the European Economic Area (EEA) with 380 million people, a GDP of some US$ 6.87 billion and accounting for 40 per cent of world trade. This agreement, in force from January 1, 1993, provides for the elimination of all obstacles to the free movement of goods, people, services and capital as well as increased cooperation in environment, transport, education and research and development. EFTA will contribute US$ 1.8 billion in soft loans to the EC and will donate US$ 500 million to help the poorer EC members.[4] In return, it expects increased economic growth, a drop in prices, creation of new jobs and access to new markets as a result of liberalization measures taken.

The creation of the EEA has put the EC under pressure to open membership to other countries. The East European countries—Czechoslovakia, Hungary and Poland—have initiated action and are expected to conclude an agreement with EFTA. EFTA sent a fact-finding mission to the Baltic states and signed a free trade agreement with Turkey. It is negotiating with Israel and is scheduled to start discussions with the Gulf states.

The ACP countries are gradually becoming marginalized as a result of these initiatives. From the viewpoint of the EC, the Central and Eastern European countries pose an immediate problem to its economic stability, which requires comprehensive and urgent solutions. The democratization process and the abandonment of the centrally-planned economic systems by these countries as well as by the USSR have been accompanied by far-reaching institutional changes, rapid moves to market-based economic systems and further integration into the world economy, the factors which have undermined established systems and accelerated social and political tensions. These developments, it is feared, could provoke massive immigration into the EC and thereby accentuate unemployment and impair future growth. For the EC, this poses a real threat which requires swift and decisive action as the costs of the transition are now likely to be considerably higher than previously anticipated, both in terms of political and economic stability, as well as in resources for development and social welfare.

The strong support being given by the EC and the OECD countries to the process of reform underway in these countries, as well as their response to urgent Soviet humanitarian needs raise many concerns. These are heightened by the realization that, far from being maintained at their current levels, trade, aid, investment, loans and technology flows could be diverted away from the ACP countries.

The abrupt changes taking place in these countries as well as in East-West relations and the emergence of the EC as a viable alternative to the dominant role of the United States in world affairs should prompt the ACP Group to undertake a fundamental examination of its place in the emerging configuration of political and economic power. Indeed, there is a danger that, apart from instances where strategic concerns of the EC are directly affected, the vital interests of the ACP countries would continue to lose their salience on the EC's ever increasing priority list. This elimination of geopolitical rivalries could make the EC inward-looking and thereby reduce its effectiveness in international actions to redress poverty and underdevelopment. As the USSR disintegrates, developed countries in general are likely to pursue their particular interests in a less inhibited fashion so that intensification of conflicts over trade, exchange rates and macroeconomic policies could ensue. These developments, if realized, could have far-reaching consequences for the ACP Group and are likely to have irreversible implications for the future of ACP-EC cooperation.

Bibliography

1. World Economic Survey 1988: United Nations 1988.

2. The Geographical allocation of the EDF under the Lome Conventions: Dr. M.K. Anyadike-Danes, December 1990.

3. Cambridge Economic Policy Review, Vol 6(3): December 1980.

4. World Debt Tables, External Debt of Developing Countries: 1987-1988 Edition.

5. The Common Agricultural Policy: Peter Gakunu, 1988.

6. The Single European Market: An ACP-Viewpoint: Peter Gakunu, November 1991.

8

The African Economic Community: Political, Economic and Social Prerequisites for Success

H.M.A. Onitiri

The world is going through political and economic changes of monumental proportions. At the same time, Africa, apart from digesting the consequences of these changes, has to cope with new political situations, along with its continuing search for new ways to promote economic recovery and future growth.

The political, economic and social prerequisites for the success of the African Economic Community (AEC) has to be considered against the background of these developments. The signing of the AEC treaty in June 1991 was accompanied by hopes and expectations that the new organization will provide a framework within which some of the present concerns of African countries can be resolved. Though such hopes have been tempered by a realistic assessment of the capacity of African institutions to cope with the gigantic tasks and new structures envisaged in the AEC treaty, the overall outlook is still one of cautious optimism.

The purpose of this study is to examine the prerequisites that can create a favourable environment for the implementation of the objectives of the AEC treaty, and to assess the prospects for fulfilling those prerequisites during the 1990s and beyond. While those prospects would depend primarily on the actions, or inactions, of African governments themselves, the implications of the current trends in the international environment should not be under-estimated, given the openness and continuing dependence of most African economies.

Implications of major developments in the world economy
The world is in the throes of major developments that will have profound effects on production and trade and on the distribution of incomes between rich and poor

countries. Without doubt, these developments will further intensify during the 1990s. How they will affect the African continent will depend on the linkages of African countries with the global economy through international trade, interest rates, capital flows and commodity prices. It will also depend on developments in major areas of international economic policy, particularly developments in international trade policy in the context of current multilateral trade negotiations under the Uruguay Round; policies affecting real interest rates; debt relief policy and efforts to increase capital flows to countries with a heavy debt burden; and policy on international commodity prices.

It has been emphasized that the outcomes at the global level in these four areas will have a significant bearing on the growth prospects of African countries, through their effect on growth of industrial country markets, the international cost of capital, the terms of trade and the availability of external capital, particularly export-oriented foreign direct investments (World Bank, 1991).

Although the successful ending of the Uruguay Round negotiations depends on whether a number of crucial outstanding issues will be resolved, an indication of what a successful ending will mean for African countries can be glimpsed in the 'complete and consolidated' draft agreement presented by the Secretary-General of GATT to the Trade Negotiating Committee (TNC), the main negotiating body in the Round, in December 1991, in the form of a Draft Final Act.

No matter what exceptions and safeguards are made for developing countries in the final agreement, African countries are likely to find themselves saddled with new obligations in many areas. Apart from stronger pressures for even more trade liberalization beyond what has already been forced upon them by the Structural Adjustment Programmes (SAPs), they will be required to accept new obligations for the liberalization of their trade in services under the General Agreement on Trade in Services (GATS). Also, there are new constraints on investment policies under the agreement on trade-related investment measures (TRIMs) and new obligations that may adversely affect their acquisition of technology under the agreement on trade-related aspects of intellectual property (TRIPs). These new obligations would have to be accepted without any clear gains, because in all these areas, African countries simply do not as yet have the capacity to take advantage of new opportunities under the new agreement. Such capacity will not be easily developed without the kind of concerted efforts that can be mobilized under the AEC. While a few African countries will benefit from tariff reductions on tropical products, most will suffer a net loss of advantage, because the general extension of liberalization will erode the margin of preference that they enjoy at present under the Lome Convention.

124

The lumping together of the various issues for negotiation in a single Final Act, to be administered by an umbrella organization—the Multilateral Trade Organization—poses a number of problems for African countries. In particular, there is the possibility of cross-retaliation between, for example, trade in goods and trade in services, or between these and policies on TRIMs and TRIPs.

Rapid changes in technology

Rapid changes in technology will have profound effects on international competitiveness and on the distribution of world growth and prosperity. The spectacular changes in technology are the most obvious and undoubtedly the most important. The present relentless speed of technological change should leave no doubt as to what to expect in the future. It is a generally accepted fact that the next century will be largely a technology-driven world. It is also widely believed that the frontier of technology will extend much further in the present decade than in the last, and that most of the foundations for the technology-driven world of the 21st century will be laid in this decade. The predictable outcome is that those who are not in the race will be pushed further to the margin of world development and prosperity. African countries will have to ensure that they are part of this development rather than fall victims to it. It is not likely that there will be a half-way house. Every aspect of life will be touched by new technologies. Information technology, robotics performing complex manufacturing functions, synthetic substitutes for a growing list of natural products, new processes using less raw materials per unit of output and the extensive application of biotechnology techniques in agriculture and other spheres of life are already facts of life.

The march of technology cannot be stopped. In the coming years, it will be the most important determinant of relative productivity among nations in virtually all spheres of goods and services. It will have a profound effect on the structure of international trade. Indeed, it is already having a noticeable impact on the relative prices of manufactured goods and primary commodities. In order to cope with the impact of these developments, trading countries must develop the capacity to respond with maximum speed to changing situations in world markets that would depend essentially on the level of development and the stage of technological advancement. It need not be stressed that such a capacity for domestic economic adjustment is at present beyond the reach of most African countries.

Future trading blocs

Also important is the growing division of the world into trading blocs. While the outcome of the negotiations in the Uruguay Round is still uncertain, there are indications that, whatever the outcome, the future trading world will be dominated more by the interactions among the major trading blocs than by the principles of free trade and unfettered competition which the negotiations are trying to promote. It is no surprise then that the participating countries are hedging their bets by consolidating their trading blocs or forming new ones. The European Community is laying plans for 1992; the US and Canada have concluded a Free Trade Agreement; Australia and New Zealand have concluded an Agreement on Closer Economic Co-operation. Plans have been mooted for an OECD type of arrangement among the Pacific rim countries. There will be more developments as other countries try to align themselves with the success stories. Many of the Eastern European countries are likely to have various forms of association with the EC, and the possibility of Mexico joining the US-Canada axis should not be excluded. The world is on the threshold of major economic alignments.

African countries have not ignored these developments. A report prepared for the African Development Bank by a Committee of Ten draws attention to these developments. It notes that new trading blocs may seek to dominate the trading scene by the time the Uruguay Round agreement goes on effect. The implication is that the trading blocs would be in a stronger position to defend their interests. The losers would be those areas including Africa where economic integration is yet to be fully developed. Therefore, it will be necessary for the present integration schemes to consolidate their positions: hence the proposed African Economic Community is an urgent necessity and not just a distant dream.

Reduced investment to Africa

The global demand for capital will slow down or even reduce foreign investment to Africa and raise real interest rates. It is likely that the decline in the flow of foreign resources to Africa will be reversed without the development of a large number of multinational projects that will attract foreign investment, particularly in the fields of industry and infrastructure.

It has been estimated that real interest rates in the 1990s are likely to remain near the high levels of the 1980s. This is because of the vast increase in global demand for capital arising from the social and infrastructure needs of unified Germany and Eastern Europe, the post-war reconstruction of Kuwait and Iraq, and the expected surge in investment as Europe moves to a single market.

For these reasons, it is important that Africa take more decisive steps to mobilize domestic resources for investment and to substantially improve efficiency in the use of both domestic and foreign investment resources. With more decisive steps towards economic integration, African countries will be able to make more efficient use of foreign investment and foreign assistance. New strategies to attract foreign investment should therefore give increased attention to multinational projects. In this connection, the World Bank notes that what is needed is harmonization of macroeconomic policies as part of a phased programme of trade liberalization favouring African products. Rationalizing regional institutions should be high on the agenda. This would promote economic integration and regional cooperation across issues, such as education, research and watershed management. Consistent with the priority proposed for capacity building and technology training, particular attention should be given to creating regional centres of excellence (World Bank, 1989a). Mr. Jacques Pelletier, a former French Minister of Co-operation and Development, urged African countries to establish regional markets along the lines planned in Europe, in order to increase their competitive potential and to prepare to take on trade opportunities in European markets.

Future world growth

Sharing in future world growth and prosperity would require effective participation in global linkages and interdependence. Over the last four decades, the growing interdependence of the world economy, which has been an intrinsic part of world development, has gathered increased momentum. Interlinkages between production process and ownership of enterprises have gone so far as to make it difficult to decide who owns which enterprise and to which country a particular end product should be attributed. While the process has undoubtedly contributed to world economic growth, the benefits have largely bypassed those countries, including a majority of African countries, that have been able to join in this global process. For example, from 1965 to 1989, average *per capita* GDP of East Asia grew by about 5.2% a year, compared with 0.4% in sub-Saharan Africa. Improvements in infrastructure, particularly communications, an enabling environment for foreign investment and capacity to adjust rapidly to sudden adverse changes in the external environment are prerequisites for effective participation in this global process.

The 1980s saw a sharp divergence in economic performance across developing regions, and it has been estimated that regional disparities in growth will continue. The analysis of alternative scenarios shows that the chances of significantly reducing these disparities are remote in the 1990s. Hence there is a great risk that the number of absolute poor in the world will rise greatly, with the percentage increase being greater in Africa than elsewhere. Africa needs to re-orient its links with the world economy.

Relevant conditions for a favourable political atmosphere

Peaceful resolution of internal and inter-country conflicts will free resources for development and create an enabling environment for investment. Against the background of current world developments, the primary risk for African countries is to reduce the needless waste of human and material resources caused by internal and inter-country conflicts. Hence, the overriding need of the continent is peaceful resolution of conflicts, without which no economic plan or programme can succeed, and without which Africa cannot attract the foreign investment that it needs for development.

Three principles are enshrined in the AEC treaty to encourage the creation of a favourable political atmosphere. These are:

(1)   peaceful settlement of disputes among member states, active cooperation between neighbouring countries and promotion of a peaceful environment as a prerequisite for economic development;

(2)   recognition, promotion and protection of human rights in accordance with the provisions of the African Charter on Human and Peoples' Rights;

(3)   accountability, economic justice and popular participation in development.

In recognition of these principles, the OAU Assembly of Heads of State and Government in 1990, adopted the Declaration on the Political and Socio-Economic Situation in Africa and the Fundamental Changes Taking Place in the World. In that Declaration, the African leaders expressed their commitment to work together towards the peaceful and speedy resolution of all the conflicts on the continent, as well as towards greater democratization in African countries. This was, in fact, the first time the issue of internal conflicts had been addressed by the Assembly. Hitherto, the OAU, on the basis of principles of sovereignty and non-interference, had regarded such conflicts as outside its mandate.

At a meeting of the OAU's Council of Ministers in February 1992, a number of important decisions were taken to approve the Secretary General's proposal to restructure the Secretariat with a view to establishing a Division for Conflict Management. During the meeting, the OAU Secretary General drew attention to the need for a permanent mechanism to backstop initiatives and actions on conflict anticipation, management and resolution. He called for the establishment of such mechanism which will enable the OAU to respond swiftly and decisively to crisis situations. He considered it vital that Africa be in the forefront in the efforts to resolve conflicts which bleed people and squander resources. Africa urgently and badly needs peace, stability and security.

Necessary conditions for a favourable economic and social environment
Harmonization of policies and integration of programmes is at the heart of the integration process. On the economic and social fronts, the heart of the matter is the

principle of "inter-State cooperation, harmonization of policies and integration of programmes", also enshrined in the AEC Treaty. It is this principle that underlies most of the economic objectives of the treaty, such as economic self-reliance and endogenous and self-sustained development, mobilization and utilization of the human and material resources of the continent, harmonization of national policies in order to promote community activities, particularly in the fields of agriculture, industry, transport and communications, energy, natural resources, trade, money and finance, human resources, education, culture, science and technology.

In some respects, the AEC will merely be underlining or strengthening cooperation arrangements that were already in existence or under discussion in various spheres, such as the UN Transport and Communications Decade for Africa (UNTACDA) and the African Environmental Agenda (AEA). The question that is now being asked is how these arrangements can make better progress within the framework of the AEC and in the light of the multitude of pressures to which African countries are now subjected as a result of the momentous changes on the world scene.

Implementing current strategies

The signing of the AEC treaty has had significant effects on the programmes of the major African institutions and organizations, and there are signs of a convergence of programmes towards the implementation of the treaty. The OAU has concentrated its strategy for implementation on three main objectives, namely, popularizing the treaty; preparing some of the important protocols to be appended to the treaty; and establishing suitable institutional mechanisms, including a restructuring of the OAU secretariat, for the implementation of the treaty.

A sustained mechanism to popularize the treaty coupled with successful implementation of treaty objectives in a few key areas will promote the high level of awareness required for continental integration. In December 1991, the OAU Secretariat organized a meeting of press and media experts, including information and public relations experts from the agencies of the United Nations to discuss strategies for the popularization of the objectives of the AEC. There are also plans to hold popularization seminars at regional and subregional levels.

In pursuing the popularization objectives, the organization is drawing on its experience in the implementation of the Lagos Plan of Action (LPA). In this connection, it is generally believed that efforts to disseminate the objectives of the LPA fell far short of what was needed to assure the success of the Plan. Hence many informed observers believe that if the AEC is not to go the way of the LPA, and if the African population is to be convinced that the AEC can bring about changes in their lives and the lives of their children, the two-prong strategy now being pursued by the OAU would have to be supplemented by more action at regional, sub-regional and national levels.

The OAU is aware that, while it can do its utmost to popularize the AEC treaty, its efforts will be in vain if they are not complemented by similar efforts by Member States at national level. Furthermore, there is also general awareness that an elaborate popularization programme will achieve little tangible results without at least few successful initiatives by the AEC.

Swift ratification of the treaty and the priority protocols will enhance the process of implementation. Of the almost thirty protocols envisaged by the treaty, the Permanent Steering Committee (PSC) of the OAU has identified a priority list on which initial work should concentrate: These include the relations between the Community and regional economic communities (RECs); elimination of trade barriers; free movement of persons, right of residence and establishment; and agriculture; industry, science and technology; energy and natural resources; environment; human resources, social affairs, health and population; education, training and culture; monetary, financial, and payments policies; and solidarity, development and compensation fund. These protocols cover a wide range of subjects and will provide a framework for the activities of the AEC. Work has already been completed on the protocol on the relations between the AEC and the RECs and it has already gone through initial discussion by the PSC. It is expected that at least four more protocols will be completed. In each case, the central theme is cooperation, coordination and integration, and the basic issue is how to overcome the difficulties of pursuing these objectives that have become manifest even at the subregional level.

Work on the protocols is in addition to pursuing the central objective that the treaty has identified as the major task to be accomplished during the first five years of the AEC, namely the strengthening of the RECs. Strengthening implies essentially two main activities: support for the efforts of the RECs to rationalize and strengthen their institutional structures, and new initiatives to promote cooperation among the RECs in areas where more rapid progress requires extensive interregional linkages. As regards the first, all the RECs are currently grappling with three main problems: rationalization of the inter-governmental organizations (IGOs) within their respective domains, exploration of measures to achieve financial viability and promotion of arrangements for subregional coordination of national programmes in critical economic sectors.

Strengthening and restructuring the OAU Secretariat is a fundamental requirement for the successful implementation of the AEC treaty. The establishment of the AEC has added a new dimension to the functions of the OAU and the relationship of the organization to African regional institutions and organizations. The decision of the Heads of State and Government of the OAU to create a single OAU/AEC Secretariat means the OAU's traditional structure has to be transformed to focus primarily on the implementation of the AEC treaty. This implies that new duties and functions have to be defined for the organization, and new relationships established with other African regional and sub-regional organizations. In particular, the organization, in its role as the Secretariat of the AEC, would have to implement, along with the treaty, a large number of protocols covering a wide range of subjects on Africa's socio-economic development.

Two other developments will further enhance and supplement the capacity of the OAU Secretariat to cope with the new tasks. The first is the institution of regular meetings of the heads of three important agencies—the OAU, ECA and ADB—that are the primary actors in the implementation of the AEC treaty. The second is the institution of "Joint Secretariat" whose main purpose is to assist the PSC of the OAU, particularly in the implementation of the AEC treaty.

Mobilizing international support for the AEC

Effective mobilization of international support for the AEC requires clear articulation of the needs and priorities for the implementation of the AEC objectives. Most of the international institutions of importance for African development have now accepted the fundamental importance of economic integration to African development. Hence their current programmes reflect a willingness to respond to requests for support for the implementation of projects and programmes to promote cooperation and integration.

In his speech to the 21st Summit of the OAU in June 1991, the President of the World Bank pledged that the World bank would do everything in its power to support the realization of the objectives of the treaty establishing the AEC. He noted that the signing of the document was an important first step, but it was even more important that concrete, pragmatic measures be taken—by African countries—to implement the treaty and make the idea of an African Economic Community a reality.

This commitment of the World Bank should be seen against the background of new interest of the bank in regional integration in Africa (World Bank, 1989a, b). It is also significant that the growing interest of the Bank in economic integration in Africa has come at a time that the Bank has embarked on the African Capacity Building Initiative (ACBI) for improved policy analysis and development management, an initiative co-sponsored by the ADB and the UNDP.

The new interest of the international community in African economic integration should also be seen against the background of new efforts by the ADB to fulfill its primary mandate to promote multinational projects; and the emphasis on economic integration in the new orientations for the UNDP fifth programming cycle. How the new interest of the international community in African economic integration can be mobilized to promote the implementation of the AEC treaty has been the subject of several meetings, and more such meetings are planned in the near future. However, it has now become necessary to ensure that these rounds of meetings focus on the critical issues of the integration process rather than on conceptual issues of what kind of integration is best for Africa. As regards the latter, African countries have defined their own strategy in the AEC treaty, and the way forward is to articulate strategies and options for implementing the provisions of the treaty.

Naturally, it is for Africa's development partners to decide what kind of support they wish to give to the process of integration. However, it should be recognized that the continent has the responsibility to define its own priorities. This principle should run through the round of dialogues on African development and the role of the AEC in the coming years. The introduction to a recent report of the Global Coalition for Africa notes that Africa will need sustained support to avoid hardship. This support should not diminish Africa's' right to determine what happens on the continent, but it should respond to the concerns and insights of the external development community (GCA, p. 1). The African intellectual community should organize themselves to play a major role in articulating strategies and policy options for the future within the framework of the AEC treaty.

African institutions and organizations
Now that the AEC treaty has been signed and a number of important protocols are being prepared, African institutions and organizations should begin to look into the hard reality of how the institutional and legal framework of the treaty can be used to promote specific programmes and projects at regional and continental levels.

The present period of political and economic transition calls for continuous intellectual debate and close analysis of policy options. Apart from national institutions, which unfortunately, have been weakened by SAPs, Africa is not short of regional and subregional institutions and organizations (IGOs and NGOs), that can make major contributions in this sphere. The issue is how to strengthen these organizations, particularly through rationalizing their activities, so that they can play a more effective role in articulating new options and strategies for coping with Africa's development problems.

The African intellectual community needs to develop capacities and mechanisms to meet the new challenges posed by current developments. In the economic field, and in particular content of the AEC treaty, several issues pose great challenge. These are, among others:

(1)   How far should Africa carry the doctrine of economic liberalization in a world which liberal economic principles are more honoured in the breach than in the observance? An elated question is what trade policy should Africa pursue in this context?

(2)   What institutional arrangements should be established for financing and operating multinational projects?

(3)   How should the issue of distribution of the gains from cooperation arrangement be tackled within the framework of the AEC?

(4)   What role should the AEC play in the elaboration of Africa's response to global economic and social issues that are of relevance to African development?

All such questions call for continuous debate and the elaboration of policy options, in the context of the AEC treaty. A few examples will illustrate the importance of these questions.

The first set of questions is perhaps the most fundamental. While economic liberalization is at the heart of the SAPs now being implemented by most African countries, it is now generally accepted that the present conception of the programmes has serious drawbacks, most especially in its impact on income distribution and the alleviation of poverty. Hence special programmes for the alleviation of poverty, including some by the World Bank, have become the vogue. Indeed, the recent *Poverty Guidelines* issued by the World bank underlines the need to emphasize poverty alleviation in future loan programmes. The question that African scholars must ponder is how far *ad hoc* programmes to alleviate poverty can succeed if the original designs of the SAPs themselves are biased against poverty alleviation.

This is actually part of a general question concerning the limits to economic liberalization that is now exercising the minds of intellectuals around the world. As one writer recently put it, "The urgency about the limits of communism is over. Communism is lost. The argument about the limits of capitalism is just beginning" (Rogaly, 1990). Another recent publication, drawing attention to the adverse impact of liberal economic policies on income distribution in the United Kingdom argues that the decade which ended with the collapse of the socialist countries was not one of great success for capitalism (Mitchie, 1992), Africa has joined this debate in the African Alternative Framework to Structural Adjustment Programmes for Socio-Economic Recovery and Transformation (AAF-SAP) proposed by the ECA. This debate must now continue in the context of the AEC.

Nowhere are the limits of economic liberalization more apparent than in the trade policies of the developed countries, The conclusion of the Uruguay Round negotiations was held up for more than one year, and there is a risk that the whole process with be aborted, not by the intransigence of the developing countries, but by the reluctance of the developed countries to liberalize imports in those areas, notably agriculture and textiles, where the developing countries have a clear comparative advantage. Furthermore, the developed countries have devised new ways of protecting their domestic industries, such as voluntary export restraints (VERs), and various ways of supporting domestic industries indirectly with low interest loans and defence contracts which poor countries do not have the economic leverage to employ. To appreciate the prevalence of such practices, one only has to recall the controversy in GATT between the EC and the USA over the breach of competition rules in their support for local airplane industries.

What kind of trade policy should Africa adopt in these circumstances, particularly in the context of the AEC? Since it is not likely that present conditionalities, which include a large dose of trade liberalization, will be easily relaxed, the battle must be fought on the terrain of reasoned arguments on the consequences of the present conditionalities. One possibility that could be explored is the rationalization, within the AEC or the RECs, of whatever protective measures are considered necessary to promote growth without adverse consequences on income distribution. The best environment for such possibility to the credible is that the RECs must make speedy progress with their programmes for custom unions at the regional level, as a basis for gradual establishment of such a union on a continental scale.

Conclusion

This study has done little more than skip through what is undoubtedly a large subject. Though the AEC treaty is still relatively new, African intellectuals should not lose time in exploring the various possibilities that the new treaty provides to think afresh on the critical economic and social issues which can be tackled within its framework. However, the successful translation into practical actions of the ideas and policy options resulting from such exercise would depend on the creation of a favourable political, social and economic environment for the implementation of the AEC treaty. This, in the final analysis, depends on the political decisions of African governments.

Note

The author is Chief Technical Adviser of the UNDP/OAU project on the African Economic Community. The views expressed in this paper are his personal views.

References

World Bank. 1991. *Global Economic Prospects and the Developing Countries.*

World Bank. 1989a. *Sub-Saharan Africa: From Crisis to Sustained Growth.*

World Bank. 1989b. *Intra-Regional Trade in Sub-Saharan Africa.*

Global Coalition for Africa. *Documents on Development, Democracy and Debt.*

Rogaly, Joe. 1990. Towards the limits of capitalism. *Financial Times*, March 2.

Mitchie, J. (ed). 1992. *The Economic Legacy: 1979-1992.* New York: Academic Press.

9

Towards Monetary Cooperation in West Africa

S. Tomori

Abstract

The importance of economic integration is seen in its adoption by both the developed and developing countries in the 20th century. Its popularity stems from the perceived economic benefits which include increased production arising from specialization according to comparative advantage and better exploitation of scale, greater efficiency and increased competition. Monetary integration, which involves exchange rate union and capital market integration, are special areas of economic integration. The expected gains of monetary integration are exchange rate certainty, reduction in misallocation of resources, economies in the use of foreign reserves, reduced cost of financial management, as well as price level stability. Additional benefits are the stability of the economies of the union and better effectiveness of monetary control. The growth of monetary integration in the ECOWAS sub-region is considered, and the inherent problems of economic cooperation in West Africa is surveyed. The impediments which must be addressed before the laudable goal of economic integration is achieved is then considered in some considerable detail, with appropriate policy recommendations.

Introduction

Economic integration between sovereign states is one of the leading aspirations of international economic policy in the late 20th century. This era has been termed "the age of integration" (Robinson, 1967). Economic integration, which embraces several forms of international economic cooperation, includes free trade, which is a form of economic integration whereby tariffs and quantitative restrictions are abolished on trade in local products between the participants, while each country retains its own tariff against imports from non-members. Customs union involves not only free trade between its members, but also a common external tariff. Common market is a more developed form of integration in which obstacles to the movement of some or all of the factors of production are also removed; and where fiscal, monetary and other instruments of economic policy are harmonized or integrated. This is the order of the day among developed and less developed countries.

In the developed world, the desire for integration is reflected in the formation of such groupings as the European Economic Community (EEC), European Free Trade Association (EFTA) and the Council of Mutual Economic Assistance referred to in Western Europe as COMECON and in the Eastern Europe as CMEA. The EEC, which is a common market form of integration was founded in 1957 under the Treaty of Rome by France, West Germany, Italy, Belgium, Netherlands and Luxembourg. It was enlarged in 1972 by the accession of the United Kingdom, Ireland and Denmark. The EFTA was proposed by Britain in the mid-1950s in order to allow European countries to enjoy the benefits of free trade in industrial products if they were not prepared to commit themselves to a common agricultural policy, or to other political and economic objectives envisaged in the establishment of the EEC. Because of its unacceptance by the founding members of the EEC, the establishment of the organization was delayed until 1960 when UK and other smaller West European countries, namely, Switzerland, Austria, Denmark, Norway and Sweden, decided to integrate. CMEA was established in 1949 by USSR, Bulgaria, Czechoslovakia, German Democratic Republic, Hungary, Poland and Rumania together with Cuba and Mongolia. It was established to accelerate the pace of economic development and a more rational division of labour among its members.

In the less developed countries, there is the Union Douanière et Economique de l' Afrique Centrale (UNDEAC) which links the People's Republic of the Congo, Gabon, Cameroon and Central African Republic; the Communauté Economique de L'Afrique de L'Ouest (CEAO) which was set up in 1974 under the Treaty of Abidjan by the Ivory Coast (now Côte d'Ivoire) Mali, Mauritania, Niger, Senegal and Upper Volta (now Burkina Faso); the Mano River Union (MRU), a custom form of integration established in 1973 between Liberia and Sierra Leone; the Economic Community of West African States (ECOWAS) which was established in 1975 by the signing of the Treaty of Lagos by fifteen West African countries. It is envisaged to be a customs union form of economic integration. Others include the East African Community (EAC) which embraced Kenya, Uganda and Tanzania before its break-up in 1978; Economic Community of the Countries of the Great Lakes (CEPGL) formed by Zaire, Rwanda and Burundi in 1976; the Southern African Customs Union (SACU) made up of Botswana, Lesotho, Swaziland and the Republic of South Africa. The Latin American Free Trade Association (LAFTA) was established under the Treaty of Montevideo in 1960 by

Mexico and the countries of the South American continent (except Guyana): Jamaica, Trinidad and others.

According to Robson (1980), the need for economic integration is always borne out of various political, economic and social factors. Some of the economic benefits that could be enjoyed by members of an organization include increased production arising from specialization according to comparative advantages; increased output arising from better exploitation of scale economies; improvements in terms of trade of the group with the rest of the world; forced changes in efficiency arising from increased competition within the group; and integration-induced changes affecting the quality or quantity of factor input, such as increased capital inflow and changes in the rate of technological advance.

Monetary integration

Monetary integration has two essential components: the first is what might be called an exchange rate union, that is, an area within which exchange rates bear a permanently fixed relationship to each other even though the rates in the union may vary relative to non-union currencies. The second is convertibility, the permanent absence of all exchange controls whether for current or capital transactions within the area (Corden, 1972; Ingram, 1973; Robson, 1980).

Convertibility for capital transactions, including interest and dividend payments, is the principal element in what might be called capital-market integration, the establishment of a unified capital market with no geographical restrictions of any kind on capital movements (or the rewards to capital) within the area. Essentially, monetary integration can be regarded as an exchange rate union combined with capital-market integration (Corden, 1972).

Exchange rate union

There are basically two types of exchange rate union: pseudo-exchange rate union and a complete exchange rate union. In the pseudo-exchange rate union, member countries agree to maintain fixed exchange rate relationship within the union, but there is no explicit integration of economic policy. There is no common pool of foreign exchange reserves and no single central bank. The union members determine what the reference currency should be (one of their currencies might be used, or they might establish a new accounting currency for the purpose). Then each of the member partners agrees to keep its exchange rate fixed relative to this reference currency.

Each country has its own foreign exchange reserves and conducts its own monetary and fiscal policies to achieve its macroeconomic objectives. For effective monetary integration, the required exchange rate system is the complete exchange rate union. This is needed because of the problems associated with the pseudo-exchange rate union. For example, the finance minister of each member country may fight for that common exchange rate that would be most appropriate to his balance of payments situation. This could lead to disagreement among the representatives of member countries. The pseudo-exchange rate system does not allow for the possibility of the reference currency floating relative to outside currencies, or even fluctuating within a band. It is possible that a complete exchange rate system will help alleviate these problems.

In the complete exchange rate union, there is a complete pooling of foreign exchange reserves of the union currency. The community balance of payments is regulated at the community level with the outside world. A single member nation will no longer be able to compute its balance of payments with the outside world. A union central bank is then established to manage the common fund. This common reserve fund would have the incidental by-product of economizing on foreign exchange reserves, since all the countries could not tend to be in deficit and surplus at the same time, and surplus countries would automatically be helping deficit countries (Corden, 1972; Robson 1980). The union central bank would operate in the market to permanently maintain the exchange-rate relationships among the various union currencies.

Capital market integration

Exchange rate union is one aim of monetary integration, while convertibility is the other. In this case, convertibility may be for capital transactions or, more generally, for capital market integration. Capital mobility may be fostered by the harmonization of legislation affecting investment, by ending any legal discrimination against foreign securities or against the export of domestic securities, and so on. The claims of a single central bank may become readily marketable within the union. Direct and portfolio investment within the union may be fostered, if company law and relevant tax laws are harmonized (Corden, 1972).

A high mobility of capital means a high elasticity of substitution on the part of creditors between assets in one country and those in another. The higher the degree of intra-union capital mobility, the greater the shift in capital flows induced by potential differences in earnings (Robson, 1980). Scitovsky (1962) also shared this view when he argued that free capital among regions or nations will bring the equilibrium role of the capital market on the balance of payments.

It should be noted, however, that capital mobility may not completely solve the problems of balance and adjustment in a union, because such flows may be either equilibrating or disequilibrating (Fleming, 1971). Considering the disequilibrating situation first, increased capital mobility may exacerbate the adjustment problem in a monetary union. The mobility of capital movements may lean investors to invest in member states where the marginal productivity of capital is relatively high. The outcome may then be further unemployment and reduced national income in the area of initial high unemployment (Robson, 1980). On the equilibrating function, Ingram (1973) argued that monetary union facilitates adjustments within countries as a result of high short-term capital mobility. If, for instance, the demand for a region's exports falls, then in the short-run local banks may sustain their customer's operations with short-term loans themselves by borrowing in turn at short term on the open market. or through inter-bank transfers. Likewise, firms that are branches of national firms can borrow from the parent concern. Such borrowing could not continue indefinitely, however, except to finance productive investment, and eventually the region's income, output and employment would have to fall. The argument that the higher degree of capital mobility found in a monetary union is capable of overcoming the adjustment problems of the regions within it, is therefore, applicable only in the short-run (Robson, 1980).

Just as capital market integration is essential for monetary integration, there is also the need for labour market integration. Mundell (1961) in his pioneering article that introduced the concept of "optimum currency area" argued that high degree of factor mobility is an essential criterion for the establishment of a single currency area. Meade (1957) also argued that factor mobility is necessary for solving disequilibrium situations within a free trade area. Thus, effective labour mobility will help to ameliorate, to some extent, the problems of monetary integration.

Gains from monetary integration
Many gains are claimed in the literature for monetary integration. Some of these include exchange rate certainty, reduction in misallocation of resources, economies in the use of foreign reserves, reduced cost of financial management, stability of price level, stability of the economics of the union and better effectiveness of monetary control.

Scitovsky (1992) summarized succinctly the case for a common European market, which should modify the nature, scale and geographical distribution of Europe's manufacturing equipment. This could be done by influencing the investment decisions of private business, who need to know that a free all-European market is long-term and will not be disturbed by trade restrictions, exchange controls or exchange-rate revision.

The second argument for monetary integration rests on its contribution towards reducing the misallocation of resources that may otherwise occur if speculative influences, through their impact on exchange rates, distort the price of raising capital in the union. Resource allocation gains may be obtained from increased intra-union trade securities as a result of returns to different kinds of capital coming close together in the member countries (Robson, 1980). Sodesten (1983) simplifying this point under discussion of the "optimum currency areas" said that two countries might want to form a currency area to improve resource allocation. This would eliminate exchange rate risks. Producers would regard not only their own country but the entire common currency area as their marketing territory. If increasing returns to scale are present, producers would expand productive capacities, capital would be allocated more efficiently and labour would become a more homogeneous factor of production. Hence an optimum currency area would lead to improved resource allocation.

A third source of gain may arise from economies in the use of foreign exchange reserves. When a common currency is established and a common pool of foreign exchange is created, the quantity of reserves required will be reduced. Since members will not normally go into deficit at the same time, a pool of reserves will economize them, so long as the formation of monetary union does not itself increase fluctuations. Also, foreign exchange would no longer be needed to finance intra-union trade (Robson, 1980).

A further source of gain may arise from reduced costs of financial management. Integration should make it possible to spread the overhead costs of financial transactions more widely, and in addition part of the activities of foreign-exchange-dealing institutions could be dispensed with, thus generating resource savings (Robson, 1980). Sedesten (1983), arguing on another important aspect of an optimum currency area, said that it would lead to a more stable price level for two reasons. The larger an area is, the less disturbance would be caused by random shocks. A decline in incomes in one region could often be compensated by an increase in another region. Thus the impact of any single specific disturbance could be less as the size of the area increases. Larger currency areas are less dependent on external trade. Changes in the foreign exchange rate would have a comparatively minor impact since the share of tradeables would be relatively smaller.

Monetary integration would also improve the stability of the economies in the union. Its formation would produce positive externalities referred to as the externalities associated with an increased use of money. In essence, the more stable the price level and the better the foresight regarding changes in the price level, the more useful money will become. Money would perform its static as well as its dynamic functions in a much better way. The use of money would improve the welfare of the citizens.

Lastly, other possible sources of gain may result from the enhancement of any initial trade effects that less costly payment adjustments could be expected to bring about, and from the greater effectiveness of monetary control that could be expected to accompany the elimination of exchange rate speculation among union members.

Losses from monetary cooperation

The major cost of monetary integration has been summed up by Fleming and Corden in the existence of a trade-off between inflation and unemployment. According to Fleming (1971) and Corden (1972) price inflation may co-exist with unemployment, and there may be a direct link between the rate of unemployment and the rate of change of money wages such that low levels of unemployment are accompanied by high rates of changes of money wages and vice-versa. This relationship involves the analysis of disequilibrating situations and was first developed by Phillips (1958).

The two writers argue that if member countries of the union experience the same rate of change of costs and prices at their respective points of internal balance, and if it is assumed that external equilibrium exists initially and that structural shifts in demand and supply over time are absent, then relative exchange rates need not change. On the other hand, if optimal domestic policies require different rates of inflation in member countries, some countries will have to depart from their optimal positions if a uniform change on costs is to be ensured. Some countries will be compelled to accept more inflation than they would choose, while others will have to accept more unemployment. For those obliged to suffer unemployment, the excess, valued by the loss of output that it represents, will be one measure of the cost of monetary integration (Robson, 1980).

Thus, under monetary integration, there will be a tendency for the relationship between unemployment and price inflation for the union as a whole to be less favourable than in a situation in which members retain the ability to alter their relative exchange rates. That is, if the average rate of inflation is to equal the average of the separate country rates, the level of unemployment will have to rise more in deflating country than it falls in the inflating country. Integration will, therefore, tend to increase the amount of unemployment required to hold inflation at any given rate and will increase the rate of inflation corresponding to any given rate and will increase the rate of inflation corresponding to any given rate of unemployed. Although certain counter-tendencies may operate, they are unlikely to predominate (Robson, 1980).

It is also significant to note that the pursuit of an independent monetary policy to achieve some national objectives in member countries may be in conflict with policies associated with monetary integration.

The ECOWAS sub-region

ECOWAS is the largest economic integration group in West Africa in terms of membership. It was established on May 28, 1975 when the Treaty of Lagos was signed in Lagos by the West African Heads of State and Governments. The aims of the Community are to promote cooperation and development in all fields of economic activity, particularly in the fields of industry, transport, telecommunications, energy, agriculture, natural resources, commerce, monetary and financial questions and in social and culture matters for the purpose of raising the standard of living of its 200 million peoples, of increasing and maintaining economic stability, of fostering closer relations among its members, and of contributing to the progress and development of the African continent (ECOWAS, 1989).

The decision for ECOWAS monetary union was taken during the Conakry meeting of the Heads of States and Governments in May 1983. A study group was set up, and in 1984 the group submitted a report titled "Report on Proposals for an ECOWAS Monetary Zone," based on the following terms of reference given by the Committee of Governors of Central Banks of ECOWAS Countries:

(1)   Economic implications and prerequisites for the establishment of the monetary zone;

(2)   Critical evaluation of the experience of the West African Monetary Union (WAMU) founded by Benin, Burkina Faso, Cote D'Ivoire, Niger, Senegal and Togo;

(3)   Management framework and institutional arrangements for ECOWAS monetary zone;

(4)   Discussion of the appropriate policies and the adjustment measures required by each member country for adhering to the monetary zone;

(5)   Examination of the visibility of the various possible approaches of the monetary zone, e.g. a single monetary zone, an enlargement of WAMU alongside two or three sub-regional monetary unions and if several monetary zones are to co-exist, establishment of a regional co-ordination mechanisms.

The basic issues highlighted by the study are the need for a common currency with a common exchange rate policy and common monetary policy. Also important are control of foreign exchange reserves in a common reserve pool and external links to give credibility to the system by providing an external convertibility guarantee for the common currency. These might require external financial assistance for short-term balance of payments purposes. Other factors fiscal harmonization, defined to include a centralized fiscal policy in terms of the overall targets for budgetary deficit financing determined by the central monetary authority, and commitment of the member countries to the permanence of the monetary union, as well as a clearly defined and easily enforceable unambiguous rules to govern the system of fiscal and monetary management (Nemedia, 1990).

The study gave strong preference to a single monetary system in the ECOWAS region and proposed an administrative structure of an ECOWAS monetary union with a Conference of Heads of States as the supreme political authority for broad policy guidelines and an ECOWAS Monetary Council (Finance, Planning and Economic). Ministers would provide the link between political direction and economic decision-making. An ECOWAS Central Monetary Authority under a Board of Executive Directors would be chaired by the Union Governor. There would be a specialized ECOWAS Development Bank and a Regional Monetary Authority.

In a paper presented to the Consultative Group on West African Integration, Nemedia (1990) reported that the Committee of Governors of the Central Banks in the ECOWAS region accepted in principle the concept of an ECOWAS monetary zone ununciated in the preliminary study. The committee called for further studies in specific areas relating to adjustment measures, reserve management and convertibility guarantee. The terms of reference for a study are given as the need for adjustment measures and policies by each member and the process spelt out in a stage-by-stage programme over a transitional period; modalities for external reserve pooling; external linkage and convertibility guarantee; institutional and operational aspects; the functions and nature of coordinating and monitoring bodies; and the draft monetary zone (Union) Treaty. According to Nemedia, the study was completed in 1986. It highlighted the problem of the multiple currencies, exchange and payments systems and varying degrees of convertibility of currencies. It traced the evolution of monetary disharmonies, analysed trends in domestic credit and exchange rate divergences and determined the levels of over-valuation and under-valuation that have developed in each currency.

The results of the study formed the basis of the monetary cooperation scheme programme adopted by the Abuja Summit of ECOWAS Heads of States and Governments in 1987. The study suggested a fixed transitional period of five years within which adjustment measures required to achieve limited convertibility and ultimate establishment of a single monetary union are to be undertaken. It recommended the strengthening of the West African Clearing House mechanism to facilitate increased intra-region trade and payments transactions through greater use of national currencies. The coordination and implementation committee (CIM) has not been set up to see how a single monetary zone with limited convertibility would work out. CIM is still beset with a number of problems, notably staffing matters. It does not have the assistance of full-time and experienced technical and professional staff to implement the original and up-dated versions of the 1987 study.

Problems of economic cooperation in West Africa

Economic cooperation is beset with a number of problems, both economic and non-economic. In a paper presented to the Consultative Group on West African Integration during the meeting held at Otta, April 9–10, 1990, Asante discussed extensively the non-economic elements which have bedeviled the progress of many Third World integration schemes including West African economic integration (Asante, 1990).

The crucial elements highlighted in his paper relate to political instability, security, sovereignty, jealousies and fears of dominion. He identified political instability as one of the significant factors militating against the effective implementation of the provisions of the ECOWAS Treaty. He added that the internal insecurity of many member states of ECOWAS has been reinforced by the epidemic of military coups, counter-coups and threats of coups, which have significantly influenced the "political will" of member states to implement ECOWAS programmes. Concerning security, he argued that in Africa, integration systems tend to be highly vulnerable to regime changes mainly because integration efforts are generally sustained by the actions of political splits. He added that whenever revolutions topple the governments of countries belonging to an integration scheme, the scheme's future is usually jeopardized. Military take-overs reinforce the feeling of insecurity in political leaders and make them more inward-looking and less likely to regard any increased integration with favour.

The existence of overlapping economic groupings is another obstacle to monetary integration in the sub-region. These groups not only make claim on the limited resources of their members but also compete with one another in objectives and operations. It is often not enough to agree upon a decision that is based on purely economic analysis and which is a product of difficult political negotiation. There is no legal structure capable of implementing the decision and giving practical content to it. In this regard, the diverse legal systems in West Africa constitute an obstacle to the harmonalization of policies and promotion of community interests. Other factors inhibiting economic integration include the decision-making process in relation to staff matters and institutional obstacles. Furthermore, human factors in various forms can also constitute obstacles to the integration process in the West African sub-regions.

Which way ahead?

The multiplicity of inter-governmental organizations for economic cooperation and integration in West Africa has seriously impeded the process of sub-regional integration. Part of the disappointing results achieved are attributed to the absence of a coherent overall framework for achieving this objective in the sub-region. The absence of an effective central coordinating mechanism at the sub-regional level, which is reflected at the national level, has aggravated the objective of economic integration in West Africa. For example, many ministries are responsible for making and implementing policies with considerable degree of variation from one country to the other.

A number of internal and external factors are hindrances to the process of economic integration. Some of these include the misdirected economic relations of many member states which are outward-looking. There has been a general neglect of the role which could be played in economic integration by mass organizations, such as trade unions, women's associations and students, given the widespread belief that economic integration is the exclusive business of governments.

The unequal economic strength of the countries in the sub-region has also explained the reluctance of some countries to surrender their sovereignty. Many countries have given strong preference to their national interests over community goals. As such, many recommendations and decisions have not been implemented, because of fear of supranational authority over country economies. There has been a general lack of financial resources to promote community goals, and many members are in arrears of their financial contribution.

To achieve the laudable goal of economic integration, the above impediments must be addressed. A political decision is required to re-start the process of economic integration. The first step that has been to be taken is the political decision to rectify and re-model the existing machinery of economic integration. The need for the gradual elimination of the negative external forces is mandatory, and a bold attempt should be made to set in motion the process of monetary cooperation for a future unified monetary zone with a single currency within the Community. Efforts should be made to promote and strengthen the integration of the productive sector of member countries, while Heads of Governments should be continuously persuaded of the long-term benefits of economic cooperation. Attempts should be geared towards the mobilization of mass organizations for economic integration and the development of modalities for the implementation of the Lagos Plan of action at national levels.

The Community should be seen by member states as the only economic unit within the sub-region. The multiplicity of other organizations should be rationalized and restructured under its authority. The various protocols and conventions which have been agreed to by members should be implemented without further delay. Member states should be urged to urgently meet their outstanding financial obligations and ensure regular payment of future ones. In particular, it should be stressed that since monetary cooperation is an essential step towards effective economic integration, there is an urgent need for establishing a West African banking system. Such a system should have branches in member countries, assist in facilitating economic and financial transactions and help remove some of the obstacles to inter-community trade.

Some other economic groupings in Africa have made substantial progress in comparison to the experience in West Africa. The Southern African Development Co-ordination Conference (SADCC) and the Preferential Trade Area for Eastern and Southern African States (PTA) are notable examples in this regard. The PTA has succeeded in implementing the first customs tariffs reduction through the publication by its member states of PTA tariffs. Also, non-tariff barriers such as prohibition, quotas, restrictions, advance import deposits and taxes on foreign currency transactions have been eliminated. Between 1987 and 1989, those products eligible for preferential treatment among PTA countries increased from 312 to 700. All the member states serve as the PTA clearing house, whose utilization rate exceeds 75% of total trade in the sub-region. Almost all the member states of the PTA now issue PTA traveller's cheques which are in circulation in the region.

Summary and conclusions

Some of the issues raised in this study may be summarized. Full monetary integration involves complete exchange rate, capital and labour market integration. When countries form a monetary zone, they enjoy such gains arising from economies in the use of foreign exchange reserves, stable prices and reduced costs of financial management. Apart from these gains, they can also incur losses such as that arising from the departure of internal balance and loss of independence in pursuing independent monetary policy.

Monetary integration, as a high form of economic integration, is nevertheless the desire of most economic groupings. Countries of West Africa have considered the need to form a single monetary union with limited convertibility and have taken some steps on how this union could be promoted. However, the CIM, set up to see how this monetary union would work, is still besieged with the problem of adequate and experienced staff.

There are many strong economic and non-economic obstacles inhibiting the progress of integration in the ECOWAS sub-region. It has been found that monetary union is an ideal form of economic integration which economic groupings should strive to achieve in order to benefit immensely from the fruits of economic integration. Concrete effort has been made within the EEC and the PTA, but similar effort within the ECOWAS has been hindered by economic and non-economic obstacles. It is only when these problems are minimized that the desired monetary union among West African countries can be achieved. Professional economists must strive relentlessly for the abatement of these problems in order to bequeath to posterity, an economic well-being that ranks among the highest in the world.

As a panacea to these enormous problems, there is need for rationalization of the economic groupings in the West African sub-region. It is necessary to have a single economic group which will help rationalise the existence of various inter-governmental organizations that compete unfavourably for the available scarce resources within the sub-region. Secondly, member states should think it wise to implement ECOWAS protocols. Thirdly, there is need to re-organise the specialized institutions of the Community and recruit competent staff to run the Community affairs. Fourthly, adequate measures should be taken by member states to involve more of their citizens in the implementation of ECOWAS protocols. Also, member states should always endeavour to contribute regularly to the up-keep of the Community. It is obvious that if these measures are not implemented, the objective of economic cooperation with its numerous benefits will be a mirage to the West African sub-region.

References

Asante, S.K.B. 1990. Non-economic obstacles to economic integration. *A paper presented to the Consultative Group on West Africa Meeting* 9-10 April 1990, Otta, Abeokuta.

Sodesten, B.O. 1983. *International economics.* 2nd ed. London: Macmillan.

Corden, W.M. 1972. Monetary integration. *Essays in International Finance* 93: 1-41.

ECOWAS. 1989. Objectives of the Lagos Treaty. *ECOWAS Contact,* 2.

Fleming, M. 1971. On exchange rate unification. *Economic journal,* 81:467-88.

Ingram, J.C. The case for European monetary integration. *Essays in International Finance,* 98: 1-28.

Meade, J.E. 1957. The balance of payments problems of a European free Trade Area. *Economic journal,* 67:379-96.

Mundell, R.A. 1961. The theory of Optimum Currency Area. *American economic review,* 55:657-665.

Nemedia, C.E. 1990. Monetary co-operation issues in the West African sub-region. *A paper presented to the Consultative Group on West Africa Integration Meeting*, 9-10 April, 1990, Otta, Abeokuta.

Phillips, A.W. 1958. The relationship between unemployment and the rate of change of money wages in the United Kingdom, 1862-1957. *Economica*, 15:283-299.

Robson, P. 1967. *Economic Integration in Africa*. London: George Allen & Unwin.

Robson, P. 1980. *The Economics of International Integration*. London: George Allen & Unwin.

Scitovsky, T. 1962. *Economic Theory and Western European Integration*. London: Unwin University Books.

10

Towards Monetary Integration in Africa: Options and Issues

African Center for Monetary Studies (ACMS-Dakar)

Introduction

Throughout Africa vigorous efforts are being made to promote adjustment development and regional integration. Macroeconomic policy is recognized to be a crucial
element in the success of these efforts. Partly as a result, in all sub-regions there have
been initiatives that look towards the establishment of new monetary unions. Parallel
and in some cases, wider, initiatives look towards other means of strengthening
monetary harmonization and cooperation.

In the light of these efforts and initiatives and the specific proposals for monetary
harmonization in the PTA in the Maghreb and in ECOWAS, it was decided that leading
issues and options involved should be discussed at this meeting. This paper is intended
to provide a background for that discussion. It focuses on alternative forms of monetary
union and integration the options that might be followed in pursuing such objectives
and on certain crucial policy and management issues that have to be resolved if
monetary integration and certain other forms of cooperation are to be durable.

More particularly, the paper is concerned with the monetary and financial aspects of
different forms of monetary union and alternative mechanisms for monetary harmonization and financial cooperation. It thus does not set out to discuss basic structural
factors which, it must be recognized, should be taken into account in determining
whether or not a group of countries should aim at monetary union at a particular time.
These structural factors traditionally analyzed in optimum currency area theory
include: the openness of prospective union economies, intra-union factor mobility, the
degree of diversification of production, the importance of intra-bloc trade and the
degree of fiscal integration. In the context of monetary union the significance of these

structural factors is that they affect the need for real exchange rate variability on the part of potential members in the face of shocks.

As a result, monetary integration is thus usually seen as more appropriate for already well-integrated and indeed developed regional economies, and as therefore suited to advanced phases of a process of economic integration. Existing African monetary unions have not followed this pattern, however, and their successful operation refutes any interpretation of the structural conditions that have been mentioned as pre-conditions for monetary union, though of course they will affect the size and character of the benefits.

Certainly, regional monetary integration alone will not resolve the development problems of any African state nor guarantee that countries following such a path will adequately integrate their real economies. Equally although monetary integration once established can itself reduce or even eliminate the risk of later emergence of internally induced macroeconomic disequilibrium, there is a need to assure union members of access to appropriate adjustment assistance mechanisms to alleviate external shocks affecting them. But with those provisos independently of its possible contribution to market integration and viewed purely as a vehicle for the re-establishment and maintenance of convertibility and exchange-rate stability, the various options for monetary integration merit serious consideration, because of the contribution that convertibility and stability can afford to economic development.

The paper falls into the following five parts:

(1)   Part one identifies different forms of monetary union and discusses their respective costs and benefits.

(2)   Part two examines options for the implementation of full monetary union on the one hand and for cautious movement towards it on the other.

(3)   Part three examines certain important technical management and policy issues that have to be addressed in the operation of a monetary union in the African context.

(4)   Part four examines the possible implications of monetary union for the integration of other policies and institutions with particular reference to fiscal policy.

(5)   Part five considers some alternative mechanisms for financial and monetary cooperation that might yield some of the benefits of monetary union.

(6)   The concluding part summarizes some of the main conclusions that emerge from the paper and draws attention to certain areas where research or more specific evaluation would be desirable in order to clarify the economic signifi- cance or operational implications of some of the options.

One conclusion of the paper is that where there exists a firm resolve on the part of governments to embark on monetary union a direct path such as is set out in the PTA and ECOWAS reports would be strongly indicated. Other approaches to monetary integration would be advantageous in the event that countries are not finally commit- ted to monetary union.

The implications of structural conditions and accompanying economic integration arrangements both for the size and range of benefits from monetary integration and for its continuing viability once established, must clearly be borne in mind. The existing African monetary unions though no doubt special cases, do demonstrate that the conventional structural conditions already referred to and sometimes viewed as preconditions do not in fact have to be satisfied for a monetary union to work and to yield significant benefits.

Information on the current exchange-rate systems of African countries and other relevant economic data are presented in Annex 1.

Forms of monetary union

The essential characteristics of monetary integration are on: (a) fixity of exchange rates between the members of a union and (b) full convertibility for current and capital account transactions within the union. In other respects, however, there is a variety of possible types of monetary integration: it will therefore be convenient here to distin- guish in abstract terms three basic types and then to locate existing African monetary unions with respect to them before going on to look at the relative costs and benefits of the different forms of monetary integration.

Basic types of monetary integration

(1)   In an informal exchange rate union (ERU), exchange rates are fixed between members currencies and all intra-union transactions are convertible but sepa- rate national currencies managed by separate central banks exist. There is no pooling of foreign exchange reserves and their management is undertaken by separate central banks. The current European Monetary System (EMS) which started life as an adjustable peg system has evolved more recently into a *de facto* example of this type of monetary integration.

(2)   In a formal exchange rate union, exchange rates between member countries are fixed and intra-union transactions are fully convertible. Separate currencies and central banks exist, but the latter are strongly coordinated by a central institution of some kind. Foreign exchange reserves are pooled and their management is undertaken by a single agency. An example of this type of monetary union would be the European System of Central Banks envisaged in the Delors Report for the third stage of European Economic and Monetary Union (EEMU).

(3)   In a full monetary union (MU) there is a single currency managed by a single central bank which also controls the pooled reserves and intervenes in the foreign exchange market as appropriate. This arrangement corresponds to the more developed form of errant integration which is now being increasingly advocated in discussions of European Monetary Union.

Any form of monetary integration limits the scope for monetary policy at the national level (and consequently to fiscal policy as is discussed below). These limits are obviously more strict in the cases of the formal exchange rate union and the full monetary union; in the latter in particular national monetary policy would be limited to the implementation at national level of policy decisions of the central bank. At the same time the acceptance of monetary integration does not in itself imply any change in the actual techniques of monetary policy that is to say the use of interest rates of recent requirements for banks or of sectoral lending ceilings.

The key differences
The main features of the three basic types of monetary union are summarized in Table 1. Between the informal and formal exchange rate unions the key difference is the existence in the latter of a central institution which coordinates the activities of the various separate central banks and manages the foreign exchange reserves. In addition exchange rates in the formal exchange rate union would be expected to fluctuate within narrower bands or even within zero bands. Between the normal exchange rate union and the full monetary union the key difference is the replacement in the latter of separate currencies and central banks by a single currency and a single central bank.

Several further points may be noted at this stage. First there are a number of technical issues to be resolved in connection with the establishment of an informal exchange-rate union. Members would have to decide on the numerate with reference to which exchange-rate parities will be fixed; the permissible margin of fluctuations around those parities; the form in which countries could be obliged to interfere in order to

Table 1: Characteristics of different types of monetary union

	Current a/c convertibility	BETWEEN MEMBERS Capital market integration	Exchange rate fixity	Exchange rate credibility of parties	CURRENCIES	CENTRAL BANKS	RESERVE POOLING	FOREIGN EXCHANGE MARKET INTERVENTION UNDERTAKEN
Informal exchange rate union	yes	yes	yes (within margins)	no	separate	multiple, independent	no	separately
Formal exchange rate union	yes	yes	yes (narrower or zero margins)	yes	separate	multiple, strongly coordinated	yes	by single agency
Full monetary union	yes	yes	yes (zero margins)	yes	single	single	yes	by single agency
UMOA and BCEAC	yes	yes	yes (zero margins)	yes	common	single	yes, but individualized accounts	by single agency

155

maintain their exchange rates within the margins.[1] Pegging to an external anchor currency (which also served as the numeraire) would simplify both the definition of exchange-rate parities and the form of intervention; without an external peg, member countries would have to fix their parities in terms of some basket of their various currencies (as with the ECU in the EMS) and to agree on a set of rules on the currencies in which intervention is to take place in different circumstances. Similar problems would arise on a smaller scale with a formal exchange-rate union operating non-zero margins of fluctuation.

Second, the existence of separate currencies and central banks in the informal exchange rate union means that monetary integration is not final and could be reversed. The financial markets will not therefore perceive the exchange rates as irrevocably fixed and there would be a recurring danger of speculative runs on one or other currency in the expectation of a devaluation or revaluation. In the European context the term inconsistent quartet[2] has been used to refer to the impossibility of enjoying at the same time free trade capital mobility exchange rate fixity and national monetary autonomy. It is a recognition of this problem which is driving the countries of the European Community to proceed from the present EMS to a higher form of monetary integration. In a formal exchange rate union, by contrast, the coordination of the various central banks by the supranational central institution is strong enough to convince the financial markets that existing exchange rate parities are permanent. In a full monetary union the existence of a single currency obviously excludes any possibility of intra-union exchange rate changes.

Third, in the informal and formal exchange rate unions, any intervention in the foreign exchange market involves both external currencies and those of member-states, but in a full monetary union, only external currencies and that of the union. Similarly in the first two forms, but not in the third, foreign exchange reserves include the currencies of member countries.

The African monetary unions

The two African monetary unions (UMOA and BCEAC), represent formally similar variants on full monetary union. There is in both cases a single central bank and a common currency and reserves are pooled. The note issues of each country are separately identifiable, separate balance of payments accounts are drawn up, and changes in individual countries reserves are used in the determination of the country-specific lending ceilings set within the framework of the Union-wide monetary and credit policy.

A similar form of monetary union is recommended for ECOWAS in the 1987 report and for the PTA in its 1990 Monetary Harmonization Programme. Is there any economic (as opposed to political or historical rationale for this special form of monetary union? Should its use be imitated elsewhere in the continent?

The two African unions and the Common Monetary Area of Southern Africa (CMA) were not set up as a result of a process of monetary integration in which national central banks were replaced by a single central bank and multiple currencies by a single currency, but are a legacy from the colonial period when effectively the currency of the metropolis was in use as elsewhere in Africa. They have since undergone major reforms. Nevertheless they operate now and then against a background of a relatively low degree of economic integration amongst their members and the scope of the unions is not coterminous with that of regional economic communities. For instance Togo (and Benin until recently), are not part of CEAO and Mauritania, though a member of CEAO is not a member UMOA. There were and are no union-wide (and few rational) organized capital markets, financial intermediaries are strongly segmented along national lines, and within countries public and private sectors are largely self-contained. In practice the main function of the existing unions even after the reforms of 1974 has been to provide a framework for macroeconomic stability for each country. The particular arrangements involved, separately identified banknotes reserves and credit ceilings and provide a guide to credit policy for each country geared to external balance. At the same time the arrangements permit each country to have individualized access to the resources of the World Bank and the IMF along other funders, which would not be feasible in a full monetary union.

It would unquestionably be a major achievement if similar monetary cooperation arrangements for promoting macroeconomic stability could be generalized in Africa. However, the present context of debate is even more ambitious. Monetary integration is viewed as potentially contributing to closer economic integration and hence to economic growth and development in wider sub-regions. That would seem to point to a more far-reaching integration of money and capital markets. Nevertheless, several reasons suggest that present or similar arrangements to those found in present African unions may have a natural and continuing role to play in Africa. Firstly, as a result of information asymmetries which mean that the borrower is better informed than the lender about the likely return to the projects to be financed, market failure is inherent. These asymmetries explain the existence of equilibrium credit rationing whose origin is the behaviour of the financial intermediaries themselves rather than controls exercised, by the monetary authorities, and the persistence even in advanced countries of indirect finance (financial flows passing through financial intermediaries), rather than direct finance (funds passing directly from lender/investor to borrower through e.g.

the issue and purchase of equity). Secondly, the costs of setting up new markets and of carrying out financial transactions in general cannot be ignored and are increasingly recognized to be very significant.

Thus, the absence of organized capital markets in Africa and even of money markets and markets for wholesale funds in the existing unions will, and should persist. It derives from significant informational imperfections and high transaction costs and the generally less developed business infrastructure.

In the longer term, African monetary unions may be well advised to work towards a greater use of market mechanisms and it is possible that the UMOA countries at least may already be nearing the point where such mechanisms could assume a rather more prominent role even without a higher degree of economic and fiscal integration. In the shorter term however, country-specific lending ceilings modified by reference to the external positions of each member and the ability of each country to make good use of credit[3] would seem to be an appropriate and perhaps indispensable mechanism for the allocation of credit within any African monetary union and for its continued viability. They also ensure and demonstrate that no one country gains at the expense of its fellow members. In this way the mechanism serves a political role and may contribute to the preservation of the union.

Relative costs and benefits
A number of costs and benefits of monetary integration can be identified. Most are difficult to quantify particularly in the African context. However, the net benefits of different forms of monetary integration can be ranked, because while the *ex ante* costs are similar for each form, the benefits are larger for higher forms of monetary union. Later in this paper it will be argued that any monetary union that is set up should peg its currency (or currencies) to an external anchor, preferably the ECU which would provide the best guarantee of price stability over the medium term. It is therefore assumed at this point that such a peg is adopted in each case; this assumption simplifies the analysis without affecting the rank. The focus of the analysis is on the relative costs and benefits of different forms of monetary integration rather than on the case for monetary integration *per se*. The absolute size of the benefits and to some extent their range will depend on the degree of regional economic integration that exists, but that qualification does not affect the ranking either. The analysis is summarized in Table 2.

Costs
Three different costs can be distinguished as follows:
(1)   **Loss of exchange rate as an instrument.** Any of the forms of monetary integration discussed in this paper implies that countries will no longer be able

Table 2: Costs and benefits of different forms of monetary integration

COSTS	INFORMAL ERU	FORMAL ERU	FULL MU
Loss of exchange rate as instrument *vis-à-vis* other members	yes	yes	yes
Initial disinflation where necessary	yes	yes	yes
Loss of seigniorage and inflation-tax revenue from lower inflation	yes	yes	yes
BENEFITS			
Improved price stability (actual and expected)	partially	yes	yes
Reduced exchange rate variability (actual and expected) leading to increased trade and investment flows within union	partially	partially	yes
Reduced transaction costs and improved price transparency leading to increased trade and investment within union	–	partially	yes
Interest savings on government debt from lower nomina interest rates and reduced exchange rate risk premium	partially	partially	yes
Resource saving from pooling of foreign exchange reserves	–	partially	yes
Resource saving from centralization of monetary policy	–	partially	yes
Dynamic gains	–	partially	yes

ERU = Exchange rate union
MU = Monetary union

to use the nominal exchange rate freely if at all as a policy instrument for the adjustment of imbalances with the rest of the world and with other members of the union. The union as a whole will of course still in principle be able to use the exchange rate as an instrument to adjust imbalances between itself and the rest of the world. The loss of the exchange rate as a policy instrument is today generally considered less serious than it was a few decades ago, since it is widely believed that nominal exchange rate changes are quickly passed through to domestic wages and prices, so that they have only limited and temporary effects on competitiveness. At the same time the flexibility today attributed to wages and other prices suggests that with a fixed exchange rate automatic market mechanisms may be more effective in dealing with imbalances than previously thought, both in advanced and in many developing countries. In any case any cost that is involved arises from the fixity of the exchange rate, and is therefore necessarily common to all forms of monetary integration.

At the current level of economic integration amongst African countries it is of course their exchange rates *vis-à-vis* external currencies rather than with respect to potential fellow-members of a monetary union that would be principally significant for adjustment. That rate would as already noted still be open to change on a uniform basis in a monetary union.

(2)   **Initial disinflation.** The need to bring about a prior convergence of inflation rates means that countries with relatively high initial inflation will have to undergo deeper recessions with larger rises in unemployment and larger foregone production. However, since each type of monetary integration requires the same convergence of inflation rates on the part of any country the exchange costs of the alternative forms will be the same for any given country. It is also worth noting that for most African countries a significant part of these costs is likely to be borne in the course of externally supported country-specific structural adjustment programmes.

(3)   **Loss of seigniorage and inflation tax revenue.** Monetary integration also involves some loss of seigniorage from the issue of notes and coin and the increase in the commercial banks reserves at the central bank. With slower inflation, the demands for these assets from the private sector on the one hand and the banks on the other will grow more slowly and the government's (central banks) ability to obtain real resources by issuing them will be lower. However in each form of monetary integration the loss depends on the envisaged reduction in inflation and it is therefore the same for all forms.

Benefits

On the benefits side seven different mechanisms may be identified as follows:

(1)   **Price stability.** The improvement in price stability (reduction in inflation) both actual and expected should produce a better allocation of resources due to the more efficient working of the price mechanism. Actual price stability should be the same for each type of monetary integration, but the greater confidence of financial markets in the formal exchange rate union, and the full monetary union implies a larger reduction in expected future inflation in those types. Therefore, this benefit would be greater for higher types of monetary integration.

(2)   **Reduced exchange rate variability.** The reduced variability of exchange rates both actual and expected should facilitate increased trade and investment flows within the union. More importantly perhaps to the extent that monetary union is accompanied by external convertibility a significant effect on inward investment can be expected. Since exchange rates vary within narrower margins in a formal exchange rate union, compared with an informal union and within zero margins in a full monetary union, the benefit is larger for the higher forms of monetary integration.

(3)   **Reduced transaction costs.** The reduction in the transactions costs is usually considerable when changing from one currency to another and the improved transparency of prices should also have positive effects on trade and investment flows within a union. The benefit will be greatest for the full monetary union with its single currency.

(4)   **Interest savings.** A move to monetary integration can be expected to lower the interest payable on any internally held government debt, firstly, as nominal interest rates fall with the (actual and expected) reduction in inflation, and secondly, as the greater confidence in exchange rates reduces the exchange rate risk premium. These savings in the cost of debt service will again be larger in the higher forms of monetary integration. In the African context, the private sector is typically largely self-contained, there is little net lending to the public sector and to that extent the size of this gain will be small.

(5)   **Resource saving from pooling of foreign exchange reserves.** The pooling of foreign exchange reserves in the formal exchange rate union and the full monetary union will generate a saving in real resources: to the extent that the various members of the union are subject to different and unsynchronized fluctuations in their balances of payments and provided that the creation of a

union does not lead to an unwarranted relaxation of monetary policy. The union's overall need for reserves will be smaller than the sum of individual members' reserve needs in the pre-union stage and in the full monetary union intra-union imbalances no longer need to be financed out of reserves. Thus, the benefit is largest for the highest form of monetary integration .

(6)   **Resource saving from centralization of monetary policy.** The centralization of monetary policy in the formal exchange rate union and particularly in the full monetary union should also release some real resources, notably in the form of skilled manpower and top level management.

(7)   **Dynamic gains.** The complex of static gains listed above and particularly the benefits (1) to (3) may well generate significant dynamic gains in terms of an increased rate of economic growth over the medium term, where there exists a significant degree of prior economic integration and interdependence. In the African context, however, any such effect can be expected to be small (though not negligible), while integration remains low.

Conclusion

The conclusion is that in general terms there would be greater gains to be obtained from a full monetary union than from any other form of monetary union. In the African context there are strong reasons for preferring the variant of this form of monetary integration that is represented by the West and Central African monetary unions for the reasons discussed above. However, no concrete recommendation can usefully be made for adopting any of these options (or indeed any other form of monetary integration), except in specific cases.

Strategic issues in monetary unification

A preliminary distinction must be made between: (a) the question of how to get to a full monetary union when governments are firmly committed to that objective and (b) the question of what steps could usefully be taken if governments favour some form of monetary harmonization, but are not yet firmly committed to full monetary union. This section addresses each of these questions in turn and evaluates the main alternative strategies.

The direct route

If governments are firmly committed to the objective, the needed steps for monetary unification itself, that is the establishment of a full monetary union, are well understood. A *preparatory period* during which economic convergence would be brought about would be succeeded by a *transitional period* for the actual exchange of currencies and adoption of the new unit of account.[4]

During the preparatory period countries would need to bring their inflation rates into line, stabilize their exchange rates, and remove all restrictions on current and capital account transactions amongst each other. The length of the period would depend on the extent of the disequilibria, the strength of rigidities, and the firmness of government policy, but might be expected to last between two and five years. Once a firm decision has been taken, there is much to be said for creating and sustaining a momentum towards monetary union and moving relatively rapidly towards it, even if that means a sharp initial recession for some countries and inflation rates that are not completely harmonized at the start of the transitional period.

The new union-wide central bank would be set up during the preparatory period and existing national central banks prepared for their transformation into subordinate agencies. After union the national agencies would still be required to perform important functions. They would manage the national payments clearing systems, administer the prudential supervision of national commercial banks and operate any country-specific elements of the monetary policy set by the union-wide central bank in terms of interest rates reserve requirements and/or credit ceilings. The new union-wide central bank for its part would inevitably draw heavily on the existing central banks for its managerial expertise and technical staff.

The Central Bank should be given a specific policy mandate namely to pursue the objective of price stability and/or the maintenance of the exchange rate of the new currency in terms of an external anchor currency if (as suggested later), a fixed peg is adopted.

Consistently with this, its policy makers should be appointed in such a way that they would be free from political pressures in acting in pursuit of their mandate. Such insulation from political interference may well be easier to ensure in a monetary union of several countries than for a central bank in a single country.

In the transitional period the new single currency would be introduced and existing national currencies phased out. Banks would replace old notes and coin both automatically and on demand with new ones. On a certain date the old currency would cease to be legal tender and all transactions and accounts would be conducted in the new currency. Experience of similar exercises suggests that a short period of between three and six months might suffice for its completion.

It should be emphasized that no "currency competition" would be involved in the transitional period. The temporary coexistence of old and new currencies would occur only as the mechanism for reaching the preordained goal of a new single currency.

A currency reform alternative

In cases where one or more of the intended members of a full monetary union were currently experiencing very high rates of inflation—in excess perhaps of 100% per annum—it might be preferable not to undertake a costly disinflation of the existing currency but to opt instead for introducing the new currency directly in the country (or countries) concerned. The old currency would depreciate rapidly against the new one and this would complicate the mechanics of the transition. The monetary authorities would face difficulties in controlling the overall rate of monetary expansion, while price-setting economic agents would have to set prices in both currencies, maintaining the appropriate relationship between them. Nevertheless for countries with very high rates of initial inflation, the costs of currency reform might be less than those involved in bringing about price stability first.

Progress without commitment

If governments are interested in some form of monetary integration, but not yet willing to commit themselves to monetary union, the question may be posed as to whether there is any way in which they can seek to obtain at least some of its benefits, and to manoeuvre themselves into positions from which they might later be willing to make the commitment?

One solution would be for countries to make a start through monetary harmonization by mutually fixing their exchange rates or agreeing on common inflation objectives. Generally major operational difficulties would confront such an approach not so much in agreeing on common inflation objectives or exchange rate parities, but in determining the appropriate macro policies. The relationship between monetary policy and such targets is not sufficiently precise or stable to guarantee their attainment.

In the African context, however, these difficulties can be avoided, because of the existence of external anchor currencies or of currency baskets to which most African countries can and do peg their currencies. These anchors are so strong relative to any actual or prospective African currencies that they are unaffected by developments in the latter. The existence of such potential anchors together with the lower intra-African mobility of capital due to the relatively underdeveloped nature of the financial markets in African countries, suggests that a policy of pegging currencies to the same external anchor would constitute a useful and viable first step towards monetary harmonization. The policy issue would be to determine what would be the optimal peg.

With the development of the EMS in recent years (including the consolidation of the French franc/Deutschemark parity and the more recent accession of sterling to the exchange rate mechanism), the European Currency Unit (ECU) to which in turn the

French franc the Deutschemark the pound Sterling and other currencies are pegged has a claim to be regarded as the optimal peg. Its adoption would allow African countries to peg to a large and solid bloc which accounts for the bulk of their external trade. Pegging to such an external anchor evidently means that countries must accept implicitly or explicitly the inflation objective which is implied (i.e. the inflation rate in the anchor currency). This is likely to be satisfactorily low for the EMS over the medium term.

Thus African countries can relatively easily take initial measures towards both monetary integration and economic convergence. The next step would be to make trade and capital transactions between the members of a prospective union fully convertible, a process which could be installed if so desired in gradual stages and at varying speeds.

Once convertibility had been accomplished countries would find that they had arrived at arrangements which differed from those of an informal exchange-rate union only insofar as: (i) they were operating different degrees of convertibility on their transactions with outside countries, (ii) their explicit exchange-rate commitments were to the common anchor currency rather than to each other's currencies, and (iii) they retained the right to change their exchange rate parities.

At this point, then, countries would have to decide whether they wished to go further. One persuasive reason for doing so would be the difficulties already mentioned of ensuring that the harmonized macroeconomic policies of each country would remain consistent with the peg. If countries did decide to proceed, the course promising the largest benefit would be to embark on the direct route to full monetary integration described earlier.

Other options

The only other options for moving towards monetary integration that have been at all widely discussed, notably in the European debate, are the free currency competition and parallel currency approaches. The first of these would involve making every national currency legal tender in each member country and allowing the currencies to compete until one emerges as the dominant currency. The second option involves the introduction of a new currency parallel to the various existing national currencies; it is presumed that competition, possibly assisted by endowing the parallel currency with superior characteristics in terms of price stability, would then lead to its emergence as the dominant currency throughout the union .

An objection to the first of these strategies is that it might well exacerbate national rivalries; an objection to the second which may also apply partly to the first; is that the problem of controlling the overall rate of monetary expansion and therefore of inflation would be aggravated by the greater number and/or substitutability of currencies.

A further objection derives from the "public good" and "externality" characteristics of money. The usefulness of a given money to a transactor depends fundamentally on the extent to which other transactors are using that money; transactors therefore tend to gravitate towards the same money. In the context of multiple currencies this consideration suggests that only a major shock would induce people to switch to another currency. The only obvious possible example of such a shock is a major divergence in inflation, but for many transactors the loss from higher inflation on average money holdings would be outweighed by the transaction costs of changing into another currency, unless the inflation differential was much larger than is likely after the preparatory period—or indeed for the vast majority of African countries before it.[5]

Advocates of currency competition argue that it "allows the market to decide" the extent and the speed of monetary integration and that this is to be preferred on welfare grounds. However, reliance on the market produces efficient outcomes only if economic agents have full information about the goods or assets amongst which they are choosing. In the case under discussion, uncertainties about the extent to which other transactors are using which money and the longer term properties of different currencies (e.g. the likely inflation rates), are surely so large as to make that argument lack force.

The most recent policy proposal of this sort, the "hard ecu" scheme put forward in the EC context by the UK Government has been criticized on several counts. Apart from the points outlined above, it has also been argued that the hard ecu would either create greater potential instability (by increasing the number of currencies in use within the EC) or would make no contribution at all to monetary integration (because transactors would not choose to use it).

Issues in the management of a monetary union
Any form of monetary union that does not merely involve a *de facto* arrangement resting on the hegemony of a pivotal currency, will be based on a treaty that sets out its constitution and management. The efficacy of any union that is established among a group of sovereign states in Africa, as elsewhere, the distribution of its costs and benefits, and its ability to survive, will depend on the arrangements agreed on and adopted for dealing with a number of technical, managerial and policy issues. Some of the more important of these are discussed in the following section.

The pooling of external reserves

The pooling of external reserves is an integral part of both a formal exchange rate union, and of a full monetary union. An equitable basis of contribution will need to be devised in the formative stages. While national currencies remain, the pooling of reserves not only generates economies, but can also serve as a useful element in the pragmatic operation of monetary policy by indicating the need for changes in policy at the individual country level. In a full monetary union on the other hand, the reserves would be unified and have no intra-union management significance.

External convertibility

A suitable external anchor can be found in the form of a currency (or set of currencies), that has both a dominant influence on a sub-region's trade and investment flows and a low inflation rate. Assurance by the union's central bank of free convertibility of the union's currency into the anchor currency would encourage external confidence and inward investment.

The use of an external anchor currency also confers a number of more technical advantages: (a) exchange rate parities can be defined against the anchor rather than against a basket of the currencies of the union's members, (b) there would be no need for the development of a "divergence indicator" such as that created for the EMS (which turned out to be technically flawed and superfluous), and (c) there would be much less danger of a single dominant country moving the whole union in a direction in which the other members did not wish to go—a particularly important danger in the African context. The use of an external anchor would therefore avoid a number of the problems which have arisen in the EMS.

An external guarantee of convertibility

The currency of an African monetary union could be given still greater credibility if an external guarantee of convertibility could in addition be provided. In the cases of the UMOA and the BCEAC such a guarantee is provided by the French Treasury through the medium of the operations account.

In the context of the new importance attached by the European Community (EC) to supporting regional integration in the framework of Lome IV and the prospect of an EMU being established, it is not inconceivable that a similar kind of monetary cooperation to that which currently exists between France and the African unions might be developed between the EC and some at least of the other countries of Africa. The idea of such cooperation was indeed evoked by the Community itself a decade ago.[6] This prospect could encourage solid progress towards further monetary cooperation. For instance African countries wishing to follow the strategy suggested earlier, and to progress towards monetary union without commitment could be encouraged to attach themselves to the new European monetary unit or meanwhile to the ECU. For all but the handful of currencies that presently float, this would formally entail only a change in the reference currency.

The effect would be to stabilize nominal effective exchange rates between African currencies. The incentive for any country to do this will depend on the number of countries that make the same decision. To induce African countries to take this step, it would be useful if the EC could be persuaded to guarantee the convertibility of the currencies in question.

The amount of aid required to support such an initiative would depend on how it is structured. Unlimited assistance for any major sub-regional monetary initiatives through an operations account on the lines of that provided by the French Treasury for UMOA and BCEAC, is hardly likely to meet with much support from the EC or any other funder.[7] Other systems limiting potential liability to some maximum level could fairly readily be devised and could for certain blocs be valuable. No external guarantee of convertibility is likely to be negotiable, except within the framework of monetary cooperation agreements that would inevitably limit the monetary autonomy of the countries in question perhaps severely. However, such restrictions would strengthen the position of the Central Bank against pressure from union member governments and would reinforce the credibility of the union in financial markets.

External funding to support sub-regional integration initiatives of all kinds is limited. It is thus important that African states should determine the priority they attach to the provision of aid for any monetary integration initiatives by comparison with others, relating for instance to trade and infrastructure.

Finally, it should be mentioned that where external guarantees are already in force as is the case in West and Central Africa, these must pose a major obstacle to any extension of monetary cooperation or union on a wider sub-regional basis unless any wider union is able to offer, at least as favourable guarantees and arrangements.

Exchange rate adjustments
A monetary union would have to retain the ultimate right to adjust its exchange rate *vis-à-vis* the anchor currency in the event of a marked acceleration of inflation in the anchor currency area or an exceptional real shock in either area.

This right exists in the two existing African unions on the basis of unanimity on the part of the Council of Ministers, but has never been exercised. One reason for this, specific to those unions, is the implication that the exercise of this right might have for the future of the external guarantee. But even apart from this, the differing interests of the member countries in terms of their need for changes in real exchange rates to deal with imbalances, and their extent would itself render agreement on change difficult. This would not necessarily apply to other sub-regional groups in which structural characteristics might be more convergent. In any case, no single member of a full monetary union can devalue or revalue, except by leaving the union as did Mali in the case of UMOA.

In recent years African monetary unions and some African countries have experienced episodes of persistent overvaluation. It is, however, far from clear that exchange-rate adjustments can provide more than a temporary palliative to such overvaluations. In so far as it is amenable to policy its cure should be sought elsewhere, notably in firm monetary and fiscal policies.

Seigniorage

The profits that result from the seigniorage of the union's central bank would be distributed according to an agreed formula. The choice is between attribution on the basis of relative shares in the currency issue or else on a redistributive basis resting on some other formula. In the case of the BCEAO, profits are distributed equally amongst the members. Formally this implies a distribution of the benefits that is biased towards the smaller poorer members, but the true situation bearing in mind the elements on profits of the country distribution of subsidized central bank credits and the effects of insolvencies on loan recoveries is likely to be different.

In the case of Southern Africa, in the Common Monetary Area which includes the Republic of South Africa, Swaziland, Lesotho and Namibia, initially under the 1974 Agreement, compensation was paid to Swaziland and Lesotho in proportion to the circulation of Rand currency notes in those countries. With the establishment of central banks in Swaziland, Lesotho and Namibia and the abolition of the Rand's legal tender status in Swaziland, compensation is no longer paid to the latter country (Agreements of 1986). The arrangement with Namibia is under negotiation.

Ceilings on credits to governments by the monetary union

To the extent that domestic non-monetary financing of budget deficits is limited by the underdeveloped nature of capital markets in most African countries any national budget deficits have ultimately to be financed by monetary means or by foreign borrowing. In a full monetary union (and in the African variants) some degree of credit creation may be consistent with compliance with the Central Bank's basic mandate. The central bank must then set ceilings on the credit to be made available to each government. An appropriate formula or guidelines would have to be devised and agreed in advance. In UMOA for instance an upper limit of 20% of the previous year's tax revenue is laid down for the total credit to any member state's government and overall financing limits are fixed for each country in the light of the evolution of its external position.

Nationally differentiated money and credit policies
In the context of full monetary union, an important issue concerns the possibility of the use by the central bank of country-differentiated monetary policy either to facilitate adjustments to shocks affecting a particular member state or to take account of specific structural features in national economic conjunctures or goals. If capital market integration in the union's monetary area is complete in the sense that there are no regulatory or other barriers to the movement of money and capital such differentiation would clearly not be possible. A full monetary union is probably a necessary (but not sufficient) condition for a perfect capital market. In such a market, credit would automatically flow to countries in transitory difficulties. If, however, significant market imperfections remain as for instance is to be expected even in a formal exchange rate union then the central institution should be able to some limited degree to affect the incidence of monetary policies on the member states at least in the short run by means of credit controls that are country specific. In particular, if economic integration is limited with respect to trade, any spillover effects of credit creation in one country on demand conditions in another, will be limited.

In the African context, even if regulatory barriers to financial flows are eliminated significant imperfections in capital market integration are likely to persist as a result of imperfect information and high transactions costs . A full monetary union with a near-perfect capital market may in any case be unattainable or if attainable, undesirable, unless there is a very high degree of economic integration or even full economic union.

The operation of existing monetary unions in Africa can throw some light on what has been achieved with these forms, with respect to financial market integration. At present, there are no effective union money markets in either of the unions. There are virtually no private banking flows between member countries even between affiliates, so that independent credit objectives can be pursued for each country by the Central Bank. Interest rates on loans made by the Central Bank are not market clearing rates but are administered. Its loans are discretionary and depend on policy considerations other than the purely prudential.

If in such monetary unions more perfect financial markets were to be desired by the authorities, many informational and institutional obstacles would as already noted have to be overcome. One of the ingredients for overcoming present limitations would be a much more effective prudential supervision of the commercial banking system than has so far been attempted such as is now in prospect for the countries of BCEAC. That apart, certain institutional changes can be envisaged at the level of the central bank that could help—for instance by giving such international financial intermediation as it itself performs a firmer market basis. Reforms on such lines have been advocated by the World Bank in its Regional Reform Programme for UDEAC. But the trade-off would be a reduced ability to separate national credit conditions. Likewise more effective sub-regional money markets would also imply some rethinking of certain country-specific objectives of the Structural Adjustment Programmes of international agencies—for instance in relation to credit—which could not then be made effective.

The implications of monetary union for the integration of other economic policies and institutions

Introduction
The necessity for a centralized monetary policy in a monetary union and the close relationship that normally exists between monetary policy and certain other policies in particular fiscal policy, leads to the question of whether it is necessary or desirable that in African monetary integration any of these other policies should be centralized, and if so through what instruments and to what degree.

If the monetary union is seen as one facet of a programme of economic and monetary integration, perhaps selling as a catalyst for economic integration, the question is partly a matter of sequencing and timing. If however, monetary union is seen more as a free standing policy designed essentially to provide macroeconomic stability, whose benefits derive principally from the advantages of convertibility and fixed exchange rates for development generally, the appropriate question would be what is the minimal degree of integration, harmonization or co-ordination of these other policies that is consistent with the viability of monetary union once established. Moreover, where countries wish to maintain as much national autonomy as possible, which may be the appropriate scenario in Africa? The issue is, what mechanisms are appropriate to secure purely national goals?

The answers to these questions will depend partly on the forms of monetary union adopted and the extent to which they are encouraged to result in highly interrelated money and capital markets. It will also depend on the structural characteristics of the member states themselves, on the extent to which they are structurally interdependent (which will determine the significance of economic and policy spillovers), on the extent to which any shocks affecting them are likely to be internal or external, symmetric or asymmetric, transitory or of long duration, and finally on the extent to which product markets and other factor markets—notably that for labour—are integrated.

Measures to improve the working of the capital market
The development of effective sub-regional money and capital markets will necessarily require the removal of intra-bloc controls over the movement of money and capital within the union area, but such measures would not in themselves be sufficient. It would in addition be necessary for the members to adopt on a concerted basis a range of positive integration measures targeted at harmonizing national financial regulations and structures.

Capital market liberalization will also demand a consistent harmonization of certain aspects of fiscal (tax) policies with respect to capital and savings if highly integrated financial markets are to result from any form of monetary union.

Conceivably, tax harmonization requirements in terms of rates might in certain circumstances—e.g. free trade—be left to market forces to induce, but experience in Europe suggests that many other needed changes would have to be addressed by concerted public action. This would be facilitated if they could be implemented directly under the aegis of sub-regional economic groupings. In the African monetary unions, the conduct of the central banks themselves would also be material.

Fiscal harmonization
A crucially important issue in relation to monetary integration arises in connection with the extent of the control needed over national budgets of member states. It is essential that national fiscal policies should somehow be made consistent with the monetary and exchange rate objectives of the union. To attain this goal, several options might be envisaged.

One option would be for binding rules to be imposed that would impose uniform upper limits on deficit financing by member states and limit public sector recourse to sub-regional capital markets and external borrowing. The theoretical justification for introducing such uniform rules in terms of the imputable effects of national fiscal policies on union reserve positions is not convincing.

Another option would be to leave the market to resolve the issue, that is to permit member states to utilize sub-regional or international capital markets to finance any desired deficit beyond what may be financed through the central bank. But even in Europe, where the Community's money and capital markets are already highly integrated and efficient, it is not generally thought to be consistent with the macroeconomic objectives of EMU to leave such fiscal policy choices in the hands of member states to that degree. The debate has not yet been resolved, but the Delors Plan itself places strong emphasis on the need for the Community to impose binding constraints on national fiscal policies.

In the two African monetary unions, the principal formal means of fiscal harmonization is provided by the statutory limit on credit accorded to member governments by the central banking system. The binding constraint, however, is provided by the national credit programmes which are determined in the light of the needs of external balance. As a result, fiscal policy stances have not been uniform, some members having incurred substantial deficits, in part financed by foreign debt.

On the whole, unless and until highly integrated regional economic communities should be developed in Africa, it seems both desirable and inevitable that some flexibility should be built into African systems to reflect national conjunctural situations and, in particular, the ability of particular countries to service their external debts. The task is to do this in such a way that the monetary stability of the whole system is not threatened. Can an operational yardstick be provided? In the end it may be desirable for African monetary unions to adopt a so-called golden rule of public finance, namely that national public borrowing should not exceed investment. But this is unlikely to rule out the need for other pragmatic controls.

Like the proposed European Monetary Union, many African unions will operate for the foreseeable future in a context in which it will be the fiscal stances of member states that determine the fiscal stance of the blocs. This is because none of the actual economic communities in Africa possesses any of their 'own' revenues or a budget of a sufficiently large size and scope to be significant in terms of macroeconomic policy. In the EC, this consideration has provided additional grounds for arguing for the imposition of fiscal harmonization upon member states of the proposed monetary union (for instance, because of the need to take joint account of the spillover effects of expansionary fiscal policies in determining optimal national fiscal policy stances). These additional arguments appear to have no immediate relevance in the current structural conditions of African economies, given in particular their highly open nature and the limited degree of intra-African trade. In the longer term, as structural transformation succeeds, they may become so. In the meantime, the basic argument for fiscal policy harmonization in actual and prospective monetary blocs in Africa in terms of the requirements of monetary and exchange rate stability considerations, has overriding force, though its precise operational implications for African blocs can only be determined pragmatically. It is clear from the previous section, however, as well as from the evolution of the

173

reserve positions of African unions during the decade of the eighties, that although the fixing of credit ceilings is an important instrument of fiscal harmonization, it may not on its own be sufficient.

Intra-regional adjustment issues
The major problems under this head are likely to present themselves in connection with post-union adjustment problems and shocks that are unexpected in their severity or character and at the same time asymmetrical. Some mechanisms must be provided for alleviating these problems if a union is to be durable. It will in general be easier to deal with a number of these problems if the monetary union coexists with a well-functioning economic community that possesses some degree of fiscal centralization. Indeed, if a union should exist without significant economic and fiscal integration, it may not be possible for the bloc itself to deal with any adjustment problems satisfactorily since the central banking mechanism will have a strictly limited capacity for doing so. To that extent, it is not a matter of indifference whether full monetary union precedes or follows a significant process of economic integration. It must, however, be noted that if a coexisting economic community is based upon a customs union, certain other possible national adjustment mechanisms, for instance those that operate through trade policy interventions, will also be unavailable to member states on an individual basis.

If monetary union takes the form of an informal exchange rate union, asymmetrical adverse shocks will give rise—in one or more member—states to a loss of reserves, and ultimately a reduction in the money supply, and will also require relative changes in prices and incomes. If a formal exchange rate union or a full monetary union exists, the need to settle intra-union deficits and surpluses in foreign currency, would not arise, but intra-union deficits would still have to be adjusted by a fall in the deficit country's wage and income levels. The need for such adjustments might be postponed by a redistribution of private financial assets within the union through the commercial banking system, but would not be eliminated.

Outside Africa, monetary unions hardly exist except in federations or in unitary states. In these cases, fiscal policy brings about automatic or discretionary transfers of resources within the union, that compensate to an extent for the inability of states or regions to conduct their own trade and exchange-rate policies for the purpose of dealing with their adjustment problems. If full monetary union comes about in Europe, it will be the first major example of a monetary union of independent states.

Many critics argue that even in Europe, a monetary union could not be viable without a substantially increased role for the EC budget and a corresponding transfer of certain major existing national expenditure functions such as social security to the Community so as to enable it to undertake similar transfers and policies to those undertaken in unitary and federal states.

Since such a prospect does not seem to be realistic when considering new or extended African monetary unions, if such unions are to be acceptable and viable, some alternative means, even if limited, may have to be in firm prospect to ease their potential adjustment problems and to promote the cohesion of the bloc, even if the union or bloc is not itself the source of emergent problems.

In Africa, unlike the case of Europe, a persisting segmentation of capital and money markets, even if formal exchange-rate or full monetary unions should be established, is likely to leave room for some time to come for the operation of a limited degree of country-differentiated credit policy without impairing the overriding objectives and mandate of the central bank. The danger of overloading monetary institutions with inappropriate functions to the detriment of their central objectives is, nevertheless, to be avoided.

But in any case, if adjustment problems should arise that take the form of long-term problems for certain members, perhaps resulting from a polarization of development, facilitated by capital market liberalization, these could not be dealt with in the framework of monetary mechanisms since they would involve a need for long term financial transfers. Other devices would then have to be found.

Possibly, appropriate sub-regional vehicles for dealing with them might be developed, either through sub-regional development banks, such as the West African Development Bank, or through funds akin to those already established by ECOWAS and CEAO. The likely continuing need on the part of African countries to rely for adjustment assistance on external funders and donors would, however, argue strongly for the adoption of the special form of monetary union represented by UMOA and BCEAC, rather than full monetary union.

Alternatives to monetary union
If it is concluded that certain sub-regions do not constitute suitable single or even common currency areas, or if, although they may be potentially suitable, there is no immediate prospect of needed macro-adjustment policies being implemented, no alternative mechanisms are available that are capable of fully capturing the benefits of monetary union. There do, however, exist some institutional arrangements that in principle are capable of generating some of its subsidiary benefits. Three such mechanisms are considered below:

Sub-regional clearing arrangements

One important advantage of a monetary union is that it eliminates the costs of foreign exchange dealing with respect to intra-union transactions. Even with highly developed banking and foreign exchange markets such as exist in Europe, these costs can be considerable.[8]

It may be possible for groups of African countries to procure part of this gain without establishing a monetary union by establishing a clearing institution. Three have already been established with this in mind. The object would be to channel payments among the members through this institution instead of through other institutions outside the sub-region. Such a clearing house could reduce transactions costs by limiting the need for convertible currencies (on the basis of which intragroup trade would otherwise take place) to the net balance of any country with the group. The extent to which real gains would actually be generated would depend on the extent to which the gains from economizing in the use of foreign exchange would be offset by the administrative costs involved in operating such an institution.

Three such arrangements are already in operation in Africa, namely the West African Clearing House (WACH), the East and Southern African (PTA) Clearing House, and the Clearing House of the Economic Community of Central African States.

The WACH, the longest established of the three, is recognized to have performed poorly because of a number of problems which also concern the other two institutions. The share of sub-regional trade handled—never high—has declined markedly. Although as much as 40% of sub-regional trade could potentially have been paid for in the eighties with regional currencies, only 2% was so cleared, because of persistent imbalances in regional trade handled by the system. Large debit positions have accumulated, requiring settlement in convertible currencies. The widespread delays and failure to settle debts have inevitably curtailed the use of the system.

Many suggestions have been made for improvement. Provision for direct access on the part of commercial banks is one. Another is to utilize parallel exchange rates for transactions through the clearing houses. This proposal, designed inter alia to promote regional convertibility and the greater use of official channels, is fraught with difficulties and does not go to the heart of the problem. Multilateralizing the settlement process could be an important improvement. This, however, would have to be linked to the formal provision of credit which would in any case be desirable.

A sub-regional payments union

Clearing houses are not designed to provide credit, apart from interim finance between settlement dates. A more developed form of monetary cooperation that might overcome some of the settlement difficulties experienced with existing clearing houses and so encourage their wider use, is the payments union. This links an automatic credit arrangement with a clearing arrangement. Such a union would require a capital fund made up of part of the reserve assets of member countries. This fund might be supplemented by donors. This kind of union is on the point of being re-established for Central America, with EC funding, to underpin the Central American Common Market, and has effectively been recommended for WACH. The PTA Clearing House is also pursuing the issue. In the case of WACH still more ambitious proposals envisage a parallel assumption of additional functions as a path to monetary integration.

It has to be recognized, however, that clearing and payments institutions, though useful, cannot be expected to perform adequately without a reform of present trade and exchange-rate policies that significantly impede sub-regional integration. Effectively, liberalization is a pre-condition of their successful operation.

Reserve pooling
A third form of monetary cooperation that has been suggested to enable some of the gains associated with monetary union to be secured is the institution of a freestanding arrangement for reserve pooling by this means. There could in principle be a reduction in the size of the reserves that need to be held in relation to the character and size of the trading position of the group to the extent that the members of the union experience different and unsynchronized fluctuations in their balance of payments. Without an agreed framework to coordinate the macro policies of its members, however, immense practical difficulties would be likely to arise in operating a reserve pooling arrangement and these would almost certainly rule it out as a realistic option in advance of arrangements for monetary harmonization. The same difficulty could indeed apply to certain forms of payments union with provision for automatic credit, since members could effectively be called upon to finance the deficits of others from reserves. With built-in sanctions, however, or, more ambitiously, in conjunction with effective arrangements for monetary harmonization in appropriately chosen blocs, a well-designed payments union could constitute a useful mechanism to adopt on the way to fuller monetary integration.

Conclusions
The main conclusions are as follows:

(1)   If monetary union is sought, full monetary union is generally to be preferred, since while the *ex ante* costs of all three basic types are the same, the benefits of full union are higher. In African conditions, however, given the low level of bloc fiscal integration, the dependence of African countries on external funders,

and the financially self-contained nature of the private sector, the more limited African form resting on a common currency would be strongly indicated.

(2)   The achievement of any form of monetary union would, however, require a preparatory period of macroeconomic adjustment during which exchange restrictions are removed, exchange rates are stabilized, and inflation rates are brought broadly into line in the countries of the prospective union.

(3)   If countries in certain sub-regions are interested in monetary union, but not prepared to commit themselves, a useful and viable first step would be for them all to peg their currencies to the same external anchor currency. During a second stage, intra-union current and capital transactions could be gradually liberalized, not necessarily at a uniform pace.

(4)   Other possible strategic options, including the creation of a parallel currency, such as a "hard" Africans, would not be recommendable.

(5)   If the formation of new monetary unions is desired, or major extensions of existing ones, the possibility of procuring an external guarantee of convertibility should be vigorously pursued (perhaps with the European Community in the first instance). The benefits of union (notably its impact on inward investment), and its credibility, would be greatly enhanced. Guarantees are unlikely to be forthcoming without the acceptance of significant constraints on the monetary policy sovereignty of member states. But it has to be recognized that this sovereignty is in any case largely nominal and that the long-run real effects of its exercise, if any, are almost certainly adverse.

(6)   If new African monetary unions are established on present lines, limited scope would still exist for the operation of nationally differentiated money and credit policies within them, thus enabling account to be taken, to some extent, of the special positions and needs of member states. Such possibilities would be greater the less integrated were their money and capital markets. In this respect, there is a trade-off between the benefits of more complete money market integration and the costs of reduced national autonomy .

(7)   The development of efficient and effective money and capital markets within a sub-region, from which the benefits of monetary integration partly flow, would in any case not only demand the removal of restrictions on intrasubregional transfers, but also the introduction of a variety of positive measures, probably calling for action in concert, to overcome informational deficiencies and reduce transactions costs.

(8)   Monetary union would require limitations on access to central bank credits by member states and control over the fiscal policy stances of member states. Operational rules would need to be devised. A rule that national public borrowing should not exceed defined investment, suggests itself, but is unlikely on its own to be sufficient.

(9)   If new monetary unions are to be established, financial support to ameliorate potential long-term asymmetric structural adjustment problems would need to be available to protect their viability. These problems cannot adequately, if at all, be dealt with in the framework of purely monetary arrangements. If a monetary union were to be established in conjunction with an effective system of regional integration, to some degree some of these problems could be dealt with more readily, notwithstanding the fact that trade policy adjustment measures specific to particular member countries would at the same time often be excluded. To the extent that African countries must continue to rely for some time to come on external funders and donors to provide their main financial support for adjustment, the special form of monetary union already in operation in Africa would appear to be optimal.

(10)   Although there are no alternative mechanisms capable of fully capturing the benefits of monetary union, some of its subsidiary benefits, notably a reduction in transaction costs, could in principle be procured by the development of certain free-standing institutions such as clearing houses and payments unions, and conceivably by reserve pooling arrangements.

(11)   Among the areas where policy-orientated research is needed to carry discussion further, and to enable an informed choice to be made amongst alternative policy options, the following may be mentioned:

(i)   The implications for prospective members of potential monetary unions or of other schemes of monetary harmonization, of pegging their currencies if they are presently floating, and for those already pegged, the implications of pegging to the ECU rather than to any other reference currency or basket of currencies.

(ii)   An evaluation of the feasibility of alternative proposals for improving the contribution of the WACH and other clearing institutions to monetary integration and harmonization in Africa.

(iii)   An examination of the merits of alternative rules for coordinating fiscal policy within monetary unions in Africa. .

(iv)   The feasibility, costs and benefits of further developing sub-regional and financial markets in Africa.

    (v)   The financial costs and other implications of alternative arrangements for the provision of external guarantees of convertibility in the context of possible new African sub-regional currencies and other forms of monetary integration and harmonization.

    (vi)   The specific tax and other harmonization measures required for effective capital market liberalization and integration.

    (vii)   An examination of mechanisms that might be developed to ease regional adjustment problems within monetary unions in the specific sub-regional blocs now contemplating such arrangements, and their compatibility with different levels of economic and monetary integration.

Notes

1   Intervention may operate partly by non-monetary restrictions as is typically the case in African countries outside monetary unions. Such restrictions are precluded by convertibility.

2   Padoa-Schioppa, T., "The European Monetary System: A Long-term View" in F. Giavazzi, S. Micossi and M. Miller, eds), *European Monetary System*, Cambridge University Press 1988.

3   This can be assessed either by examining the net export of individual countries' banknotes or by comparing the growth of money holdings in each country with the expansion of domestic credit.

4   The preparatory period in effect combines Stages 1 and 2 of the Delors Report. It has been widely remarked that in that report Stage 2 is largely empty of content, and that the monetary arrangements envisaged for that stage (an informal exchange rate union) would be most vulnerable to instability and speculative pressures.

5   For a transactor who is paid monthly (weekly), average money holdings are likely to be at most $1/24$ $(1/104)$ of annual income. If the inflation differential between the existing national currency and the new parallel currency (or some other competing national currency) is 20%, the transactor then loses each year 20% of $1/24$ $(1/104)$, that is 0.8% (0.2%), of annual income by continuing to use the national currency. This figure needs to be compared with the transactions cost involved in transferring the year's income (in monthly or weekly amounts) into the other currency; that cost is likely to be nearer 5 %.

6   Memorandum on the Community's Development Policy. EC: Brussels 1982

7   Equatorial Guinea has been admitted to BCEAC and it is believed that there would be no objection on the part of the French Treasury to the admission of The Gambia to UMOA. The admission of large countries, or of large numbers of small countries would, however, clearly pose many difficulties for the present guarantor.

8   For instance, the average time taken for bank transfers is five days and the effective cost of clearing a Eurocheque for 150 Ecu is about 7% (according to the Christophersen Report). However, in "One Market, One Money" (*European Economy*, no.44 Oct 1990), the Commission gives a somewhat lower cost for clearing a Eurocheque.

Annex 1
Exchange rate systems, origin of imports, inflation rates and GDP of African countries

	One currency $US	FF	Currency basket Rand	SDR	Others	Flexible systems	Year	EC Canada	USA & Canada	Africa	1965–80	1980–87	$million 1987
Exchange rate established by reference to								**Origin of imports: % of total**			**Average annual inflation rate (%)**		**GDP**
Algeria					x		1987	60.3	8.9	2.8	9.8	5.6	64,600
Angola							1981	56.8	10.0				1,570
Benin		x					1984	54.8	5.1	10.5	7.4	8.2	
Botswana				x						8.1	8.4		1,520
Burkina Faso		x					1983	44.9	10.8	28.8	6.2	4.4	1,650
Burundi				x			1986	56.4	2.7	12.2	8.5	7.5	1,150
Cameroon		x					1987	64.7	3.8	5.8	8.9	8.1	12,660
Cape Verde					x		1985	67.9	2.0	4.7		13.9	
Central African Republic		x					1982	64.9	4.3	14.5	8.5	7.9	1,010
Chad		x					1983	59.2	5.7	31.0	6.3	5.3	980
Congo		x					1985	72.1	6.8	5.5	6.6	1.8	2,150
Djibouti	x												
Egypt						x	1988	40.8	12.7	1.3	7.3	9.2	34,470
Ethiopia	x						1985	35.6	19.3	1.4	3.4	2.6	4,800
Gabon		x					1983	74.6	11.2	1.5	12.7	2.6	3,500
The Gambia					x		1980	51.6	2.0	8.4	8.3	13.8	
Ghana						x	1983	48.4	9.8	21.7	22.8	48.3	5,080
Guinea						x	1983	51.1	9.2	12.4	2.9		
Guinea Bissau						x	1981	50.0	7.5	8.2		39.2	
Equatorial Guinea		x					1982	89.7	1.0	3.9			
Ivory Coast		x					1985	54.1	7.9	21.4	9.5	4.4	7,650
Kenya				x			1984	37.1	5.3	1.2	7.3	10.3	6,930
Lesotho			x								8.0	12.3	270
Liberia	x						1984	40.0	22.5	13.5	6.3	1.5	990
Libya				x			1981	64.8	6.9	1.0			

Annex 1 (continued)
Exchange rate systems, origin of imports, inflation rates and GDP of African countries

| | Exchange rate established by reference to | | | | | | Origin of imports: % of total | | | | Average annual inflation rate (%) | | GDP $million |
| | One currency | | Currency basket | | | | | | | | | | |
	$US	FF	Rand	SDR	Others	Flexible systems	Year	EC	USA & Canada	Africa	1965–80	1980–87	1987
Malawi					x		1986	41.7	3.9	7.4	7.0	12.4	1,110
Mali		x					1982	43.8	4.0	41.3		4.2	1,960
Mauritania						x	1986	74.6	3.4	6.9	7.7	9.8	840
Morocco						x	1988	52.4	12.1	2.1	6.1	7.3	16,750
Mozambique					x		1983	50.0	5.7	1.2		26.9	1,490
Namibia			x										
Niger		x					1985	42.0	13.6	18.0	7.5	4.1	2,160
Nigeria						x	1986	57.8	12.3	1.2	13.7	10.1	24,390
Rwanda				x			1986	45.4	5.3	21.3	12.4	4.5	2,100
Sao Tome & Principe					x		1983	18.2	4.1	16.2		4.9	
Senegal		x					1984	44.1	6.5	25.9	6.5	9.1	4,720
Sierra Leone	x						1984	40.5	4.2	38.0	8.0	50.0	900
Somalia					x		1985	43.2	14.2	6.7	10.5	37.8	1,890
Sudan	x						1983	38.3	9.6	3.4	11.5	31.7	8,210
Swaziland			x								9.1	10.2	
Tanzania					x		1985	42.6	5.4	6.3	9.9	24.9	3,080
Togo		x					1984	44.2	6.0	11.4	6.9	6.6	1,230
Tunisia						x	1988	66.7	9.4	5.6	6.7	8.2	8,450
Uganda					x		1983	36.0	2.5	43.0	21.2	95.2	3,560
Zaire						x	1982	64.6	13.2	3.1	24.7	53.5	5,770
Zambia				x			1984	26.4	7.5	7.8	6.4	28.7	2,030
Zimbabwe					x		1986	32.2	9.3	3.4	6.4	12.4	5,240

Source: UNCTAD, Handbook of International Trade and Development Statistics, 1987 and 1989 supplements; World Bank, World Development Report 1989.

11

Towards Monetary Integration in Africa: the Strategic Monetary Policy Issues

M.I. Mah'moud

In recent years, summit-level decisions have been taken among various African governments in support of monetary integration or coordination in their respective sub-regions. For some of the decisions, integration is to pave the way for the eventual establishment of sub-regional monetary unions. In the Economic Community of West African States (ECOWAS), the decision to create progressively a single monetary zone was taken by the Heads of States and Governments in 1983 and confirmed by the adoption in 1987 of the ECOWAS Programme on Monetary Cooperation. In the Eastern and Southern African sub-region, monetary harmonization endeavours, whose ultimate objectives are the establishment of a common market and a monetary union, are being pursued under the auspices of the Preferential Trade Area (PTA). There is a similar parallel effort among the countries of the Southern African Development Coordination Conference (SADCC).[2] While the decisions have come out of careful consideration of the perceived net benefits for monetary integration, the strategies for implementing monetary integration or the methods for coordinating monetary and fiscal policies among the various countries in the transitional period are still not clear. Yet the importance of choosing the right strategies for monetary integration cannot be overemphasized because the good intentions of governments can turn into disaster when integration is implemented with bad methods and around bad policies. Welfare improvements for the people in the sub-region are not automatic, simply because national policies are changed in recognition of sub-regional economic interdependence.[3]

It is also worth explaining that proper coordination of monetary and fiscal policies is only one of the conditions required for successful monetary integration (ACMS, 1981).[4] Another important requirement would be for countries in the sub-region to liberalize trade in order to facilitate freedom of movement of goods and services. Countries would also have to grant each other preferential tariff reductions to encourage intrasub-regional trade. In addition, restrictions on intrasub-regional movements of capital and labour should be removed.

This study, however, focuses on some of the issues that arise in search of the correct methods for coordination of monetary and fiscal policies among African countries and does not concern itself with arrangements towards the achievement of the other conditions for successful monetary integration (Mah'moud, 1991). The backdrop of the discussion will be coordination arrangements other than those for full monetary union, which are rather well-known and well defined. The study, therefore, discusses the merits and demerits of alternative methods such as rules versus discretion, single versus multi-indicator (and/or target) approaches and hegemonic, versus symmetric systems in the coordination arrangements such as are made for the transition to full monetary unions. Related to these are also the issues of appropriate margins for fiscal independence and of rapid versus gradual implementation of the necessary adjustments.

While the above issues also emerge in domestic policy discussions, their consideration in sub-regional policy coordination efforts may come up against some difficulties. Though monetary policy goals are normally considered by all African governments to include price stability, sustainable economic growth, balanced economic development, high (if not full) employment, sustainable balance of payments positions and, in general, stable financial system, the priorities accorded to these goals differ among various governments, and for any given country, intertemporally. However, since the mid-1980s, because of the widespread external debt problems, many governments have tended to put emphasis on the need for maintaining sustainable balance of payments positions. Yet policy responses to current account imbalances will differ among countries, because of differences in the origins and reversibility of the imbalances as well as in available foreign support.

The various bargaining governments may also have different assessments of the effects certain policy changes can have on policy targets. These differences may go beyond the size to even the direction (or sign) of the policy impacts. Such controversies are more likely to arise especially with regard to the efficacy of price instruments such as interest rates and exchange rates and the extent of use of quantitative restrictions to correct structural problems. Such disagreements on how the African world works may also frustrate bargaining on what common objectives to adopt. If policy instruments are also to be treated as targets, as would be the case for exchange rates in currency arrangements in the transitional period to the establishment of monetary unions, the bargaining can be very complicated.

The transitional arrangements towards monetary unions would normally require, for example, that following exchange rate adjustments to appropriate levels, countries endeavour to maintain stable exchange rates. Thus, progressively there will be loss of the nominal exchange rate as a policy instrument. One condition for ability of countries to accept this loss is the availability of a transfer system to accommodate reversible current account imbalances, but it is unlikely that such arrangement (say from pooled reserves), will be established in the transitional period.[5]

Another difficulty in the sub-regional coordination efforts is that in terms of national priorities, sub-regional (or regional) bargaining comes after domestic bargaining. African countries are undertaking various reforms, which have been the outcome of discussions with such powerful international institutions as the International Monetary Fund and the World Bank and with domestic political pressure groups. Therefore, sub-regional coordination efforts will come at the back of domestic commitments, because the bargaining governments cannot afford to adopt objectives and instruments that are likely to be rejected by domestic political pressure groups, especially in the present era of political reforms, nor conflict with the policy directions desired by the supporting external financial institutions. These difficulties are important to bear in mind for the discussions here.

Rules versus discretion

The discussions for coordination in an emerging monetary union or in any arrangements for monetary integration are likely to touch on the issues of setting of monetary policy instruments such as interest rates and exchange rates as well as the extent of use of direct controls to achieve the objectives for coordination. However, instrument settings have been the source of long continuing debate of the relative merits of rules versus discretion at the domestic economic policy level, and the debate cannot be avoided among bargaining governments. While some governments may favour rules being imposed to guide conduct of monetary, fiscal and exchange rate policies, others may want commitments to coordination to be implemented by discretion.

At the international policy coordination level, the case for rules reflects the success in the management of the existing monetary unions, which are anchored with rules (Guillaumont and Guillaumont, 1988). The rules-based system decreases the need for frequent coordination and, therefore, limits negotiation costs and burden-sharing conflicts that are inherent in more discretionary systems. Such conflicts raise the need for more negotiations for proper coordination. However, if there is an excess demand for coordination, the appropriate response should not be the increase in the supply of coordination. Rather, the excess demand for coordination should be eliminated by agreement on rules. Related to the above argument is the fact that rules can provide a viable mechanism for imposing discipline on economic policy-makers who could otherwise manipulate instrument settings for their own objectives and to the detriment of the community. Rules also enhance the predictability of policy directions and, therefore, help the private sector to make better informed decisions for their economic operations. Finally, recalling a monetarist argument for rules-based domestic economic policies, the case for rules can also be made in African countries on the basis of the need to provide protection against the lack of knowledge about how the economy operates by pre-empting destabilizing fine-tuning.

The counter-arguments in favour of discretion can, however, rest on an important distinction that needs to be drawn between the situations of the monetary unions where the member governments have given up sovereignty in the area of monetary policy formulation and that of the transitional or other coordination arrangements in which sovereignty in the area of monetary policy formulation and that of the transitional or other coordination arrangements in which sovereign rights are maintained. In the latter situation, there can be no guarantee that rules will be followed in the face of intense domestic pressures to depart from the community's agreement. The likelihood that rules may be broken anyway will be high to the extent that the community arrangement does not impose sanctions on rule-breakers. In any case, the rigid adherence to rules will trade off the governments' abilities to adapt their policies to changes in the economic environment.

In an African country such discretionary adaptation appears to be important for three reasons. First, the kind of shocks that hit African economies are mostly real rather than monetary. In contrast to the shocks of developed market economies, which are more likely to be endogenously-caused *ad cyclical*, the shocks affecting African economies are mostly exogenous and not inherently reversible (Mah'moud, 1988). In such situations, discretionary policy intervention is necessary to reverse a steadily deteriorating situation. Second, because of structural rigidities in African economies, exogenous economic shocks can have very severe impact and long-term effects which would require resetting of policy targets and instruments. Third, recent empirical work undertaken for developed countries (Friedman, 1989) shows that there is a weakening in the link between narrow monetary aggregates and the ultimate monetary policy targets in the face of large-scale financial innovation and institutional changes. Such a weakening of link, which reduces the usefulness of rules, is also likely to be found in African countries because of the ongoing structural adjustment programmes and radical financial sector reforms. Therefore, there is great attraction in coordinating economic policies in an African sub-region (or community) in a framework that leaves some discretion in policy formulation to the individual governments.

Rigid versus flexible fiscal policy coordination

Although this study relates to monetary policy issues in the context of monetary integration efforts in Africa, a special discussion of fiscal policy, especially in connection with the issue of rules versus discretion, would not be out of place. Indeed, a profound lesson of monetary policy formulation and implementation in post-colonial Africa is that for many years, in several countries, fiscal policy remained undisciplined and uncoordinated with monetary policy, causing the goals of stabilization policies, especially efforts to promote price stability and sustainable current account balances, to be seriously compromised. In the context of monetary integration, undisciplined budgetary policies have the added danger of generating international spillovers with adverse effects on the efforts of the community. Therefore, some mechanism for enforcing budgetary discipline would be necessary to reinforce the strategies for monetary policy in arrangements for monetary integration in Africa.

While the potential mechanisms for fiscal discipline could be either domestic (market mechanism or self-imposed rules) or external (the country's international political or economic relations), in Africa the former mechanisms have not been effective. The conditions for market-imposed fiscal discipline, via increasing cost of borrowing or the pressures to avoid higher taxes, do not exist, mainly, because of imperfect financial market conditions and the existence of banking systems that are compelled to bail out the government (Frenkel and Goldstein, 1991). At the same time, the post-independence development strategies and economic recourse to borrowing from the banking systems, made it difficult to adhere to nationally-imposed rules for fiscal discipline.

As explained by Collier (1991), the effective mechanisms for fiscal discipline in Africa have been available only through the external relations of the various countries. For countries in the African monetary unions (the Franc Zone), the constraints are in the form of lending ceilings from the monetary authorities. They are, therefore, rules based and participatory. For the other African countries, external restraints for fiscal discipline are related to donor leverage and operate through IMF and World Bank conditionality, which are largely non-participatory and therefore subject to criticisms by the African governments. Thus, in the efforts toward monetary integration in Africa, fiscal discipline cannot be left to IMF/World Bank conditionalities, and neither are union-type rules enforceable in the preparatory stages.

A plausible mechanism for fiscal discipline in the emerging monetary unions, as suggested by Frenkel and Goldstein (1991), could be fiscal policy coordination that is encouraged through community (or peer group) surveillance. If coordination is to prepare the way for the eventual establishment of a monetary union, then the mechanism should foreshadow the union rules. Yet, in the absence of mechanisms for transfers or reserve pooling, rigid rues may not be desirable because of relevant intercountry differences—say, in private savings rates, outstanding debt stocks, initial fiscal positions, budgetary objectives and/or available foreign assistance. Therefore, coordination can likely be achieved only through a discretionary format.

Quite apart from the normal obstacles to effective discretionary fiscal policy action (for example, the existence of long and variable lags, the need for appropriate application of changes in taxes and expenditures for the desired effects on macrovariables), a key issue in the design of fiscal policy coordination in search of fiscal discipline in the emerging monetary unions would be the formulation of the format for coordination. As hinted above, the formats often chosen foreshadow union rules. In the existing African monetary unions, the rules are in the form of ceilings on fiscal deficits to be financed (specifically, ceilings on the stock of debt with the union central bank) relative to fiscal receipts.[6] Such ceilings would be useful in preventing overexpansionary budgetary policies, and cannot limit excessive budgetary contractions (see Bovenberg et al., 1991). Therefore, there is some merit in allowing fiscal flexibility within specified bands (ceilings and floors) of fiscal deficits or stocks of debt financed by the national central banks (Buiter, 1981). However, as argued below, the most appropriate surveillance methods should be based on multi-indicators so as to give considerable scope for discretion in policy diagnosis and prescription.

Single indicator target versus multi-indicator target
Indicators are the variables that provide a quick measure of a country's economic performance. With respect to economic policy coordination among countries, the indicators signal how the thrust of a country's economic policies are consistent with the commitments made for coordination. Therefore, the indicators chosen will depend on the objectives for economic policy coordination. For example, in the European Monetary system, where the objectives relate to the achievement of exchange rate stability and greater convergence of financial and economic policies among the participating countries, the indicator chosen is the divergence of the countries' exchange rates from given parities. The flashing of a warning from a divergence indicator triggers consultations, and the country concerned is expected to take corrective measures. In the Franc Zone system, where exchange rates among members are fixed, indicators relate to movements of foreign exchange reserves at the French Treasury.

While indicators are not necessarily goals to be achieved by economic policies, it is possible for some indicators to also be used, combined with targets of economic policy. This is particularly likely in sub-regional economic coordination arrangements. In such arrangements, the objective of establishing monetary unions or promoting sub-regional trade, for example, may require countries to set targets on one or a combination of exchange rates, credit to government and some fiscal and monetary policy variables. While some of these targets are instruments of economic policy, they become indicators of how to measure a country's economic performance with respect to commitments under the sub-regional coordination arrangements.

Apart from the problem of choice of indicator(s), which depends on the objective of the coordination arrangements, there is often the issue of how many indicators to use. A single indicator approach may focus on exchange rate movement alone, whereas a multi-indicator approach may focus on a number of other monetary and fiscal variables. The advantage of the former is that it avoids over-coordination by preserving freedom of action over the other policies not selected as indicators, thereby increasing the likelihood that the sovereign states would abide by their commitments for coordination. The single indicator approach has the added advantage of giving economic operators a clear signal as to the future policy direction. For example, a sub-regional commitment on fixed (or given levels of) exchange rates could give economic operators one clear economic signal and provide monetary authorities with a clear guide for economic policy formulation.

However, the single-indicator approach is not without risks. While giving clear signals about policy actions on the chosen indicator, it can weaken surveillance of other variables not chosen even if their changes have important implications for the objectives of coordination. On the other hand, multi-indicator approach commits the authorities to pay attention to a set of important indicators. For example, with respect to possible arrangements for monetary policy harmonization in the African sub-regions, although a commitment on the exchange rate as an indicator would have merits as explained above, the adoption of additional indicators such as credit to government and/or some measure of financing of budget deficits would be appealing, because the vast cause of misaligned exchange rates is inappropriate fiscal/monetary policy stance. Besides, as indicators also act as warning signals to the authorities, the chances of false signals would decrease with a set of signals rather than with one signal.

Hegemonic versus symmetric system
The method of coordination (or harmonization) also has to settle the question of whether one country (or group of countries) should have a predominant influence on

the sub-regional policy direction (hegemonic system) or whether that influence should be shared among the participating countries (symmetric system). For example, under the European Monetary System, Germany provides an informal leadership with macroeconomic policies that impart price stability to the others. The United States of America also provided such leadership under the Bretton Woods system. Closer to home, South Africa was a leader for the Rand Monetary Area (now Common Monetary Area), while France dominates the Franc Zone.

Consideration of the hegemonic system could have some attraction for arrangements being discussed in various African sub-regions. This is especially so in sub-regions with monetary union enclaves such as ECOWAS (with the West African Monetary Union), Central Africa (with the Banque des Etats de l'Afrique Centrale) and SADCC or PTA (with the rand-led Common Monetary Area). The issue is whether the other countries in the sub-region should, provided this were possible, simply join the existing monetary unions, which are operating relatively successfully or whether these monetary unions should be dismantled for new unions which, for all practical purposes, would be on trial in their initial stages. Further complicating the issue is the existence of economies (for example, Nigeria in the ECOWAS or Zaire in Central Africa), which by themselves are big enough in population or resources to want to replace the existing monetary unions as leaders and which may not therefore accept positions as satellites to the existing unions in the sub-regional monetary integration efforts.

However, a hegemonic system is not necessarily an issue of a number of countries that can combine to provide leadership or sizes of economies. Rather, it is based on an implicit contract between the "leader" and the follower (or satellite) countries for the leader to promote the interests of the group. The arrangement requires that the leader combine an *unblemished* record for economic stability, a *dominant* position in international trade and finance (relative to other members of the community) and a *readiness* to undertake the requisite responsibilities. It is against these criteria that one should measure the existing monetary unions (or any other African country) as a leader or model in the context of sub-regional monetary integration efforts. Such measurement would be complicated by the fact that the monetary unions in turn are somewhat (exchange rate-wise) satellites to the monetary system of France.

Empirical work has shown clearly that the African Franc Zone countries (which form the monetary unions) have had faster growth rate with less inflation and lower trade restrictions compared to the non-Franc Zone countries. According to Collier (1991), the rate of GDP growth in Franc Zone Africa over the last 15 years has been double that of non-Franc Zone Africa; prices have risen seven-fold in the former group since 1960, compared to 21-fold in the latter group. In no country in the latter group has inflation rate been as low as any country in the former; the current average inflation rate in the former group is negative compared to 30% in the latter (Guillaumont and Guillaumont, 1988). However, the Franc Zone performance has, in recent years, exhibited some weaknesses inherent in the system. The mechanism of restraining recourse to central bank borrowing has encouraged governments to borrow heavily from commercial banks and foreign sources, thus causing many commercial banks in the zone to become insolvent; many of the countries suffer heavier external debt problems compared to the non-Franc Zone countries. Second, while many non-Franc Zone countries have recently effected steep exchange rate adjustments to improve upon their external competitiveness and to lower real wages, the Franc Zone countries have their exchange rates rigidly fixed to the French Franc. They therefore have to rely on cumbersome fiscal proxies that have not succeeded in restoring external competitiveness. Therefore, the adoption of the Franc Zone model by the other African countries in the sub-regional monetary integration efforts, would require that commercial banks be protected from government interference and that the exchange rate parity system be modified.

Another limitation of the Franc Zone monetary unions as potential leaders is that they do not have dominant positions in international trade in their respective sub-regions. In this regard, they are themselves satellites to France's economic system, which dominates their trade and finance. Linked to this fact is a more complicated aspect of the Franc Zone model for their respective sub-regions: the guarantee of CFA convertibility by the French Treasury. France may not want to undertake the convertibility of the exchange rate of the currency of the larger sub-regional monetary union.[7] It has been indicated, however, that if the Franc Zone model were to be adopted by the sub-regional groupings, the resulting monetary unions would be tied to the European Monetary Union (EMU). While the EMU countries have a good record of economic stability and also dominate trade and finance in Africa, the crucial condition for the arrangement would be the readiness of the European Community to underwrite African sub-regional exchange rate arrangements. It is suggested that such an underwriting could be arranged through the EC's aid budget (Collier, 1991; Guillaumont and Guillaumont, 1989).

A link between monetary integration in Africa and that of Europe in the way suggested above would be a blend between symmetric and hegemonic systems. As a symmetric system, each participating African country's policy action would have some influence on the policy direction of the group and no country's policy direction would be assumed to be necessarily the best for the group to follow. However, that symmetric system among the African countries would be related in some way to an external leader—in this case the EMU.

However, if for any reason, tying to the EMU is ruled out, it would still be possible for the African countries to work out a symmetric system. In this case, a possible way around the problem of existing Franc Zone monetary union enclaves would not be to require their member countries to coordinate their monetary policies right at the onset with those of other countries in the sub-region. Such an approach would run the risk of engendering passive resistance from the Franc Zone (union) member countries that could handicap the implementation of the sub-regional monetary integration programme. Rather a "two-track", two-stage approach could be adopted. In the first stage, one track would consist of the monetary union member countries which would continue to maintain intra-union coordination and the other track would consist of the non-Franc Zone countries, which would harmonize their monetary and fiscal policy conditions.[8] In the second stage, negotiations could then be effected to harmonize monetary and fiscal conditions in the "two tracks" on a symmetric basis.

Related considerations

The need to strike a proper balance between rules and discretion as well as establish an acceptable set of indicators in a symmetric system would suggest that the policy indicators could best be defined in terms of target ranges (or zones) rather than specific or given levels. Strictly speaking, target zones have been used to refer to the acceptable or expected ranges for floating exchange rates in coordination arrangements among developed countries (Frenkel and Goldstein, 1988). However, the concept can be stretched and adapted for discussion of coordinating arrangements among African countries. In that regard, target zones need not be limited to some indications of ranges for exchange rate fluctuations, but could also cover ranges of other monetary and fiscal variables that provide indications of policy thrust for financial stability.

The authorities may also need to go further to choose between the so called "hard" and "soft" target zones. The hard version, which requires greater commitment from governments, would entail that economic policy actions be taken to maintain the indicators within narrow, infrequently revised and publicly announced zones or ranges. However, where there are no certain or firm commitments, the authorities may want to opt for the soft version of the target zones which have wide zones that are frequently revised and kept confidential. The choice in each sub-region would depend on the commitment to the coordination efforts relative to domestic economic policy objectives.

One firm recommendation that can be made irrespective of the choice made with respect to the above methods is, however, that both the likelihood and effectiveness of coordination will be enhanced within a regular, on-going process. This is because multi-period bargaining expands the opportunities for policy bargains by, for example, facilitating phasing of policy measures. The welfare effects of the sum total of the various discussions may far exceed the impact of a single final agreement. Furthermore, when bargaining is repeated and reviewed frequently, the role of reputational considerations (which encourage members to implement decisions) will be strengthened, whereas infrequent or one-time agreements run the risk that commitments will never be implemented. Moreover, if coordination is established on an ongoing basis, it provides the opportunity for participants to submit their individual constraints and problems for group consideration. In contrast, agreements reached in a rush or crisis atmosphere may not properly reflect all the constraints (present and prospective) of participating countries. This last consideration is particularly important in the African economic setting, where exogenous factors have strong and unpredictable impacts.

Coordinating arrangements organized on an ongoing basis would require a permanent committee or council of competent authorities to follow up effectively and advise on the policy direction of the member countries. The formulation of the coordination arrangements or changes therein should not be effected without having been considered by the committee. In the areas of sub-regional exchange rate or monetary and fiscal policy coordination, it is advisable that the central banks of member countries, by virtue of their important role in the formulation and implementation of domestic monetary policies, should constitute (or at least be associated with the decisions of) the committee. Such a filtering of decisions before their adoption by the Heads of States would help avoid serious errors of formulation and minimize difficulties of implementation.

Notes

1 The author is Director of Research at the African Centre for Monetary Studies. He would like to express gratitude to colleagues in the Centre for helpful comments.

2 In the North African and Central African sub-regions decisions for the establishment of sub-regional monetary unions have not been taken, although grounds are being prepared for closer monetary cooperation. For example, in the North African sub-region, the establishment of the Arab Maghreb Union (AMU) in 1989 has been followed by the creation, in 1990, of a Council of Governors of Central Banks of AMU. In the Central African region, a monetary union enclave already exists (Banque des Etats de l'Afrique Centrale), but efforts are also being made to expand monetary cooperation with other countries outside the monetary union.

3 For an analysis of the effectiveness as well as costs and benefits of policy coordination among developed countries, see for example Horne and Masson, 1980.

4 For details on the Structural Requirements of Monetary Integration, see various articles on the theory of optimum currency areas by Mundell (1961) and McKinnon (1963).

5   This condition should be distinguished from those that would determine the need for stable exchange rates (or greater monetary integration) such as the objective of increasing intraregional trade or, generally, supporting the larger objectives of regional integration.

6   Such a rule on budget deficit was also proposed in Delors Report (1989).

7   Collier (unpublished data) reported that while Equatorial Guinea was admitted to membership of the Franc Zone because its economy is so small that the costs to France are negligible, Ghana with a far larger economy, failed to gain admission in the mid-1980s.

8   Such a two-track approach was adopted for the implementation of the European Monetary system, which allowed the Italian lira a greater margin for exchange rate fluctuation at the onset.

References

African Centre for Monetary Studies. 1991. Towards monetary integration in Africa: Options and issues. *Paper presented at the Twelfth General Assembly of the Association of African Central Banks, held in Harare.*

Buiter, Willem, H. 1981. The superiority of contingent rules over fixed rules in models with rational expectations. *Economic journal,* 91.

Bovenberg, A. Lans, J.M. Kremers and Paul R. Masson. 1991. Economic and monetary union in Europe and constraints on national budgetary policies. *IMF staff papers,* 38 (2).

Frenkel, Jacob A. and Morris Goldstein. 1986. A guide to target zones. *IMF staff papers,* 33 (4).

Friedman, Charles. 1989. Monetary policy in the 1990s: Lessons and challenges. In *Monetary policy issues in the 1990s.* Kansas, USA: Federal Reserve Bank of Kansas City.

Guillaumont, Patrick and Sylviane Guillaumont. 1988. Strategies de développement comparées: zone franc et hors zone franc. *Economica.*

Guillaumont, Patrick and Sylviane Guillaumont. 1989. The implications of European Monetary union for African countries. *Journal of common market studies,* 28(2).

Horne, Jocelyn and Paul R. Masson. 1988. Scope and limits of international economic cooperation and policy coordination. *IMF staff papers,* 35(2).

Mah'moud, M.I. 1988. Strategies for monetary policy in African countries. *ACMS staff papers,* 1(1).

Mah'moud, M.I. 1991. Coordination of financial policies among African countries: Some operational issues. *Financial news analysis,* 4(5).

McKinnon, R.I. 1963. Optimum currency areas. *American economic review,* September.

Mundell, R.A. 1961. A theory of optimum currency areas. *American economic review,* September.

12

Aspects Monétaires de l'Intégration en Afrique au regard du Traité d'Abuja

Salah Mouhoubi

La volonté de coopération monétaire en Afrique a été manifestée dès les premières années des indépendances. L'Afrique indépendante s'aperçoit que le continent est morcelé entre diverses unités monétaires autonomes ou rattachées "des monnaies-pivots" (franc français, livre sterling, dollar). Le commerce intra-africain ne dépasse guère 5% du total du commerce du continent.

En recherchant les causes qui font que l'Afrique ne commerce pas avec l'Afrique, il a été prouvé que les obstacles au commerce continental sont d'ordre économique (extraversion des économies davantage orientées vers les ex-métropoles que vers les pays voisins) et monétaire (inconvertibilité des monnaies, détour dans les règlements nécessitant un passage par Paris, Londres ou New York). Tous ces facteurs constituent encore les véritables freins au processus d'intégration des économies africaines.

C'est pour lutter contre les obstacles d'ordre monétaire que des initiatives furent amorcées d'abord au niveau sous-régional et ensuite au niveau continental, dans le but d'instaurer entre les pays africains une coopération monétaire. Parmi tous les projets de coopération initiés, nous voulons souligner ici celui de la Commission Economique des Nations Unies pour l'Afrique (CEA) et de l'Organisation de l'Unité Africaine (OUA). Ce projet a conduit à la création de structures comme l'Association des Banques Centrales Africaines (ABCA), le Centre Africain d'Etudes Monétaires (CAEM) et les chambres de compensation de l'Afrique de l'Ouest, du Centre, de l'Est et de l'Afrique Australe.

On se rappelle que lors de sa cinquième session, la CEA a adopté la résolution 87 (V) priant le Secrétaire Exécutif de cette Organisation, d'entreprendre une étude sur les possibilités de créer un système de compensation au sein d'une union des paiements entre les pays africains. La même invitation avait été formulée en 1963 par la Conférence au sommet des Etats africains à l'endroit de la CEA et de son Secrétaire Exécutif.

Le professeur Triffin qui avait été chargé, à titre d'expert-consultant, de présenter un rapport relatif aux techniques de coopération monétaire entre pays africains, avait fait trois propositions essentielles:

(1) une charte de coopération monétaire africaine;

(2) un conseil monétaire africain; et

(3) des accords de compensation et de paiements.

Le rapport TRIFFIN avait ouvert la voie à d'intenses discussions entre techniciens et politiciens. On connaît les résultats de ces débats. L'approche sous-régionale de l'intégration a été retenue aux dépens d'une approche continentale. Le Plan d'Action de Lagos de 1980 avait entériné cette démarche. Le Traité signé à Abuja en juin 1991 instituant la Communauté Economique Africaine a définitivement consacré l'approche progressive et par cercles concentriques de l'intégration en Afrique.

Ce rappel liminaire avait pour but de rappeler que les aspects monétaires de l'intégration en Afrique n'ont pas été perdus de vue au moment où les pays africains avaient commencé à s'interroger sur le cadre de leur coopération économique. Si cette interrogation est restée comme un leitmotiv, peut-on malgré tout affirmer qu'une attention marquée a été accordée à ces aspects monétaires? La baisse persistante de la valeur des transactions passant par l'intermédiaire des différentes chambres de compensation, la lenteur dans la mise en place de la zone monétaire unique en Afrique de l'Ouest, par exemple, le recours plus fréquent au flottement des monnaies, etc., sont autant des facteurs qui font douter de la volonté des pays africains à accorder la priorité à ces aspects monétaires de l'intégration. Pourtant, il existe plusieurs raisons qui devraient pousser les pays africains à accélérer le processus de création de systèmes monétaires sous-régionaux, pierres angulaires de la future union économique et monétaire panafricaine prévue dans la sixième étape de la mise en place de la Communauté Economique Africaine dont l'étape ultime est la création d'une Banque Centrale Africaine unique et d'une monnaie africaine unique. Parmi ces raisons, on peut citer l'organisation monétaire de l'Europe, la menace sur l'existence de certaines monnaies africaines, le flottement des monnaies qui par définition isole les économies les unes des autres, etc.

L'objectif de cette communication n'est pas de proposer ici des solutions finales concernant le mode d'intégration monétaire en Afrique, mais d'offrir un cadre de discussions et d'échange de vues. Pour ce faire, nous avons décidé de procéder à une évaluation de deux modes d'intégration monétaire en vigueur en Afrique:

(1)   le système de compensation

(2)   les unions monétaires

La première partie évaluera le système de compensation en Afrique tandis que la deuxième partie procédera de la même façon pour les unions monétaires. Enfin, la troisième partie examinera ou plutôt énoncera un certain nombre d'implications pour la réalisation des objectifs du Traité d'Abuja.

Evaluation des systèmes de compensation en Afrique

Un système de compensation, comme on le sait, est un arrangement entre Banques Centrales impliquant l'établissement d'un système de compensation centralisé afin de fournir un mécanisme simple de règlement des transactions intra-régionales. Les transactions entre les pays membres sont réciproquement enregistrées et ne donnent lieu à des paiements qu'à des dates préfixées lorsqu'une compensation mutuelle des comptes est faite et les règlements effectués en tenant compte du solde dû.

Ainsi défini, tout système de compensation vise à atteindre un certain nombre d'objectifs. Ces objectifs sont au nombre de quatre pour les trois chambres de compensation installées en Afrique de l'Ouest, en Afrique Centrale et en Afrique de l'Est et Australe. Le système de compensation rendu possible par ces chambres est évalué ici en fonction de la réalisation des objectifs fixés et nous concluerons par une appréciation de leur contribution à l'intégration sous-régionale.

Premier objectif: promouvoir l'utilisation des monnaies des pays membres dans les transactions commerciales et non-commerciales de la sous-région. L'une des principales contraintes du commerce intra-régional en Afrique réside dans l'inconvertibilité des monnaies et de son corollaire, le contrôle des changes. Les monnaies africaines sont rarement reliées les unes aux autres. Le manque de lien est aujourd'hui aggravé par la forte tendance à adopter des taux de change flottants, le flottement étant par excellence un système d'isolement monétaire et de négation de l'unification monétaire. Le recours aux monnaies étrangères reste une caractéristique du commerce intra-africain.

Si l'on considère la Chambre de Compensation de l'Afrique de l'Ouest (CCAO), il est permis d'affirmer que l'utilisation des monnaies de la sous-région n'a pas été accrue. La preuve de cette assertion peut être tirée de l'examen de l'évolution du montant et du nombre des transactions effectuées par le canal de la CCAO.

Jusqu'en 1983–1984, le montant des transactions a évolué de manière très sensible. Après 1983-1984, le montant des transactions a connu une baisse constante passant de 195,4 millions d'UCAO[1] en 1984–1985 à 9,5 et 28,2 millions en 1987–1988 et 1988–1989 respectivement.

Le nombre de transactions a également évolué de manière décroissante depuis 1985-1986 après avoir observé une tendance nettement croissante avant cette date. Au cours des derniers exercices, le nombre des transactions est passé de 2.265 en 1985/1986 à 129 en 1987/1988, 561 en 1988/1989 et à 323 en 1989/1990.

La conséquence immédiate de ces tendances est que seule une part très faible du commerce sous-régional passe maintenant par le biais des chambres de compensation. La part du commerce intra-régional passant par la CCAO était inférieure à 1% en 1990, à comparer aux 40% en 1983. La chambre de Compensation de la ZEP a, par contre, enregistré une évolution croissante; la part du commerce intra-ZEP passant par la Chambre s'élevant de 9% en 1984 à 57% en 1987. Il convient de se garder de tout triomphalisme concernant ce dernier cas puisque la même évolution était observée au niveau de la CCAO au cours des huit premiers exercices.

Deuxième objectif: réaliser des économies dans l'utilisation des réserves extérieures des pays membres. L'inconvertibilité des monnaies africaines est généralement le résultat de la pénurie de réserves extérieures. Celles-ci ne suffisent pas à couvrir les besoins en importation de biens et services. Le rationnement des devises est alors érigé en principe de gestion et altère de plus en plus la confiance dans la monnaie nationale. Celle-ci devient de moins en moins désirée par les opérateurs qui participent aux transactions internationales.

Le système de compensation devait permettre de contourner cet écueil. Le commerce intrazonal étant réalisé désormais sans un recours systématique aux réserves extérieures, le besoins des pays en devises est diminué d'autant.

En ce qui concerne la CCAO, il faut souligner que les transactions compensées ont progressivement augmenté entre 1976/77 et 198è/81 passant de 12,7 millions d'UCAO à 29,4 millions d'UCAO respectivement. Depuis 1986/87, le volume des transactions compensées a continuellement baissé. En moyenne, le montant des transactions compensées a été de 14,7% autrement dit près de 85,3% des transactions nécessitaient le recours aux devises. L'objectif de l'économie de devises n'a donc pas été atteint.

Troisième objectif: Les pays membres s'engagent à libéraliser les échanges commerciaux. La réussite de la libéralisation dépend de l'élimination de toutes les entraves au commerce entre les pays membres. Cette élimination peut découler des gains escomptés c'est-à-dire des économies dans l'utilisation des réserves. Or, à partir du moment où ces gains ont été dérisoires, le système de compensation n'a joué aucun rôle prépondérant dans la suppression des entraves au commerce. Cette suppression découle en partie des programmes d'ajustement structurel entrepris par les pays africains.

Quatrième objectif: stimuler la coopération et les consultations monétaires entre les pays membres. Dans le cadre des réunions statutaires, les pays membres trouvent un cadre de concertation et d'échange de vue sur les questions d'intérêt commun. Cet objectif a été le mieux atteint si l'on se réfère aux discussions qui ont porté en Afrique de l'Ouest, par exemple, sur la création d'une zone monétaire unique.

En résumé, on peut raisonnablement conclure que le système de compensation n'a pas été un facteur déterminant de l'unification monétaire en Afrique. La tendance de plusieurs pays à opter pour le flottement constitue la limitation la plus sérieuse en diminuant l'efficacité du système de compensation et en créant une plus grande instabilité des taux de change.

Evaluation des unions monétaires en Afrique

Il existe trois unions monétaires en Afrique: l'Union Monétaire Ouest Africaine en Afrique de l'Ouest (UMOA), la zone d'émission de la Banque des Etats de l'Afrique Centrale (BEAC) et la zone rand en Afrique Australe. La caractéristique principale de ces unions monétaires réside dans leur origine coloniale. Dans le cas de l'UMOA et de la BEAC, ces unions ont été des structures imposées découlant de l'appartenance des pays africains à l'empire colonial français. Après les indépendances, des adaptations structurelles ont été opérées étant donné que l'accession des Etats africains " la souveraineté internationale devait nécessairement entraîner des modifications de structures plus profondes. En dehors de la Guinée Equatoriale, pays hispanophone, tous les Etats membres de ces unions sont francophones. Les deux unions appartiennent à la zone franc.

D'un point de vue purement monétaire, on peut dire que l'UMOA et la BEAC ont été une réussite. En effet, elles ont permis de maintenir la stabilité et la convertibilité du franc CFA dans un contexte africain où la plupart des autres monnaies sont soit inconvertibles, soit très instables, soit inconvertibles et instables à la fois. En matière de taux d'inflation, on peut également affirmer que les pressions inflationnistes ont été nettement mieux maîtrisées que dans le reste de l'Afrique. Toutefois, ceci est prouvé par plusieurs recherches empiriques, le maintien de la fixité du taux de change sur une longue période peut conduire à une surévaluation du taux de change, érodant ainsi la compétitivité extérieure des économies de la zone franc. Ceci a généralement réduit les prix relatifs des biens échangeables et a favorisé les importations au détriment des exportations. Cependant, certains tests empiriques ont montré qu'une dévaluation du franc CFA n'entraîneraient pas une hausse des exportations, du fait de la rigidité des structures économiques. En effet, ces pays se caractérisent toujours par une dépendance à l'égard des produits de base dont la demande extérieure est inélastique. Du côté des importations, la demande interne est incompressible.

La surévaluation est un aspect qui débouche sur des choix de politique économique controversés. Nous estimons que le véritable talon d'Achille de ces deux Unions se trouve ailleurs, en l'occurrence dans leur capacité à stimuler l'intégration économique des Etats membres. Le commerce intra-UMOA est resté très faible. En 1987, par exemple, les exportations intra-UMOA représentèrent seulement 12,6% des exportations totales de l'Union, alors que les importations intra-UMOA ne s'élevaient qu'à 7,8% du total pour la même année. Les échanges intra-UMOA approchent les 1% du total de leur commerce extérieur, alors que ceux de la BEAC ne dépassent guère les 3%.

Ces statistiques tendent à indiquer que les complémentarités ne jouent pas ou ne jouent que très peu dans les échanges de ces deux unions. Cette situation est la résultante de l'extraversion des économies nationales, souvent concurrentes sur beaucoup de créneaux. L'intégration économique de ces pays doit être repensée et fondée sur de nouvelles bases. L'unification monétaire de l'UMOA et de la zone d'émission de la BEAC n'a pas pleinement joué un rôle catalyseur dans le processus d'intégration économique.

Ce résultat mitigé a été établi par les pays africains de la zone franc qui, lors de leur réunion semestrielle, les 25 et 26 avril 1991 à Ouagadougou (Burkina Faso) ont décidé de construire une union économique et monétaire. Au niveau de l'UMOA, le Gouverneur de la BCEAO, sur la requête des chefs d'Etats de l'Union, a été chargé de mener des études et de faire des propositions, afin de renforcer l'intégration économique de l'Union.

En Afrique Australe, la zone rand est le symbole de la prépondérance de l'Afrique du Sud. Plus démocratique, multiraciale et dénuée de tout esprit de domination, la zone rand peut constituer un levier important de l'intégration économique.

En dehors de ces cas, il convient de souligner que des tentatives sont entreprises respectivement en Afrique de l'Ouest et dans la ZEP pour créer des zones monétaires. Le moins que l'on puisse dire est que les résultats attendus tardent à se matérialiser. En Afrique de l'Ouest, par exemple, la date prévue pour la mise en place de la zone monétaire unique a été repoussée. Il n'est pas évident que la nouvelle échéance fixée pour 1995 soit respectée en raison des désaccords que subsistent encore entre les tenants d'union immédiate et ceux qui prônent la convergence préalable des économies en matière de croissance, d'inflation et d'équilibres intérieur et extérieur.

En fin de compte, aucune avancée significative n'a encore été faite dans l'unification monétaire du continent résultant d'une volonté politique des Etats africains. Les Unions monétaires qui existent sont surtout le fruit de la période coloniale. Le mérite des Etats membres est d'avoir su résister aux sirènes de l'émiettement monétaire. Ces unions monétaires doivent prendre en charge maintenant l'intégration comme un tout et c'est là le but recherché par les pays africains de la zone franc.

Implications pour la réalisation des objectifs du traité d'Abuja

Les objectifs de la Communauté Economique Africaine en matière monétaire, financière et des paiements sont précisés dans l'article 44 du Traité d'Abuja. Il y est clairement mentionné que "les Etats membres conviennent d'harmoniser leurs politiques dans les domaines monétaire, financier et des paiements, en vue de favoriser les échanges intra-communautaires des biens et des services, de promouvoir la réalisation des objectifs de la Communauté et de renforcer la coopération monétaire et financière entre eux". Pour atteindre ces objectifs, le Traité prévoit, entre autres, la création de mécanismes appropriés pour la mise en place de systèmes multilatéraux de paiement et d'une union monétaire africaine, par l'harmonisation des zones monétaires.

Il découle de la lecture de l'article 44 que le Traité privilégie les deux modes d'unification monétaire examinés plus haut, c'est-à-dire le système de compensations et les unions monétaires. La stratégie prévue se fonde sur l'approche par cercles concentriques, d'abord une base sous-régionale, et ensuite un sommet continental. Pour édifier ce nouvel ordre monétaire en Afrique, des efforts importants doivent être accomplis à plusieurs niveaux dont quelques uns sont évoqués ci-dessous.

La souveraineté monétaire

En dehors des coûts réels et supposés qui naissent de l'appartenance d'un pays à une union monétaire, l'attachement à la souveraineté monétaire nationale, perçue comme un attribut de la souveraineté nationale, constitue un des principaux freins à l'unification monétaire en Afrique.

A l'heure actuelle, la souveraineté monétaire est un concept auquel sont attachés les Etats malgré l'interdépendance des économies, l'internationalisation des marchés des capitaux, le rôle des taux d'intérêt à l'étranger, et les contraintes de la coopération monétaire internationale. Nous ne pensons pas exagérer outre mesure en disant que les interventions du FMI dans nos Etats ont dessaisi la plupart de ceux-ci de la réalité de leur pouvoir monétaire. Il s'avère que dans la conjoncture actuelle, la souveraineté monétaire n'est qu'apparente et explique en partie la dégradation de la monnaie nationale dans plusieurs pays où la rigueur a cédé la place à une spéculation effrénée.

L'interconvertibilité des monnaies de chaque sous-région

L'une des causes des difficultés rencontrées dans les échanges et dans le fonctionnement des chambres de compensation tient à l'inconvertibilité des monnaies. Si les pays africains ont la ferme volonté de coopérer, ils doivent accepter le minimum, assurer l'interconvertibilité des monnaies. Les taux de change devraient être fixes afin d'éviter l'instabilité qui contrarie la compensation.

La réorientation de l'ajustement structurel

Jusqu'ici les politiques d'ajustement structurel suivies par les Etats africains sont menées dans un cadre strictement national et non régional. Après plus d'une décennie d'ajustement structurel au niveau national, il est temps que celui-ci se fasse désormais au niveau régional. Le regain de prise de conscience de l'importance de l'intégration économique en Afrique, devrait contribuer à la conception des programmes d'ajustement structurel régionaux. Une telle conversion impose une redéfinition du rôle des institutions de Bretton Woods et de la BAD. Cette dernière a déjà pris l'engagement de s'impliquer plus activement dans la promotion de l'intégration économique en Afrique.

Renforcement des systèmes actuels de compensation

Dans toutes les sous-régions, il est souhaitable que les chambres actuelles soient redynamisées et que des solutions adéquates soient trouvées aux problèmes rencontrés notamment en ce qui concerne la précarité des économies; le faible niveau d'industrialisation et le manque de complémentarité des économies; les difficultés de transport et de communication; les freins à la libre circulation des biens et des personnes; les barrières commerciales tarifaires et non tarifaires; l'absence de mécanisme de crédit; les lenteurs des systèmes de compensation, etc.

Réaffirmation de la volonté des Etats de créer les zones monétaires

La monnaie étant foncièrement politique, l'unification monétaire doit être un acte politique. Bien sûr, ceci ne signifie pas qu'il faudrait occulter toutes les contraintes réelles et institutionnelles.

Le passage à l'union africaine de compensation et de paiements et à la Banque Centrale Africaine

L'article 44 alinéa 2 du Traité d'Abuja qui trace la voie à l'intégration monétaire stipule que:

"Les Etats membres s'engagent à:

(a) utiliser leur monnaie nationale pour le règlement des transactions commerciales et financières entre eux, en vue de réduire le recours aux devises dans ces transactions;

(b) créer des mécanismes appropriés pour la mise en place des systèmes multilatéraux de paiement;

(c) se consulter régulièrement sur les questions monétaires et financières;

(d) promouvoir la libéralisation en matière de paiements ainsi que l'élimination des restrictions éventuelles de paiements entre eux et faciliter l'intégration de tous les arrangements de compensation et de paiement existant entre les différentes régions, en une union africaine de compensation et des paiements; et

(e) créer une union monétaire africaine par l'harmonisation des zones monétaires."

A terme, l'union africaine de compensation et des paiements d'une part, et la banque centrale africaine, d'autre part, seront créées. Ces deux objectifs ont des implications différentes quant au processus à emprunter.

L'union africaine de compensation et des paiements imposera des implications nouvelles relatives au type de coordination à établir entre elle et les chambres au niveau sous-régional. Sa structure devrait être légère. Elle pourrait être ouverte aux chambres de compensation des sous-régions et procéder à la compensation des transactions inter-régionales.

C'est au cours de la sixième étape que sont prévus la Banque Centrale Africaine, la monnaie unique et le Fonds Monétaire Africain. En effet, il est dit qu'au terme de 5 années au maximum, les pays africains doivent entreprendre d'abord:

(1) la consolidation et le renforcement de la structure du Marché Commun Africain;

(2) l'intégration de tous les secteurs, à savoir les secteurs économique, politique, social et culturel; la création d'un marché intérieur unique ainsi qu'une union économique et monétaire panafricaine.

La création de la banque centrale africaine nécessitera l'harmonisation des politiques de différentes sous-régions. Il est à préciser que cette banque se créera après la construction d'unions monétaires sous-régionales dotées chacune d'une monnaie unique. Lors de la création de la banque centrale africaine, il faudrait faire le choix entre la circulation parallèle de la monnaie africaine et des monnaies sous-régionales, d'une part, et une monnaie africaine qui se substituerait aux monnaies sous-régionales, d'autre part. Ce choix est fondamental puisqu'il peut influencer indéniablement la réussite de l'entreprise.

Conclusion Générale

Les expériences de certains pays africains en matière de coopération monétaire ne s'avèrent pas concluantes dans leur ensemble. Les mécanismes de compensation n'ont pas fonctionné de manière satisfaisante et les unions monétaires existantes n'ont ni engendré ni favorisé le processus d'intégration monétaire. L'exemple de la CEE à montré que des étapes sont inévitables et incontournables pour déboucher sur une monnaie unique et une Banque Centrale Commune.

Le Traité d'Abuja, qui constitue un document historique, instaure la Communauté Economique Africaine. Des étapes sont prévues selon un calendrier rigide, pour mettre en place cette Communauté. La création d'une Banque Centrale Commune et d'une monnaie unique et la constitution du Fonds Monétaire Africain représentent l'aboutissement de ce processus. Au stade actuel, des interrogations légitimes persistent. Le temps imparti à la réalisation de ces instruments est dérisoire par rapport aux problèmes à surmonter. L'intégration économique au niveau de chaque sous-région est encore au stade des balbutiements. L'UMOA existe mais sans intégration économique des pays membres.

Des entraves réelles existent. L'harmonisation des politiques économiques et monétaires est une nécessité pour poser les jalons d'une intégration économique, prélude à une intégration monétaire. Cependant, la vulnérabilité des économies africaines, le lourd endettement extérieur et les impératifs des politiques d'ajustement structurel doivent inciter les pays africains à emprunter des voies nouvelles. Par ailleurs, des défis extérieurs leur imposent de coordonner leurs efforts; sans cela c'est toute l'Afrique qui sera marginalisée.

Le Traité d'Abuja constitue une des solutions aux difficultés présentes et futures. Il importe maintenant de concilier la volonté politique unanimement exprimée avec les intérêts nationaux légitimes de chaque Etat.

13

Aspects Monétaires et Financiers de la Coopération Régionale

Pascal D Bitoumbou

Introduction

Il ne fait aucun doute que les aspects monétaires et financiers ont toujours joué un rôle déterminant dans toutes les expériences de coopération et d'intégration économiques recensées dans le monde. En la matière l'Afrique ne fait pas exception. Mieux, il est de notoriété publique que les obstacles monétaires et financiers comptent parmi les facteurs décisifs qui ont sérieusement entravé le développement des échanges commerciaux au sein des communautés économiques sous-régionales en Afrique. Aussi, est-ce à juste titre que le Traité d'Abuja met un accent particulier, dans son article 44 notamment, sur "l'impératif d'harmonisation à des politiques dans les domaines monétaire, financier et des paiements, en vue de favoriser les échanges intra-communautaires des biens et des services, de promouvoir la réalisation des objectifs de la Communauté et de renforcer la coopération monétaire et financière entre les pays africains."

Sur ces mêmes politiques en matière monétaire, financière et des paiements les Etats membres signataires du Traité d'Abuja, dans leur volonté de surmonter les difficultés chroniques enregistrées dans ces domaines sont allés jusqu'à s'engager entre autres à "promouvoir la libéralisation en matière de paiements ainsi que l'élimination des restrictions éventuelles de paiements entre eux et faciliter l'intégration de tous les arrangements de compensation et des paiements; et créer une union monétaire africaine par l'harmonisation des zones monétaires". Même s'il est vrai que certains des objectifs visés par l'article 44 du Traité d'Abuja ne recueillent pas le consensus, il y a lieu de reconnaître qu'il est urgent de reformuler les politiques monétaires et financières nationales et sous-régionales, afin de permettre à la coopération et à l'intégration économique de réaliser des avancées à la hauteur des exigences objectives du développement économique et social des pays africains.

Pour l'examen des aspects monétaires et financiers de la coopération régionale, nous adopterons la démarche ci-après. En premier lieu nous procéderons à un rappel succinct du concept de la coopération monétaire et de l'intégration sous-régionale. En deuxième lieu nous dresserons un bilan rapide de la coopération et de l'intégration sous-régionale. Enfin, nous essaierons de dégager les enseignements et les perspectives découlant des développements antérieurs. Dans le deuxième volet de notre réflexion, concernant particulièrement les aspects financiers de la coopération, nous nous efforcerons à définir le concept de financement de la coopération et l'intégration sous-régionale. Au terme de cette évaluation nous tirerons des leçons et dégagerons également des perspectives.

La dernière partie de notre réflexion sera consacrée aux conclusions générales dans lesquelles nous essaierons de situer également le rôle du Groupe de la Banque Africaine de Développement dans ces domaines.

Le concept de la coopération monétaire et l'intégration sous-régionale

La coopération monétaire peut exister à différents degrés et revêtir par conséquent plusieurs formes. Nous pouvons retenir trois formes principales, à savoir: l'union monétaire, l'union ou la chambre de compensation et le système de groupement de réserves.

L'intégration ou l'union monétaire totale suppose la réunion de plusieurs conditions dont: la fixité des taux de change entre les monnaies, la convertibilité, l'intégration du marché des capitaux, la gestion commune de la politique monétaire et d'une politique de taux de change externe de l'union, et la mise en commun des réserves.

Quant à l'union ou la chambre de compensation, c'est un mécanisme qui permet de régler plus facilement les transactions bancaires au sein d'une sous-région, en utilisant les monnaies nationales non convertibles des membres, réduisant ainsi la consommation des devises étrangères dans ces transactions. Devant la diversité des systèmes de change, il peut être établi une unité de compte, de manière à aider à l'accroissement des opportunités d'utilisation des monnaies des pays membres.

Le système de groupement de réserves est un mécanisme qui offre à chacun des pays membres l'avantage de réduire le volume des réserves qu'il est tenu de détenir relativement à la position d'échanges de l'ensemble des pays membres. Ce système tire profit, entre autres, des différences des structures d'exportation des pays membres.

Après cette présentation sommaire du concept de coopération monétaire, un bref aperçu du bilan de la coopération monétaire en Afrique nous permettra de mettre en lumière certaines des questions et des problèmes auxquels les pays du continent sont confrontés dans ce domaine.

Le bilan de la coopération monétaire en Afrique

Au niveau des unions monétaires existantes. Elles sont au nombre de deux: la zone franc qui intéresse 14 pays d'Afrique subsaharienne et la zone rand composée par des pays d'Afrique australe dont la République Sud Africaine. Il est difficile de parler de résultats spectaculaires au terme de l'examen de l'expérience de la zone franc au regard de la question de l'intégration régionale. Il serait même hasardeux d'attribuer les écarts de performances économiques entre les pays de la zone franc et les autres pays africains exclusivement ou en grande partie à leur appartenance à l'union monétaire. D'autant plus qu'au sein même de la zone franc les disparités au niveau des performances économiques sont tout aussi notables. Sur le plan factuel il est à souligner que l'intégration monétaire dans la zone franc n'a pas donné un coup de fouet extraordinaire aux échanges entre les pays membres qui, par ailleurs, n'ont pas enregistré des avancées dans la domaine de l'harmonisation des politiques économiques. Au niveau de l'UDEAC par exemple, la part du commerce intra-communautaire serait même tombée en deçà de la moyenne africaine.

Certes la zone franc a pu jouir de la stabilité relative des taux de change et d'une inflation modérée. Cependant il est difficile de montrer que l'appartenance à la zone franc a permis aux pays membres d'avoir une longueur d'avance notable sur les autres pays africains dans le processus d'intégration économique. En réalite la zone franc aussi bien que la zone rand n'a pas été conçues à l'origine pour faciliter des progrès substantiels dans la voie de l'intégration économique. Ces deux zones monétaires obéissent beaucoup plus à un schéma de coopération de type néocolonial.

Au niveau des chambres de compensation existantes. Elles sont au nombre de quatre. Le bilan est globalement mitigé. En général la part du commerce intra-communautaire qui emprunte le canal des chambres de compensation est très faible et les transactions intergouvernementales représentent la plus grande portion du total des transactions passant par ces chambres (CCAO). Celles-ci n'ont pas toujours permis de réduire les coûts des transactions d'échanges entre les pays membres et de simplifier les procédures de règlement des échanges aussi bien pour les exportateurs que pour les importateurs. De même les autres objectifs des chambres de compensation n'ont pas été atteint, à savoir réaliser des économies dans l'utilisation des devises étrangères des pays membres, accroître la libéralisation des échanges et promouvoir la coopération monétaire entre les membres des chambres de compensation. Il convient toutefois de souligner l'évolution positive des résultats de la Chambre de Compensation de la ZEP qui a vu s'accroître significativement, au fil des ans, la part du commerce intra-ZEP traitée par la Chambre (de 9% en 1984 à environ 56% en 1989). A la lumière de ce qui précède quels enseignements et quelles perspectives?

Enseignements et perspectives

Il ressort de l'expérience africaine, notamment de celle des pays africains membres de la zone franc que l'union monétaire est peut-être une condition nécessaire mais non suffisante pour faire réellement des progrès notables dans l'intégration économique sous-régionale. Dans son fonctionnement actuel les mécanismes de la zone franc ne favorisent pas le développement des échanges horizontaux entre les pays membres africains. Ce sont plutôt les échanges verticaux entre les pays africains et la France qui sont privilégiés au sein de la zone, encore qu'au fil des ans on note une diminution significative de la part des pays membres africains dans les exportations françaises.

En ce qui concerne les chambres de compensation, le mécanisme n'a pas tenu toutes ses promesses. De nombreux disfonctionnements continuent à entraver son efficacité: distorsions de change, instabilité de change, impact négatif de la dette extérieure. La surévaluation relative des taux de change constitue l'une des contraintes les plus lourdes au bon fonctionnement des chambres de compensation africaines. Mais le mécanisme semble perfectible et répond encore à un besoin réel et urgent.

Le concept de financement de la coopération sous régionale

La promotion de l'intégration économique a un coût auquel il faut faire face par la mobilisation de ressources régulières et suffisantes si l'on veut éviter de se retrouver dans l'incapacité de financer l'application des mesures d'intégration. Dans une région en développement comme l'Afrique, pour faire face au coût de l'intégration, les efforts intérieurs quels qu'ils soient, nécessitent d'être complété par des ressources extérieures à court et à moyen terme. Cela tient particulièrement au fait que dans nombre de pays africains, les taux d'épargne n'atteignent même pas 10% du PIB.

L'évaluation sommaire de l'experience du financement de la coperation sous-régionale

L'expérience du financement de l'intégration sous-régionale en Afrique se caractérise par le faible volume de ressources intérieures affectées à cette activité, le soutien modéré des organismes d'aide multilatérale, l'inexistence d'un système de ressources automatiques et indépendantes de la situation financière des pays membres, l'inadaptation des arrangements financiers et l'absence quasi-totale du secteur privé dans le financement du commerce intra-africain et des investissements régionaux.

Les Institutions Financières de Développement (IFD) sous-régionales ont constitué jusqu'ici les bras financiers des communautés économiques sous-régionales. La plupart d'entre elles ne disposent pas de politique clairement définie pour orienter leur action en faveur des projets d'intégration régionale souvent reconnus prioritaires par leurs statuts. Par ailleurs les ressources des IFD sous-régionales sont, en général, insuffisantes et inadaptées pour financer l'intégration qui nécessitent souvent des investissements massifs. Ces IFD disposent très difficilement de ressources d'emprunt sur le marché financier international et leur taille ne leur permet pas souvent de bénéficier d'économies d'échelle. Il en résulte des coûts de prêts très élevés et explique en partie leur sous-utilisation relative par les communautés économiques sous-régionales. Dans l'ensemble, leur performance en matière de financement de projets régionaux a été peu satisfaisant.

Pour sa part la BAD, qui n'est pas simplement une banque de développement mais également un organisme d'intégration, n'a cessé depuis sa création de consacrer des ressources à l'intégration. La BAD finance des projets multinationaux et nationaux à impact intégrateur. Dans les prêts multinationaux, ceux consentis aux banques régionales de développement sous-régional, ont constitué une part très importante. Durant les programmes opérationnels quinquennaux du Groupe de la BAD 1982-1986 et 1987–1991, 10% des engagements totaux du Groupe avaient été chaque fois alloués au financement des projets multinationaux. Souvent, cette allocation de ressources n'a pas été épuisée, faute de projets multinationaux à financer. La contribution de la BAD à l'intégration régionale s'est étendue à la création d'institutions favorisant cette approche telles que: Shelter Afrique, Africa-Re, L'AIAFD, la SIFIDA et la FECA.

Les principales contraintes qui ont empêché la BAD de financer davantage des projets multinationaux sont: du côté des Etats membres: la faible priorité accordée par les Etats à ce type de projets dans leurs programmes d'investissement et l'inexistence d'un fonds spécial dont les ressources seraient exclusivement affectées au financement des projets multinationaux; du côté du Groupe de la BAD: l'insuffisance de ressources concessionnelles, l'absence d'un mécanisme efficace pour l'identification et l'évaluation des projets multinationaux et l'inexistence au sein de la Banque d'un point focal solide pour la promotion des projets intégrateurs.

Enseignement et perspectives

A court et à moyen terme, étant donné la faible probabilité d'accroissement sensible du taux d'épargne, consécutive à la faiblesse et à la lente progression des niveaux de revenus, l'Afrique devrait faire davantage appel aux ressources extérieures pour le financement de l'intégration. Le changement d'attitude récent de la plupart des organismes d'aide multilatérale vis-à-vis des budgets nationaux et des Etats devraient être recherchées, afin de minimiser le problème chronique d'arriérés de contributions des Etats membres. Dans cette perspective des études devraient être effectuées afin d'identifier les ressources intérieures possibles.

Conclusion et perspectives

Au terme de cet examen rapide des aspects monétaires et financiers de la coopération régionale nous nous permettons de faire les observations ci-après:

Les impératifs de l'intégration économique en Afrique exigent une coopération monétaire beaucoup plus audacieuse et structurée. Les échanges régionaux continuent à être freinés dans leur développement par la pénurie de devises fortes et par l'inconvertibilité des monnaies nationales. La coopération monétaire devrait avoir pour objectif d'aider à atteindre la convertibilité totale des monnaies nationales. A court et moyen terme, cet objectif ne semble pas à la portée des pays africains en tant que groupe.

Dans la phase actuelle de transition vers la convertibilité totale, il y a lieu d'exploiter au mieux les différentes formes de coopération monétaire. Dans cette perspective toutes les réflexions concernant, par exemple, la convertibilité régionale devraient bénéficier de la plus grande attention.

A court et moyen terme, les chambres de compensation dotées de facilités de crédit, dans un contexte de mise en oeuvre de programme d'ajustement structurel à l'échelle sous-régionale, peuvent favoriser notablement les transactions sous-régionales. Des études devraient être encouragées dans le sens d'une mutation des chambres de compensation en Union sous-régionale de paiements. Dans tous les cas, la coordination sous-régionale des politiques macro-économiques devrait être un puissant moyen pour améliorer notablement la coopération monétaire.

Dans la réflexion concernant la coopération monétaire en Afrique, nombreux sont ceux qui pensent que l'union monétaire est la forme la plus efficace pour réaliser des avancées sensibles vers l'intégration même si des expériences aussi opposés que celle de la CEE et de l'UDEAC ne semblent pas confirmer cette idée. D'aucuns vont plus loin en n'envisageant cette union monétaire qu'à travers le rattachement à une monnaie étrangère. D'où le débat en cours sur une union monétaire euro-africaine qui semble privilégier uniquement le problème de la "reconnexion" de l'Afrique dans le commerce mondial, au détriment de la question de savoir si la zone euro-africaine pourrait constituer un facteur d'intensification du commerce intra-africain. L'Afrique doit se réapproprier ce débat, sans dogmatisme, pour clarifier sa stratégie de coopération monétaire dans la perspective de la mise en oeuvre du Traité d'Abuja.

Les impératifs de l'intégration économique en Afrique exige également une plus grande mobilisation des ressources intérieures et extérieures.

Malheureusement dans la plupart des pays africains, le potentiel d'épargne s'est beaucoup dégradé. Dans ce contexte, la mobilisation des ressources intérieures est un véritable défi. Pour mobiliser des ressources supplémentaires, il est impératif de rompre le cercle vicieux des faibles revenus, de la faible épargne et de la faible croissance. C'est-à-dire pour y parvenir, il est indispensable que les réformes économiques en cours portent leurs fruits, que la confiance à long terme dans les économies africaines renaisse et se consolide. Par ailleurs, pour relever le défi de la mobilisation des ressources intérieures, il faut que les institutions d'intermédiation financière adaptent leur mécanisme à la situation de la majorité des populations africaines. Les autres institutions financières susceptibles de contribuer à la mobilisation des ressources intérieures sont les caisses d'épargne, les compagnies d'assurance et les bourses des valeurs. Cependant à court terme, les conditions de création de bourses des valeurs de classe internationale en Afrique sont difficiles à remplir.

Au niveau des communautés économiques sous-régionales, il est urgent qu'elles se dotent d'un système de ressources propres, c'est-à-dire relativement automatiques et indépendantes de la situation budgétaire des Etats-membres.

Pour le financement efficace de l'intégration africaine par les donneurs bilatéraux et multilatéraux, il importe que ceux-ci se dotent désormais de mécanismes appropriés et puissent juridiquement et statutairement être en mesure de financer directement les communautés économiques sous-régionales. De leur côté, ces communautés, pour mieux assumer leur nouveau rôle, elles doivent avoir la capacité de contracter des emprunts dans la limite de leur capacité réelle deremboursement.

Le Groupe de la BAD, continue à rechercher les voies et les moyens pour être plus performant dans contribution à la coopération et à l'intégration économique en Afrique. En janvier 1992, la BAD a créé une division chargée de la promotion de l'intégration économique. Pour développer une plus grande capacité d'identification et de promotion de projets favorables à l'intégration, le Groupe de la BAD s'appuiera sur le secteur privé qui sera associé dès les premières phases du cycle de projet. Pour servir de catalyseur spécial à l'intégration et aux échanges commerciaux de la region, le Groupe de la BAD a choisi le financement des projets régionaux dans les secteurs des transports, des communications et de l'énergie.

Mais, en plus du financement des projets classiques, le Groupe de la BAD entend imprimer une dimension régionale plus marquée à ses opérations d'appui aux réformes, et à ses stratégies de programmation par pays. Ainsi, les efforts d'intégration menés sur le plan de l'appui aux réformes viendront compléter, comme il se doit, ceux déployés au niveau de projets; et les programmes par pays seront élaborés et exécutés, en tenant expressément compte de leur impact sous-régional et continental.

Pour soutenir ces efforts, le Groupe de la BAD dans le cadre des ressources additionnelles dégagées par suite en part de la restructuration du Fonds Spécial du Nigéria mettra également au point des mecanismes permettant de canaliser des ressources destinées à financer le commerce ainsi que des opérations de production liées au commerce et aux infrastructures. De même, l'assistance technique du Groupe de la Banque, assurée sous forme d'appui aux mécanismes de paiements régionaux, contribuera grandement à faire avancer certains des impératifs politiques de la Communauté économique africaine.

14

Les Tendances Lourdes de l'Industrie des Textiles dans le Monde

Farid Benyoucef et Naceur Bourenane

Les tendances lourdes de l'industrie "traditionnelle" se caractérisent à la fois par une profonde restructuration industrielle dans les pays développés et une politique de délocalisation soutenue en direction des Pays en Voie de Développement (P.V.D.). Le secteur des textiles n'échappe pas à ces tendances lourdes comme nous essayerons de voir dans cette contribution.

Auparavant, nous tenterons de situer l'évolution de l'industrie des textiles par rapport au contexte de l'évolution mondiale de l'industrie en général. Ceci nous permettra d'identifier la nature et l'importance des enjeux industriels à la veille du prochain millénaire aussi bien et surtout pour les textiles que pour le reste des marchandises produites et échangées au niveau mondial.

L'évolution récente de l'économie mondiale
Les mutations industrielles
On peut aisément remaquer que durant la décennie écoulée, l'économie mondiale a subi de profonds changements structurels qui tendent à bouleverser les équilibres traditionnels basés sur l'existence d'un centre industriel et technologique développé et d'une périphérie fonctionnant dans les limites d'une division internationale du travail bâtie dans le sens des intérêts bien compris de ce centre.

Si durant les années 50 et 60, la performance des entreprises américaines et européennes rythmaient tant en matière de production que d'échange, les perfomances du reste du monde, cette situation a beaucoup changé depuis le début des années 70 et a connu une accélération depuis 1980.

Quelques ratios témoignent de cette nouvelle évolution:

(1)   Durant une vingtaine d'années après la seconde guerre mondiale, la productivité du travail croissait aux Etats Unis de 30% l'an en moyenne. Entre 1973 et 1977, elle avait déchu de 1% par an alors qu'en 1979, elle déclinait de 2%.

(2)   En 1960, les Etats Unis se taillaient 25% du marché mondial des produits manufacturés, en 1979 cette part n'était plus que de 17%.

(3)   En 1960, les enterprises, aux Etats Unis, adjugeaient 95% du marché américain de voitures, d'acier et d'électronique grand public. En 1979, ces parts n'étaient plus respectivement que de 79%, 86% et moins de 50%.

Les mutations technologiques

Les mutations technologiques observées dans le monde industrialisé ont impliqué depuis 1980 une redéfinition de la croissance économique poursuivie jusque là par ces pays. Ces stratégies nouvelles visent au redéploiement des ressources disponibles vers ces nouveaux "cenrtes d'excellence" que sont les technopoles, et ceci, au dépens des industries classiques.

Les technologies "pointues" (robotique, automation, micro-machinisme, bureautique, informatiques etc...) permettent aujourd'hui aux pays industrialisés la poursuite d'objectifs de production et de gestion fondés sur l'intensification de la croissance contrairement à la stratégie de croissance industrielle basée sur l'adjonction de ressources nouvelles (croissance extensive) et qui était poursuivie jusque là.

La multinationalisation de l'entreprise et la globalisation de la production et des services

Avec la multinationalisation de l'entreprise, on assiste à une rupture totale avec les schémas classiques de production et d'échange. Les marchés sont pénétrés indirectement, les barrières douanières sont contournées, l'origine du produit final est de plus en plus inconnue, l'information se fait en temps réel et au dessus des frontières, l'investissement du capital provient de montages financiers impliquant nombre de partenaires, les élites dirigeantes se mondialisent, les prix et les taux de profits subissent une péréquation à l'échelle mondiale, les OPA, les prises de participation croisées, les fusions entre firmes se multiplient, la privatisation d'actifs industriels anciennement détenus par les Etats des pays développés s'accentue.

Le nombre des grandes fusions industrielles s'est accrû de 9% en 1986. L'Etat britannique s'est désaisi au profit du privé national et international de plus 40% depuis 1979 des ses actifs industriels créant ainsi une armée de neuf (9) millions de porteurs d'actions britanniques et étrangers, Paribas, en France comptait 150 000 actionnaires avant sa nationalisation en 1981. Reprivatisée elle compte aujourd'hui près de trois (3) millions d'actionnaires.

L'émergence de nouvelles zones de croissance rapide dans les PVD
La multiplication de "Petits Japons" en Asie du Sud Est essentiellement a été le fait marquant des 20 dernières années. Les 20 pays les plus dynamiques de la période 1970/1980 étaient des pays du "Tiers Monde" et seuls parmi ces 20 pays, l'Iran, l'Arabie Saoudite et le Koweit sont des économies pétrolières.

Ces 20 pays gagnent de plus en plus de nouveaux espaces industriels autrefois chasses gardées des pays industrialisés du Nord (acier, automobile, ferroviaire, machines-outils, constructions navales, BTPH électronique, textile etc...).

Les pays industrialisés se redéployant quant à eux, nous l'avons précédemment souligné, dans les technologies du futur (spatial, informatique et intelligence artificielle, biotechnologie, génie génétique, énergie alternative etc ...

Le Tiers-Monde ne compte plus les entreprises de certains pays qui se Multinationalisent. DAEWOO, HYUNDAI ou SAMSUNG en Corée du Sud, EMBRAER ou PETROBAS au Brésil, TATA en Inde etc ...

Les tendances lourdes de l'industrie des textiles à l'échelle du monde
Il est intéressant, croyons nous, avant de commencer l'étude de ces tendances lourdes, d'essayer fût-ce brièvement de replacer les échanges internationaux, et à l'intérieur de ceux-ci, ceux relatifs aux produits textiles, dans le contexte des législations contenues dans le cadre des accords internationaux tels que définis par des instances supra-nationales comme le GATT pour le commerce mondial en général et les tarifs, l'URUGUAY ROUND pour le commerce mondial des produits de l'agriculture et de l'élevage ou l'Arrangement Multi-Fibres (AMF) pour le commerce mondial des textiles.

Si en effet le GATT supervise le commerce mondial de plusieurs produits, à exception des produits énergétiques et des produits de l'industrie militaire, et dont le volume atteignait en 1990 quelques 4 000 milliards de dollars, les discussions menées dans le cadre de l'URUGUAY ROUND concernant presqu'exclusivement les produits de l'agriculture et de l'élevage et de tous leurs dérivés industriels; dont les textiles. Ces discussions qui impliquent surtout Américains et Européens ont débuté en Septembre 1986 à Punta Del Este en URUGUAY (d'où URUGUAY ROUND). Les tractations, serrées, menées dans ce cadre visent en substance au démantèlement progressif des mesures protectionnistes dues à la politique de subventions à l'agriculture et à l'exportation des produits de l'agriculture et de l'élevage poursuivie par les Européens surtout, et à la déréglementation totale et à terme des échanges mondiaux de ces produits et de leur dérivés industriels.

Les experts de l'OCDE ont calculé qu'il coûte aux 24 pays les plus riches quelques 250 milliards de dollars par an en subventions de toutes sortes. Ils prévoient pour la seule CEE et pour 1991 des subventions totalisant quelques 51 milliards de dollars. Si, comme il est prévu par nombre de spécialistes ces discussions échouent, un pays en voie de développement comme l'Inde dont l'industrie des textiles est essentiellement export-orientée devra continuer à passer sous les "fourches caudines" de l'AMF.

Concernant celui-ci, les "accords" qui y sont contenus règlent près de 50% soit 90 milliards de dollars en 1990, des échanges de produits textiles entre pays industrialisés et PVD dits "à faible prix de revient".

Les dispositions très protectionnistes de l'actuel AMF IV devraient, sous l'insistance des Américains, être quelque peu allégées lors de l'avènement au courant de 1991 de l'AMF V et progressivement démantelées sur une période de 10 années. Cependant la CEE, le principal visé, y met des conditions difficilement acceptables pour les PVD exportateurs de produit textile, telles que l'ouverture réciproque des marchés ou l'arrêt du "dumping".

Concernant l'industrie des textiles proprement dite, il paraît important de distinguer entre deux branches essentielles:
(1)   la branche textile, concentrée en grande partie dans les pays très industrialisés et qui concerne les activités de filature, du tissage et du finissage,

(2)   la branche de la confection ou de l'habillement basée pour presque de moitié dans les PVD.

Entre 1980 et 1988 ces deux branches ont concouru à une augmentation de l'industrie des textiles de 80% l'an. La part respective des deux dans les exportations mondiales des biens est passée de 3% et 8,8% en 1980 à 6,6% et 9,4% en 1988. En valeur les échanges mondiaux de textiles ont atteint pour 1990 un volume de 180 milliards de dollars, dont plus de la moitié réalisés par des pays développés essentiellement d'Europe occidentale. Enfin le commerce mondial des textiles représente aujourd'hui environ 5% du commerce mondial global alors qu'il n'en représentait que 2,4% au début de 1980. Ce doublement en 10 ans est dû pour une part, aux progrés techniques importants connus par ce secteur et qui à entraîné un accroissement de la productivité moyenne et pour l'autre, à la montée en puissance de PVD, surtout du Sud-Est asiatique dont les exportations mondiales en 1980, en représentent aujourd'hui plus du tiers. Cette part est appelée certainement à augmenter dans l'avenir si les discussions menées au sein de l'URUGUAY ROUND aboutissent même partiellement.

Finalement il est bon de souligner que des 5% représantant la ration du marché mondial des textiles/marché mondial de toutes marchandises, la part du textile représente les 4/5 ème alors que celle de l'habillement n'en représente que le 1/5ème.

L'industrie des textiles dans les pays développés

Sur un plan purement méthodologique, nous emploierons dans cette présentation le terme "textile" (au singulier) pour désigner le textile de base (filature, tissage, finissage), les termes "confection" ou "habillement" pour les activités aval et enfin le terme "textiles" (au pluriel) pour désigner l'ensemble des deux activités.

Le textile dans les pays développés

Comme déjà souligné, cette activité a connu depuis le début des années 80 et particulièrement dans les pays développés d'Europe Occidentale, une progression assez rapide. Ainsi la part de cette activité dans les échanges mondiaux de biens est passée de 2% en 1980 à plus de 3% en 1988. Cependant cette activité amorce un relatif déclin depuis cette date.

Lorsque nous étudions l'activité commerciale mondiale nous remarquons que les exportations d'Europe occidentale croissaient durant la première moitié de la décennie écoulée hors de la région et essentiellement en direction de l'Amerique du Nord. Depuis 1986 on a assisté à une inversion du "trend" qui a vu le commerce intra-européen passer de 74% des exportations totales à plus de 78% de celles-ci (tableau 1) Nous risquons ici l'hypothèse que l'entrée de la Grèce et du Portugal et probablement de la Turquie et de quelques pays d'Europe de L'Est dans le futur, au sein de la CEE, confirmera cette tendance à l'intraversion du marché européen, et ce, aux dépens des échanges avec les PVD. Nous émettons également l'hypothèse que les dispositions très protectionnistes contenues dans la Politique Agricole Commune (PAC) de la CEE seront reconduites à l'avenir et tendront à rendre le marché européen des textiles de plus en plus captif des membres actuels de la CEE au grand dans des libéraux du GATT et de l'URUGUAY ROUND et des PVD exportateurs de textiles. Concernant ces derniers, les zones de croissance futures de leurs exportations se situeront indubitablement en Amérique du Nord, au Japon et au Moyen Orient et dans l'aggrandissement de leur progrès marchés internes.

Tableau n° 1: Ventilation par grande région des exportations de textile de l'Europe Occidentale 1986/1988

Régions d'exportation	1986 (%)	1987 (%)	1988 (%)
Echanges intra-européens	73,3	77	78,4
Echanges avec l'Amérique du Nord	5	5	4,9
Echanges avec l'Amérique du Sud	1	1	0,8
Echanges avec l'Europe de l'Est +l'URSS	5	4	4
Echanges avec l'Afrique	6	4	4
Echanges avec le Moyen Orient	5	3	3
Echanges avec le reste du Monde	0,7	1	4,9

Rapport du GATT 1988

La valeur globale de ces exportations avait atteint en 1988 près de 45 milliards de dollars et se chiffre en 1990, à près de 75 milliards de dollars, près de la moitié du commerce mondial du textile. Le marché du textile dans les pays européens reste de loin le marché dominant puisque l'on constate que plus de 90% des exportations des pays industrialisés se font au sein de ce groupe de pays.

L'on remarque à travers la part des exportations de textile dans les exportations globales de ces pays que toute mesure protectionniste décidée par les pays importateurs de textile n'affecte pas outre mesure, à exception peut-être de l'Italie ou de la Belgique/ Luxembourg, la structure générale de leur balance commerciale.

Concernant les importations en textile des pays développés, bien à partir d'autres pays développés qu'en provenance des PVD, leur croissance est assez inégale d'un pays à l'autre. Ainsi si l'Allemagne Fédérale demeurait, en tout cas en 1988, le premier importateur (8,7 milliards de dollars américains (MD$)) de textile (elle en est aussi le premier exportateur), la balance commerciale de ce produit est excédentaire (+ 1,9 MD$). Par contre, celle des Etats Unis affichait en 1988 un déficit de près de 2 MD$ puisque ce pays avait importé cette année là pour près de 6 MD$ de textile, alors que celle de la France présentait un déficit de 1,7 MD$ en 1988 (importations 1988 = 6,3 MD$), de même que celle du Royaume Uni (3,1 MD$ de déficit). Seules l'Italie et la Belgique, à l'instar de la RFA, présentaient des surplus dans leurs balances commerciales du textile, respectivement 2,7 MD$ et 2,1 MD$. Les déficits enregistrés par la plupart des pays développés sont imputables, à notre avis, aux causes suivantes:

(1)   Les restructurations industrielles conduites par ces pays et qui ont nécessité le redéploiement des capacités industrielles en direction des technologies plus

Tableau n° 2: Principaux exportateurs de textile en 1988

Pays	Valeur: Milliards de dollars US (MD$)	Part dans les exportations mondiales de textile		Part dans les exportations mondiales de marchandises
	1988	1980	1988	1988
R.F.A.	10,6	11,5	12	3,5
Italie	7,5	7,5	8,5	6
Belgique/Luxembourg	5	6,5	5,5	5,5
France	4,6	6	5	3
Royaume Uni	3,4	5,5	4	2,5
U.S.A.	4	7	4,5	–
Pays Bas	3	4	3,5	–
Suisse	2,2	2,5	2,5	–

pointues et à plus forte valeur ajoutée. Aux Etats Unis par exemple ces restructurations ont coûté au secteur du textile de ce pays la perte de 250 000 emplois depuis 1980. Les profits dans le secteur du textile ont, quant à eux, chuté de près de 15%.

(2) L'abandon de certaines filières du textile. Le groupe Japonais Toray a racheté en 1990 les activités de la filature de l'anglais Samuel Coourtaulds qui, a son tour, se redéploie dans la fonction en rachetant la maison française de prêt-à-porter Georges Rech.

(3) La multinationalisation des activités du textile et de la confection. En France, le groupe Boussac vend des anciennes usines de filature et de tissage qui firent jadis sa gloire et racheté au passage par Christian Dior pour s'installer dans la confection de luxe. L'Anglais Coats Viyelle, numéro un europén du textile et leader mondial du fil à tricoter, s'est fortement implanté en Asie. Avec le rachat de Hart, n° 1 argentin du négoce et du peignage et la pénétration du marché australien du peignage, le français chargeur S.A. double son chiffre d'affaires et consolide sa place de numéro un mondial de la laine. Louis Vuitton-Noël Hennessy (LMVH) est racheté par le groupe anglais de spiritueux Guinness et Bernard Arnault de Dior à hauter de 43%. Yves Saint Laurent a rachéte l'américain Charles Of The Ritz pour près de un milliard de dollars.

(4) La concurrence acharnée livrée par des pays développés connaissant une meilleure productivité du travail (Allemagne, Italie) et une utilisaiton plus intensive de la technologie, l'Allemagne affichait en 1989 des coûts salariaux inférieurs de 20% à ceux de l'Italie et de 50% à ceux du Royaume Uni. Cette concurrence est plus féroce encore si on inclut les produits provenant de l'Asie du Sud-Est où les coûts de production sont plus faibles, basés qu'ils sont sur l'utilisation d'une main d'oeuvre à bon marché (faible salaires nominaux, absence d'avantages sociaux, sous syndicalisation, emploi du travail féminin et des enfants, allongement des journées de travail etc …).

(5) Les délocalisations observées dans les branches textiles. L'Americain Levi Strauss installe une partie de sa production de Jeans en Europe de l'Est en rachetant au passage une firme hongroise de production de Jeans qui perdait deux (2) million de dollars par an. Strauss qui, après avoir réduit le nombre d'ouvriers employés par cette firme produit aujourd-hui 5 000 paires de Jeans/jour et 3 000 blousons denim/mois destinés à l'exportation vers l'Afrique, le Moyen Orient et l'Europe de l'Est. Levi Strauss compte prochainement en faire de même avec une société d'Etat polonaise.

En plus de déficits, ces raisons ont conduit les pays développés à transférer vers le Tiers Monde les activités du textile traditionnel, essentiellement les activités polluantes, énergivores et à faible valeur ajoutée. Au point où pour l'année 1989 l'essentiel de la production mondiale de fibres naturelles et synthétiques est assuré par des pays en voie de développement.

Tableau n° 3: Production mondiale de fibres et synthétiques 1989

Pays ou région	Part de marché mondial des fibres (%)
Asie du Sud Est	21%
Europe de l'Est + URSS	19%
Chine	16%
Europe Occidentale	16%
U.S.A.	15%
Japon	60%
Autres pays	70

Source: L'Expansion Novembre 1989.

Tableau n° 4: Ventilation par région des exportations européennes de l'habillement

Région destinatrice	1980	1988
Marché intra-Européen	84%	82%
Marché Nord Américain	3%	7%
Marché Latino-Américain	1%	0%
Marché d'Europe de l'Est	4%	2%
Marché Africain	3%	2%
Marché du Moyen Orient	3%	2%
Marché Asiatique (Japon essentiellement)	2%	5%

Les causes des déficits que nous venons d'enumérer nous paraissent suffisamment structurelles pour conforter à l'avenir les tendances de désinvestissement graduel des pays développés du secteur du textile. Cependant concernant ce secteur en Europe Occidentale et particulièrement au sein de la CEE, il est à craindre que les parts perdues par les gros producteurs traditionnels ne soient compensées par la production de la Grèce, du Portugal, de la Turquie et de certains pays d'Europe de l'Est s'ils venaient à associer ou à devenir membres de la Communauté Economique Européene.

Il est à signaler que dans cette branche, ce sont les exportations de la Grèce, du Portugal et de la Turquie qui ont connu la plus forte progression de 1980 à 1988. (6 % du volume des exportations européennes en 1980 et 20% de ce même volume en 1988). Par contre les exportations italiennes qui représentaient au début de la dernière décennie 11 % du total des exportations mondiales de vêtements ont quelque peu chuté à la fin de la même décennie.

Quand on sait que le marché intra-européen du vêtement absorbait en 1988 prés de 82 % du total des exportations européennes, l'on mesure alors la progression entre 1980 et 1988 des exportations de vêtements de la Grèce, du Portugal et de la Turquie aux dépens de pays à forte tradition dans l'habillement tels que l'Italie, la France ou la Grande Bretagne qui, soit pour cause de restructuration ou pour cause de coûts de production plus élevés abandonnent aux premiers pays des parts du marché de plus en plus importantes.

Par ailleurs la lecture du tableau 5 révèle que nous assistons là à une distinction nette entre pays européens du Nord dont les économies sont trés diversifiées et dont les revenus d'exportations dépendent dans une faible mesure des exportations de

Tableau n° 5: Principaux exportateurs européens d'habillement

Pays	Valeur: Milliards de dollars US (MD$) 1988	Part dans les exportations mondiales de l'habillement		Part dans les exportations mondiales de l'habillement	
		1980	1988	1980	1988
Italie	9,1	11	10,2	6	7
R.F.A.	5,4	–	6	1,5	1,5
France	3,3	5,5	4	2	2
Royaume Uni	2,5	4,5	3	1,5	1,5
Turquie	2,5	0,5	2,5	4,5	20,5
Portugal	2,2	1,5	2,5	13,5	21
Pays Bas	1,5	2	1,5	1	1,5
Grèce	1,4	1	2	7,5	22

vêtements et des pays d'Europe du Sud pour lesquels les exportations de vêtements représentent une part importante de leur balance commerciale (+ de 20 % la Turquie, 22 % la Grèce et 21 % le Portugal).

Au vu de ces ratios l'on saisit mieux les réticences de ces trois (3) pays à voir la CEE (pour la Grèce et le Portugal) abandonner, fût-ce partiellement, le régime des quotas ou le régime des subventions.

Concernant les importations d'habillement, les Etats Unis et la RFA demeurent les principaux acheteurs avec respectivement en 1988, 23 MD$ et 15 MD$.

L'Allemagne présentait, à l'instar des marchés américains et nippons un marché potentiellement porteur avec un déficit de prés de 9 milliards de $ en 1988, cependant contrairement aux deux (2) autres marchés, celui de la RFA présente la particularité de s'inscrire dans le marché intra-européen où son déficit peut être comblé par des pays comme la Grèce, la Turquie ou le Portugal et par l'apport de la branche de l'habillement de l'ex. RDA.

Les textiles dans les pays en voie de développement

Dans le PVD, l'évolution de la branche a été lente quelque peu jusqu'à l'orée des années 80. Durant la décennie écoulée l'activité de cette branche s'est franchement accélérée aussi bien parce que des investissements substantiels ont été efffectués dans la branche par les PVD surtout d'Asie du Sud-Est que de la politique de décolonisation conduite par les pays développés en direction de ces pays. En ravanche, la branche de l'habillement et particuliérement la confection grand public a connu une progression beaucoup plus rapide depuis 1980 au point où des pays comme la Chine ou Hong Kong rivalisent en valeur (respectivement 6,5 milliards de dollars et 6,4 milliards de dollars en 1988/89) avec la RFA ou l'Italie. Les PVD ont contribué depuis 1980 pour 26% du commerce mondial du textile et pour 43% pour celui de l'habillement. Au surplus il nous parait intéressant de signaler que si la branche textile des PVD est presque de moitié (42%) tournée vers la satisfaction de leur demande locale, la production issue de la branche habillement est en revanche presqu'éxclusivement destinée à exportation (environ 92%).

Au vu de cette situation d'extraversion de l'industrie des textiles des PVD, on saisit mieux la nature des formidables enjeux qui transparaissent dans les dispositions très astreignantes de l'A.M.F.

Le textile de base
Comme précédemment souligné, la branche du textile dans les PVD a connu depuis 1980 une progression des exportations remarquée due essentiellement à la montée en puissance de cinq pays d'Asie du Sud-Est mais également au recul assez net enregistré

Tableau n° 6: Principaux pays développés importateurs d'habillement

Pays	Valeur des importations Milliards de dollars (US (MD$) 1988	Part dans les importations d'habillement/importation totale	
		1980	1988
U.S.A.	23,1	2,5	5
R.F.A.	14,5	4,5	6
Japon	6,7	1	3,5
France	6	1	3,5
Royaume Uni	5,5	2,5	3
U.R.S.S.	3,8	3,5	4
Pays Bas	3,8	3,5	4
Suisse	2,8	3,5	4
Belgique	2,7	2,5	3
Suede	2,1	4	4,5
Canada	1,9	1	1,5
Italie	1,9	1	1,5
Autriche	1,7	4	4,5

dans les pays développés pour ce qui touche aux exportations de la branche textile, et dont les marchés (RFA, Etats Unis surtout) se sont brutalement retournés depuis 1980 pour devenir franchement importateurs. Les importations des Etats Unis de textile ont presque doublé durant la première moitié de la dernière décennie. Les raisons majeures de ces évolutions contrastées des branches du textile en pays développés et PVD ont été déjà répertoriées dans ce manuscrit).

En revanche les importations de textile des PVD sont demeurées durant la même période assez modeste dans l'ensemble et elles concernent beaucoup plus le textile provenant des activités de chimie fine.

Par contre les exportations de certains PVD tels qu le Brésil (855 millions de $), l'Indonésie (680 millions de $) ou le Maroc (176 millions de $) sont demeureés, en dépit de grands efforts, relativement médiocres.

La confection dans les PVD
Depuis le début des années 80, plus de 3/4 des exportations mondiales d'habillement ont été assurés conjointement par les pays développés, d'Europe Occidentale et par les plus grands exportateurs d'Asie du Sud-Est (Chine, Hong Kong, Corée du Sud et Taiwan). Par ailleurs si les discussions menées dans le cadre de l'Uruguay Round, ainsi que l'avénement d'un AMF V moins contraignant se concrétisent on peut parier sans peine sur un accroissement des exportations de ces derniers pays ainsi que de celles des quelques PVD qui sauront opérer les mutations industrielles et technologiques indispensables. Par ailleurs ces tendances lourdes seront appelées à se confirmer à l'avenir compte tenu des nouvelles opportunités offertes par la baisse structurelle de l'activité habillement, surtout dans son aspect grand public, dans les pays développés. Le marché américain qui devient le marché de l'habillement le plus convoité est déjà pour

Tableau n° 7: Principaux PVD exportateurs de textile (1988)

Pays	Valeur en Milliards de dollars US (MDS) 1988	Part des exportations mondiales	Part des textiles dans la balance commerciale du pays
Chine	6,5	7,5	13,5
Hong Kong	6,4	7	10
Corée du Sud	4,7	5,5	7,5
Taiwan	4,5	5	7,5
Inde	1,7	2	14

plus de 60% entre les mains des 4 grands exportateurs d'Asie du Sud Est. Les marchés japonais et du Moyen Orient présentent les mêmes capacités d'absorption. Cependant encore une fois, il est à craindre que les parts perdues par l'Europe du Nord ne soient reprises par les pays d'Europe du Sud, en particulier ceux membres de la CEE si les dispositions actuelles de l'AMF IV sont reconduites intégralement `a parti de 1991, ou par des pays comme la Turquie et les pays d'Europe de l'Est qui tentent de rallier la CEE.

Les tendances lourdes de l'évolution de l'industrie des textiles à l'echelle du monde
Il est permis d'admettre au vu de cette présentation générale de l'industrie des textiles à échelle mondiale que tout en restant des pays du textile de base, les pays développés, et tout particulièrement ceux d'Europe Occidentale, voient progressivement leurs parts dans le commerce mondial de ce produit diminuer progressivement, même si toutefois ces pays continuent à contribuer par plus de 50% dans le commerce mondial du textile, on observe que cette part qui était beaucoup plus grande auparavant (+ de 60%) avait amorcé depuis 1980 une baisse tendancielle qui se confirmera certainement à l'avernir à la fois parce que ces pays, à l'instar des Etats Unis ou du Japon, avaient des restructurations profondes de leur industrie en général et de celle des textiles en particulier, tout en délocalisant vers le Tiers Monde le textile lourd, polluant, énergivore et à faible valeur ajoutée, que parce que des investissements importants ont été consentis depuis 1980 dans l'industrie du textile par des PVD et à leur tête ceux d'Asie du Sud Est.

Concernant la branche de l'habillement dont les pays développés assurent aujourd'hui près de 43% du commerce mondial, il est permis d'avancer qu'elle connaîtra elle aussi à l'avenir une tendance à la baisse dans ces pays. Cependant on remarque que ce qui est

Tableau n° 8: Principaux PVD exportateurs d'habillement (1988)

Pays	Valeur en Milliards de dollars US (MD$) 1988	Part des exportations mondiales	Part des textiles dans la balance commerciale du pays
Hong Kong	11,8	13,5	18,5
Corée du Sud	8,7	10	14,5
Chine	4,9	5,5	10
Taiwan	4,7	5,4	8
Thailande	1,8	2	8
Inde	1,6	1,9	14
Singapour	1,2	1,7	–

perdu, surtout pour l'Europe du Nord est dores et déjà gagné par des pays d'Europe du Sud et de l'Est; Grèce (1,5 MD$), Portugal (2,3 MD$), Turquie (2,4 MD$), Tchéslovaque (0.6 MD$), Yougoslavie (0,5 MD$), Hongrie (0,4 MD$), Pologne (0,5 MD$) et la Roumanie (0,6 MD$) ou par des pays d'Asie du Sud-Est.

Par ailleurs l'abandon progressif par les pays développés de certaines filières de cette branche au profit de la confection haut de gamme et/ou de luxe permet d'avancer que la tendance à la baisse des exportations "traditionnelles" de la branche habillement des pays développés se confirmera dans les années à venir.

A cet effet on observe que les Africains et les Européens se spécialisent de plus en plus dans la filière du haut de gamme et/ou de luxe, à plus forte valeur ajoutée.

Aux Etats Unis, des costumes "Designer Linc" de Geoffrey Beene, un des leaders américains dans la filière coûtent pas moins de 3 500 dollars à unité. En France un foulard ou une cravate Hermès coûte respectivement 200 et 100 dollars, alors qu'une robe de mariée Christian Lacroix coûte la bagatelle de 30 000 dollars US.

Chevauchant les deux continents tout en se transnationalisant de plus en plus, la marque Benetton (5000 points de vente dans le monde, dont 800 aux Etats Unis, et un chiffre d'affaires de 7 milliards de francs français en 1990) se taille un empire dans la filière haut de gamme en adoptant une stratégie commerciale, fondée sur:

(1)   une identité du produit (le même produit est commercialisé dans tous les pays, la clientèle mondiale, dans sa diversité, adaptant ses goûts au produit Benetton et non l'inverse),

(2)   des coloris adaptés à toutes les tranches d'âge,

(3)   un prix accessible grâce à la suppression des intermédiaires et de leurs marges entre la production et la distribution,

(4)   une maîtrise totale de marque sur le fond et en surface,

(5)   tous les magasins de la marque présentent la même architecture basée sur la clarté, la simplicité, l'ordre et les couleurs vives,

(6)   une publicité identique sur l'ensemble du globe,

(7)   une "culture" Benetton associant les couleurs de la marque aux couleurs des races qui composent la demande mondiale.

Par ailleurs Benetton adopte, dans ses incursions dans le Tiers Monde la stratégie dite du "merchandising" qui consiste pour lui à financer la plus grande partie des investissements de "joint-venture" avec ses partenaires dans ces pays, tout en leur faisant gérer chez eux la production et la commercialisation de son produit, sous sa marque et selon ses propres natures de production et de commercialisation. Benetton se réservant le privilège de la commercialisation mondiale de la part de la production destinée à l'exportation Benetton use également de la stratégie dite du "franchising" qui consiste à faire financer par ces partenaires dans le Tiers Monde la plus grande part des investissements et à les faire produire et commercialiser sous sa marque et selon ses canons propres, à charge pour ses partenaires de lui verser sa part du profit et à lui payer des "royalties" pour usage commercial.

Conclusion

Le marché mondial des textiles (180 milliards de dollars en 1990) est réglé par l'Arrangement Multi-Fibres qui a procédé depuis sa naissance il y a 15 ans, en vertu d'un système complexe de régulation de l'industrie des textiles, à une véritable Division Internationale du Travail entre pays développés et PVD concurrents où la part dévolue à ces derniers dans les marchés des premiers est régie par le système des quotas revus périodiquement. Cet arrangement est censé être dissous sur les dix (10) années à venir suite aux discussions de l'Uruguay Round.

Il peut être affirmé que compte tenu de la place qu'occupe l'industrie européene des textiles dans le commerce mondial des produits de cette industrie et de l'importance des échanges intra-européens, ainsi que des dispositions protectionnistes et de la montée en puissance des pays d'Europe du Sud et l'ouverture du marché européen aux produits textiles de l'Europe de l'Est, que le marché européen ne présente pas d'opportunité de pénétration suffisante pour des PVD et qu'en somme il deviendra, à notre sens, de plus en plus captif des européens eux-mêmes et de quelques autre pays asiatiques exportateurs de textiles.

Cependant nous estimons que ces opportunités peuvent être entrevues si les marchés américains, japonais et du Moyen Orient sont ciblés en premier lieu. Cela suppose cependant le maintien à un niveau élevé des invetissements. Sans quoi, ils finiront rapidement par perdre leur part de marché.

15

Les Perspectives de l'Intégration Industrielle en Afrique, les Cas de l'Industrie Textile

Mahrez Hadjseyd

Introduction

L'objet de cette communication est de présenter les politiques industrielles en Afrique dans la perspective de l'intégration régionale, illustrée par le cas de l'industrie textile. Le secteur informel ne sera pas pris en compte dans cette analyse. Par définition, il échappe à tout contrôle. Il faut rappeler, cependant que le poids économique de ce secteur est loin d'être négligeable, notamment dans la confection. C'est généralement vers ce secteur que se porte à la fois la demande des couches aux revenus les plus faibles et celle concernant le haut de gamme, pour les habits traditionnels.

Les mouvements de libération qui ont fait accéder les pays africains à l'indépendance ont, dans un élan souvent romantique et généreux (inspiré des idées de progrès technique héritées du Saint-Simonisme et en particulier des théories de développement défendant les modèles autocentrés), ont vu dans l'industrialisation le moyen adéquat le plus rapide pour transformer les sociétés africaines jugées archaïques et leur faire rattraper le retard qui les sépare des pays industrialisés. Pratiquement tous les pays africains auront connu, après leur indépendance une phase d'expansion industrielle conduite directement par l'Etat. Auparavant, durant la colonisation notamment, ils avaient connu en général une implantation industrielle extravertie, embryonnaire conduite par les multinationales. L'industrialisation en Afrique a été donc, dans la majorité des cas, l'oeuvre de l'Etat ou des multinationales et non construite, comme en Europe ou en Asie par les forces sociales dynamiques de la société.

Il semble que l'approche des pouvoirs publics dans ce domaine ait revêtu les mêmes formes que celles des autorités coloniales dans la mobilisation de la population autour des objectifs de développement en général. Elle a été autoritaire, bureaucratique et isolationniste au lieu de rassembler et de mobiliser.

L'industrialisation conduite par l'Etat a été considérée le plus souvent comme une fin en soi. Dans la plupart des cas elle est apparue comme une source de coûts dispendieux pour l'Etat et la société, connue sous le vocable "d'éléphants blancs".

Pour cette industrialisation les pays africains ont très souvent consacré une grande partie des exportations de leurs ressources naturelles et ont sacrifié également une partie importante des consommation de leur population. Elle a également servi, dans bien des cas, de source de légitimation des pouvoirs en place. De ce fait, son objectif premier qui aurait dû être la création de richesses, a été généralement perdu de vue.

L'industrie a été perçue comme une fée, qui par sa seule mise en place pouvait transformer les mentalités "arriérées", rendre disponible les biens industriels sur le marché local et surtout dynamiser les autres secteurs économiques, notamment l'agriculture.

Il s'est agi dans la plupart des cas d'une industrie rêvée plus que d'un véritable projet de développement viable et cohérent. L'échec de cette démarche, dont l'Algérie a été le prototype le plus accompli, semble infirmer l'idée que le développement puisse s'acheter ou se transférer par une simple importation d'équipement.

Les politiques industrielles suivies, qu'elles soient libérales ou étatistes, ont en fin de compte produit peu de résultats. Cependant il faudrait reconnaître qu'en dehors de l'Afrique du Nord, du Nigéria et de l'Afrique du Sud, les programmes industrielles ont été de faible ampleur.

Les caractéristiques de l'industrie textile africaine
Caractéristiques générales
La branche textile, aux côtés de l'industrie alimentaire, constitue pratiquement l'industrie dominante en Afrique. En raison de ses caractéristiques, demandant peu de capitaux et utilisant une main d'oeuvre nombreuse et peu qualifiée, elle est apparue comme l'industrie la plus adaptée au contexte africain. Ainsi, pratiquement tous les pays africains ont opté pour la réalisation d'une industrie textile parfois importante. Le plus souvent celle-ci se concentre sur l'habillement et se trouve généralement tournée vers le marché intérieur, sauf en Afrique du Nord et à l'Ile Maurice où elle possède des capacités d'exportation significatives. On relèvera que cette industrie dépasse 15% de la valeur ajoutée du secteur manufacturier dans de nombreux pays: l'Ile Maurice (51% en 1989), le Mali (40% en 1970), le Nigéria (26% en 1970), le Soudan (34% en 1970), l'Algérie (17% en 1989), l'Egypte (16% en 1989), la Tunisie (21% en 1989).

Dans bien des cas les industries textiles africaines possèdent un faible niveau de performance et de compétitivité lié généralement à des causes structurelles et organisationnelles. Elles fonctionnent le plus souvent avec du matériel vétuste, acquis parfois d'occasion lors du renouvellement des industries européennes. Elles font face à des charges salariales élevées, manquent de rigueur dans l'organisation du processus de production et souffrent de pénurie de personnel technique qualifié. Cette situation se traduit généralement par un rapport qualité-prix médiocre et des coûts de production élevés, ce qui ne permet pas le plus souvent de faire face au simple remplacement de l'équipement.

Le développement de la culture du coton en Afrique sub-saharienne est intéressant à examiner. Il est généralement considéré comme une réussite. Toutes les conditions techniques et organisationnelles ont été réunies aussi bien en surface qu'en rendement, avec une qualité appréciable. Un niveau excédentaire de production a été même observé mais il a souvent nui au maintien des prix. Toutefois, l'industrie locale n'arrive pas, le plus souvent, à rendre au niveau du produit fini la qualité de la matière cotonade utilisée, en raison essentiellement de la vétusté de ses équipements et du manque de qualification du personnel.

La faiblesse du textile africain réside encore plus dans la création et la mode.
On peut relever à ce sujet que les pagnes portés par les femmes africaines sont fabriqués et conçus en grande partie au Pays-Bas et en Angleterre. Pourtant la demande interne pour le textile est assez importante. Mais elle ne s'adresse que partiellement aux industries locales. Celles-ci sont fortement concurrencées par des importations massives de friperie et également par les articles de haut de gamme importés, pour une partie des consommateurs urbains. Seule la demande locale pour des produits de bas de gamme et à bas prix, notamment en Afrique sub-saharienne, est dirigée vers cette industrie. Partout, en Afrique du Nord, l'industrie textile résiste un peu mieux à ces situations. Malgré des barrières douanières très souvent élevées, les importations de produits textiles se sont accrues, empruntant dans certains pays les chemins de la contrebande.

Toutefois, on peut rencontrer certaines entreprises performantes, souvent favorisées par la protection du marché et les bas salaires. Elles dégagent des bénéfices importants et la qualité de leur produit est appréciable. Elles font partie, sauf de très rares exceptions, du secteur privé local ou sont des filiales de multinationales. Elles demeurent cependant des exceptions qu'il faudrait analyser si on veut établir des politiques industrielles viables en Afrique.

Historiquement, au lendemain des indépendances, dans les années 1960, l'industrie textile s'est constituée en premier lieu pour le marché local. Elle était conçue comme une industrie de substitution aux importations.

Mais ce type de développement montra rapidement ses limites, en accroissant massivement les importations ou la remontée des filières n'est pas effectuée. On se tourna, alors vers l'exportation pour soulager la balance des paiements.

Pour que ce type de développement réussisse, l'expérience des pays du Sud-Est asiatique a montré qu'il faudrait construire la filière (tissage, finissage, filature, texturation...) en amont de la production et faire la liaison avec la chimie (fibres, colorants,...) et l'industrie mécanique pour la maintenance et la fabrication des pièces de rechange et de l'équipement. L'industrialisation apparait comme un mouvement dynamique qui nécessite un élargissement permanent de la base industrielle qui peut également se faire du bas vers le haut ("reverse engineering").

La situation des pays exportateurs
Nous illustrerons la situation exceptionnelle des pays exportateurs de textile-habillement par le cas de la Tunisie et du Maroc.

La branche textile fournit environ le 1/3 des exportations du Maroc et de la Tunisie. Elle est constituée dans ces deux pays par un secteur exportateur dynamique et un secteur travaillant pour le marché local protégé par des barrières douanières élevées. Ce dernier secteur a une qualité de produit assez médiocre. Ses prix sont élevés et sa productivité est généralement basse, contrairement au secteur exportateur. Il emploie au Maroc un peu plus de travailleurs que le secteur exportateur qui compte lui, environ 75.000 travailleurs. Néanmoins les deux segments du secteur textile sont fortement tributaires de l'extérieur pour leurs approvisionnements et n'entretiennent que très peu de liens de sous-traitance entre eux. Deux produits dominent les exportations: la bonneterie, qui a connu une forte expansion au cours de la dernière décennie et la confection. Si le marché de cette dernière semble se rétrécir, celui de la bonneterie ne semble pas encore être saturé.

Le secteur exportateur maghrébin reste un secteur peu intégré. Pour exporter en 1987 1,2 milliards d'écus en produits textiles vers la CEE, il a importé environ l'équivalent de 52% de cette valeur en produits semi-finis (tissus et accessoires...) d'Europe.

Ce secteur qui fait preuve d'une compétitivité réelle, fonctionne dans beaucoup de cas comme une enclave de l'industrie européenne pour laquelle il n'est souvent qu'un prestataire de service. Généralement le circuit commercial, les modèles, les normes techniques, le développement du produit lui échappent presque totalement. Il s'agit en général d'un *perfectionnement passif.*

Malgré cette contrainte, on peut rencontrer des entreprises qui ont dépassé cette situation. Elles ont réussi à prendre leur autonomie par rapport à leurs donneurs d'ordre et ont diversifié leur marché. Elles sont certes peu nombreuses. Mais le fait est important pour être signalé. Il indique en effet que les prévisions les plus pessimistes en matière de développement ne sont pas toujours inéluctables. Depuis 1986, on note un accroissement des investissements vers la filature et le tissage, ce qui semble préfigurer l'amorce d'une remontée des filières et/ou une plus grande intégration du secteur travaillant pour la demande intérieure.

Il est à rappeler que les exportations vers l'Europe ont été encouragées par la CEE à la faveur de la délocalisation de son industrie de textile-habillement et également en guise de compensation à la fermeture du marché agricole européen à la plupart des produits agricoles maghrébins à cette époque.

Mais faisant fi des accords signés en 1976, alors que ceux-ci constituaient un engagement ferme de la part de la CEE d'ouvrir son marché à tous les produits manufacturés, celle-ci décida unilatéralement en 1977 d'interdire l'entrée sur son territoire aux produits textiles en provenance du Maroc et de la Tunisie. Depuis 1977, les produits du textile-habillement maghrébins sont placés sous haute surveillance dans le cadre du dispositif des "Accords Multifibres" et un quota dit "d'auto-limitation", leur est beaucoup plus imposé que négocié.

Cette épisode montre toute la fragilité de l'option exportatrice; elle se trouve non seulement menacée par le protectionnisme (les produits textiles sont les articles les plus surveillés dans le monde) mais également par la rude concurrence entre pays en développement.

Au Maroc et en Tunisie, à la faveur des Programmes d'Ajustement Structurel (PAS) et des politiques exportatrices, la situation économique s'est légèrement améliorée dès la fin de la décennie 1990, sans toutefois écarter les menaces sur l'avenir. En effet, les succès obtenus à l'exportation peuvent se révéler éphémères à long terme si on projette certaines évolutions probables de la branche textile-habillement.

La première de ces évolutions est qu'à la faveur des PAS, la solution exportatrice est préconisée aujourd'hui par les institutions internationales à tous les pays en voie de développement qui s'ajustent.

Les perspectives des individus à vocation exportatrice
Les perspectives générales
A la faveur de PAS dans les années à venir, beaucoup de pays disposant d'une industrie textile tournée vers le marché intérieur vont la réorienter vers l'exportation, alors que

l'offre est déjà jugée aujourd'hui largement excédentaire sur le marché mondial. Par ailleurs, si en soi cette proposition n'est pas irréaliste, il n'en demeure pas moins que dans les conditions de saturation de marché qui en découlerait, les avantages comparatifs basés sur le niveau relatif des salaires seront probablement très insuffisants pour conquérir des marchés. Et cela sans compter sur un regain de protectionnisme des pays industrialisés, en cas d'échec des négociations du GATT et l'entrée en course des pays de l'Est.

Par ailleurs, pour faire face à cette concurrence, les pays industrialisés ont procédé, au cours de la décennie précédente, à d'importantes restructurations industrielles dans la branche, au plan de l'organisation de la production et de sa délocalisation-relocalisation.

La seconde évolution probable de la branche est d'ordre technique. La branche textile est une branche réellement mondialisée aussi bien au niveau des normes de la production que de la consommation, contrairement aux autres industries classiques.

Cette industrie qui était jusque là intensive en main d'oeuvre est en train, à la faveur des bouleversements technologiques en cours, de devenir une industrie de pointe intensive en capitaux. La sidérurgie et la mécanique avaient également connu au cours de leur évolution une mutation comparable.

En réalité, on ne perçoit pas encore concrètement les transformations technologiques en cours car elles n'ont pas encore affecté significativement l'habillement et les technologies de base le concernant, elles sont restées stables et grâce à elles les pays en voie de développement peuvent encore concurrencer les pays industrialisés. Mais on peut constater que la plupart des solutions techniques sont prêtes dans certains pays industrialisés et seront mises en exécution dès que les coûts des équipements correspondants seront acceptables par le marché. Ces solutions techniques concernent le processus de production (commande numérique, fabrication et conception assistées par ordinateur, coupe au laser ...) et les matières premières (matériaux composites ...) et ont pour objectif d'affecter à la fois les coefficients de travail (diminution des quantités de travail par unité produite) et la flexibilité de l'outil de production (produite un maximum de produits diversifiés avec les mêmes outils tout en assurant la continuité des processus de production).

Dans ces conditions, la compétitivité de la branche ne proviendrait plus du niveau relatif des salaires mais du fait que le niveau de productivité va s'élever beaucoup plus vite que celui des salaires. Cette conjoncture pourrait alors se révéler favorable à une relocalisation de la branche dans les pays industrialisés et la grande majorité des PVD seraient dans ce cas rapidement distancés dans cette course, en raison notamment des coûts élevés de l'équipement et des qualifications nécessaires.

Pour toutes ces raisons, l'option exportatrice sans assise solide sur le marché interne semble être un risque à long terme, notamment la sous-traitance internationale. Dans le domaine du textile celle-ci parait assez volatile.

La place de l'Afrique
Les produits textiles font l'objet d'échanges mondiaux croissant représentant plus de 100 milliards de dollars U.S dont 20 milliards importés par les USA et 10 par la CEE.

Néanmoins, l'Afrique participe très faiblement au commerce mondial de textile. Les exportations textiles ne sont réellement significatives que dans quatre pays: La Tunisie où elles sont passées de 2% en 1965 à 35% en 1990 dans le total des produits exportés, l'Ile Maurice où elles sont passées de 0% en 1965 à 24% en 1990, l'Egypte où elles sont passées pour les mêmes périodes de 15% à 27%, et le Maroc où elles sont passées de 1% à 20%. On peut relever également les efforts remarquables dans les exportations du Malawi et de la Tanzanie qui sont passées de 0% en 1965 à 3% en 1990.

Les exportations maghrébines par rapport au commerce mondial restent modestes et représentent moins de 1% du total mondial, même si le Maroc en 1991 est devenu le premier fournisseur de textile-habillement du marché français devant l'Italie.

La CEE absorbe la quasi-totalité des exportations africaines de textile-habillement. Au plan mondiale ou même à l'échelle européenne, les exportations africaines sont assez marginales et représentent moins de 2% du volume des transactions mondiales de la branche.

Les perspectives d'intégration industrielle en Afrique
Les échanges entre pays africains demeurent insignifiants sinon inexistants dans la plupart des cas. Pourtant des complémentarités dans le textile pourraient naître, spécialement au niveau des produits de base (coton, laine ...) que beaucoup de pays importent d'autres continents. D'autre part, l'étroitesse de la majorité des marchés nationaux africains devraient inciter les opérateurs économiques à rechercher une plus grande intégration et à créer des complémentarités au niveau des sous-régions, spécialement pour les fibres naturelles et synthétiques, la filature ou la finition et pour certains équipements courants (machines à coudre, métiers à tisser, accessoires, etc) dont la technologie est stabilisée. La coopération intra-africaine pourrait aussi concerner

les marchés africains et extérieurs pour une meilleure maîtrise de l'information à leur sujet.

L'efficacité et la compétitivité industrielles dans l'industrie textile n'a pas d'explication simpliste, en termes de proximité des marchés ou d'avantages comparatifs basés sur les bas salaires.

Il est reconnu aujourd'hui que la réussite dans ce secteur est davantage fondée sur la construction d'un ensemble industriel complexe que sur un facteur bien déterminé et sur une élévation plus rapide de la productivité par rapport au niveau des salaires. Une forte croissance d'un secteur industriel qui se réalise dans le cadre d'une politique d'exportation, même si sa production ne dégage pas d'excédents significatifs permet de ne pas bloquer le développement industriel, par le déséquilibre de la balance des paiements qui freinerait les importations de certains inputs industriels.

La situation de l'industrie textile en Afrique reflète bien l'état dans lequel se débat l'ensemble de l'industrie africaine. Elle est souvent proche de l'obsolescence. Extravertie, manquant de qualification, son marché interne est grignoté par les importations ou la contrebande.

Les observateurs constatent que dans les nouveaux pays industrialisés (NPI), la greffe industrielle semble prendre, ce qui n'est pas encore le cas en Afrique où pourtant des pays comme le Nigéria, l'Algérie ou l'Egypte disposent d'une base industrielle conséquente.

Aujourd'hui dans la plupart des cas, les installations industrielles dont l'Afrique s'est dotée à grand frais au cours des années 1960 et 1970 font l'objet de restructuration, d'abandons ou cherchent désespérément de repreneurs. Elles apparaissent comme une greffe superficielle dans la société d'accueil, même lorsqu'elles ne sont pas contrôlées directement par les sociétés multinationales.

Les effets des PAS

La situation souvent difficile des entreprises industrielles africaines s'est vue compliquer par les "programmes d'ajustement structurel" (PAS). Les PAS ont agi sur l'Afrique comme un phénomène de désindustrialisation. Le leitmotiv de rentabilité financière appliqué aux entreprises publiques auparavant subventionnées et protégées de la concurrence semble avoir signé leur arrêt de mort. La brutalité et le manque d'imagination avec lesquels a été appliqué le principe de rentabilité interne a occulté certaines solutions qui auraient pu amener à moyen terme le redressement financier de certaines d'entre elles.

Même lorsque des programmes dits de "réhabilitation industrielle" ont été tentés, ils n'ont touché que les aspects internes à l'entreprise (assainissement financier, renouvellement des équipements, etc.) et ont négligé l'environnement économique et administratif en particulier. Quelque temps plus tard, les entreprises ainsi restructurées se sont retrouvés dans la même situation qu'auparavant et il allait les liquider, malgré les sacrifices consenties et l'endettement extérieur qui en a découlé et qui alourdit d'autant la charge de l'Etat.

Ces entreprises publiques déstructurées, proposées aujourd'hui à la privatisation, souvent sans un assainissement préalable sérieux, trouvent difficilement des repreneurs. Les hommes d'affaires africains n'ont pas toujours les fonds nécessaires et le capital étranger est vite découragé souvent par l'environnement politique et économique incertain de l'Afrique en général

La réhabilitation n'a de sens en réalité, que si elle agit sur les causes structurelles et sur l'environnement économique des entreprises. Elle devrait concerner toute la filière: approvisionnement, production, qualification, commercialisation, financement, etc.

En même temps, le démantèlement des barrières douanières affecte les petites et moyennes entreprises (PMI) privées et parfois des filiales de multinationales qui se sont implantées à l'abri des protections douanières. Les PMI font face à une concurrence accrue devant laquelle elles sont démunies en capitaux et en qualification. L'abandon du soutien des prix par l'Etat fait peser également sur elles dans le moyen terme un renchérissement des salaires.

Toutefois les PAS n'ont pas eu sur l'industrie que des aspects négatifs. Ils ont été dans bien des cas salutaires pour arrêter la mégalomanie d'une administration envahissante et ont surtout fait prendre conscience aux Etats, à la population et aux entreprises de l'importance de l'ouverture sur l'économie mondiale et de l'interdépendance des économies dans ce contexte.

Ils ont permis également de montrer que l'ajustement structurel, contrairement aux premières appréciations des institutions financières internationales et à celle des bailleurs de fonds n'est pas uniquement une action à court terme concernant le redressement de la balance des paiements, mais une adaptation étalée dans le temps, nécessitant l'engagement de réformes politiques, sociales et économiques profondes, pour survivre dans le monde de demain. Les PAS sont aujourd'hui "une contrainte" objective qu'il faudrait intégrer dans toute approche de développement industriel.

Quelle intégration industrielle pour l'Afrique?
Le débat sur l'intégration industrielle porte aujourd'hui sur deux approches.
La première, classique, pousse à la libre circulation des biens et des capitaux (certaines voix minoritaires réclament également celle des hommes que les représentants des Etats refusent en général). Celle-ci devrait amener d'elle même cette intégration. Il suffirait de protéger pour une courte période la sous-région de la concurrence extérieure. Généralement l'intégration n'est jugée viable que dans les sous-ensembles régionaux, considérés comme des zones économiques homogènes.

Cette approche estime également que les expériences passées de l'Afrique disqualifie le Plan de Lagos et autres programmes inspirés du combat pour un nouvel ordre économique international des années 1970, en matière d'industrie.

A cette option libérale qui évacue l'Etat, s'oppose une seconde approche plus étatiste et dirigiste. Elle préconise une intégration par la production. Chaque Etat devra garder son propre marché et ses entreprises, mais disent-ils, il faudrait définir une stratégie industrielle pour les sous-ensembles régionaux et pour l'Afrique. Cette stratégie devra désigner les industries d'intégration qui devront faire l'objet d'investissement dans lequel les Etats africains et leurs ressortissants seront actionnaires. Ces Etats ouvriront leur marché à la production des usines ainsi réalisées. Des unités de production de dimension régionale (usine automobile ou de fabrication de machines et outils par exemple) existantes peuvent avoir ce même statut et devraient alors ouvrir leur capital aux investisseurs des autres Etats membres. L'Algérie avait réussi à imposer ce schéma au Conseil Consultatif Maghrébin (CCM) en 1975 qui devait créer un espace économique maghrébin entre la Tunisie, l'Algérie et le Maroc. Ce projet a avorté à la suite de l'annexion du Sahara occidental par le Maroc.

Les reproches généralement faits à ce schéma sont que d'une part il empêche le dynamisme économique de s'exprimer. Les Etats seraient les seuls à décider de la nature et de la localisation des unités de production. Par ailleurs connaissant l'impact économique des projets industriels sur les pays et les régions, le risque serait grand de voir se répéter à l'échelle continentale ou régionale les erreurs d'implantation relevées dans les Etats membres. Par ailleurs, le choix de sites d'implantation viendrait favoriser les régions les mieux équipées, ce qui serait également source de conflits.

D'autre part il a été relevé que le choix et la promotion de filières industrielles par l'Etat restent toujours hasardeux et problématique. Même les Gouvernements des Etats développés se sont récemment "embourbés", en essayant de promouvoir des industries de pointe ou de sauver leurs industries menacées, malgré l'importance des moyens humains et financiers engagés dans cette bataille.

Entre ces deux positions extrêmes, il devrait exister à notre avis un compromis acceptable. En premier lieu, il semble nécessaire d'abandonner le manichéisme de telles approches foulées sur le choix entre l'Etat et le marché. Elles ont fait par le passé beaucoup de torts à l'Afrique. Il faudrait tenir compte de l'évolution de l'économie mondiale et des évolutions des mentalités à propos de l'industrie en Afrique même. Les limites du marché sont aujourd'hui reconnues par tous. La concurrence pure et parfaite dans une économie qui sort à peine de l'économie de subsistance relève de l'utopie. Croire qu'aujourd'hui, l'Etat en Afrique est en mesure de promouvoir des industries performantes, en corrigeant seulement quelques petites erreurs du passé est également une grande utopie.

Un certain nombre de principes devraient à notre avis guider la recherche pour une intégration industrielle en Afrique:

(1)   cette intégration doit passer tout d'abord par une harmonisation des politiques macro-économiques, du rôle et des obligations de l'Etat à l'égard des entreprises, dans le cadre des sous-ensembles africains dont il faudrait poursuivre et consolider la construction;

(2)   il est nécessaire de rechercher une coopération économique sur tous les plans en guise de soutien à l'intégration: éducation formation, recherche-développement, infrastructures, réglementations, informations sur les marchés, compensation des échanges, etc. afin de profiter des externalités qu'ils procurent, en vue d'accroître la compétitivité africaine. Il s'agira de dépasser le simple cadre commercial pour créer à moyen terme, à la fois une zone de libre échange, une union douanière et une intégration productive.

Cette dernière doit d'abord rechercher les opportunités, pour reconquérir une grande partie du marché intérieur africain et favoriser les exportations sur des marchés tiers. Elle doit se faire par des interpénétrations croisées des marchés et des sous-ensembles économiques limitrophes en particulier;

(1)   il convient d'éviter également de fixer aux entreprises communautaires des objectifs autres qu'économiques, sans pour cela négliger les leviers classiques d'orientation des investissements vers des zones ou des créneaux particuliers.

L'axe principal dans ce domaine est de détecter les initiatives industrielles viables et de les accompagner, quelle que soit la branche, dans la mesure où elles favorisent l'intégration économique;

(2)   il est également nécessaire de porter une grande attention au secteur informel pour pouvoir établir des liens de sous-traitance et de complémentarité entre ce secteur et les petites et moyennes industries;

(3)   par ailleurs, la formation demeure l'un des problèmes clés du développement en Afrique. L'industrie exige un grand effort de formation, souvent de très haut niveau que peu d'Etats pourront assurer par leurs propres moyens. Elle exige également d'énormes capitaux qui font actuellement défaut. *L'enjeu pour l'avenir reste d'ordre technologique et financier et il est impératif d'y faire face en regroupant le peu de moyens existants en Afrique, sous peine d'une marginalisation croissante.* Investir dès aujourd'hui dans la formation (en harmonisant au préalable les programmes de base), en regroupant en priorité toutes les potentialités existantes dans ce domaine semble l'option la plus réaliste qui se trouve à la portée des pays africains, notamment en coordonnant et en spécialisant les grands centres de formation universitaire et technique déjà existants. Certains de ces établissements, ainsi que certains centres d'appui industriel pourraient être dotés d'un statut africain et recevoir des étudiants de toute l'Afrique;

(4)   enfin une fois le problème des hommes réglé, il y a lieu de faire face au problème de financement.

A l'heure actuelle, dans le court et le moyen terme, l'Afrique ne semble pas être en mesure de faire face à un programme d'investissement industriel, même de faible envergure. Le cas de certaines privatisations est assez édifiant dans ce domaine. Cependant, il serait bénéfique de dépasser cette situation en intéressant le Nord au développement industriel africain, sur la base d'un véritable partenariat négocié allant vers un co-développement. Les accords doivent s'éloigner, autant que faire se peut, des logiques d'aide ou de la coopération unilatérale. L'Europe, en raison de ses liens avec l'Afrique devrait constituer un partenaire privilégié, mais les autres pôles économiques (Japon, Amérique) ne sont pas à négliger.

Conclusion

Pour réussir une industrialisation intégrée, l'Afrique doit apprendre mieux que par le passé à gérer la contrainte de l'environnement international. Il convient de considérer ce dernier comme incontournable, dans un univers économique où les interdépendances sont devenues la règle. L'actuelle division internationale du travail ne répond certes pas aux besoins africains, mais il faut rappeler que ses règles n'ont pas été faites pour les nations pauvres. Elles répondent aux logiques d'Etats et d'entreprises forts, disposant de moyens puissants, accumulés au cours de plusieurs décennies de développement.

La place que l'Afrique pourra occuper est celle qu'elle aura à construire elle-même. Le problème posé est comment tirer partie de cet environnement de telle sorte que son développement ne soit pas pénalisé et comment exploiter les brèches qui peuvent y apparaître pour avancer dans la réalisation de ses objectifs de développement.

Annexe

Valeur ajoutée et exportations de la branche textile dans les pays africains
(Classement de pays par ordre croissant du PNB)

PAYS	Valeur ajoutée du secteur manufacturier		Valeur ajoutée du textile-habillement		Part des exportations textiles dans les exportations globales	
	1970	1989	1970	1989	1965	1990
Mozambique	–	–	13	–	1	–
Tanzanie	118	212	28	–	0	3
Ethiopie	149	594	31	19	0	1
Somalie	27	47	–	6	–	0
Tchad	51	178	–	-	0	1
Malawi	–	182	–	–	0	3
Burundi	16	102	25	–	0	0
Zaïre	–	996	16	–	0	0
Ouganda	158	123	20	–	0	0
Madagascar	–	–	28	–	1	3
Sierra Leone	22	60	–	–	0	0
Mali	25	153	40	–	1	2
Nigéria	426	2365	26	–	0	0
Niger	30	124	–	–	1	1
Rwanda	8	320	0	–	–	0
Burkina Faso	–	–	–	–2	2	
Benin	–	–	–	–	0	2
Kenya	174	832	9	10	0	1
Ghana	252	525	16	–	0	0
Rép. Centrafricaine	12	–	–	–	0	–
Togo	25	114	–	–	0	0
Zambie	181	1588	9	13	–	–
Guinée	–	108	–	–	–	–
Mauritanie	10	–	–	–	0	0
Lesotho	3	49	–	–	–	–
Egypte	–	–	35	16	15	27
Libéria	15	–	–	–	0	–
Soudan	140	–	34	–	0	1
Zimbabwe	293	1384	16	16	6	–
Senegal	141	609	19	–	1	1
Côte d'Ivoire	149	–	16	–	1	2
Maroc	641	3932	–	–	1	20
Cameroun	119	1447	15	–	0	2
Congo	–	173	4	–	0	0
Tunisie	121	1460	18	21	2	35
Botswana	5	155	–	–	–	–
Algérie	682	4598	20	17	0	0
Ile Maurice	26	417	6	51	0	24
Angola	–	308	–	–	0	–
Namibie	–	80	–	–	–	–
Afrique du Sud	3892	19937	13	8	1	1
Gabon	22	279	7	–	0	0

Source: Banque Mondiale "Rapport sur le développement dans le monde 1992"

16

Stratégie de Développement Industriel et Protection Economique Régionale

L. Sangare

L'industrialisation joue un rôle capital dans l'accélération du développment économique des pays en développement. Aucun pays n'a atteint un niveau avancé du développement sans la mise en place d'une base industrielle solide au sein de sa structure économique. Cela est si vrai que le processus de développement économique devient synonyme d'industrialisation. En effet l'industrialisation a deux rôles fondamentaux à jouer dans le processus du développement économique., moderniser les autres secteurs-clefs, par la fourniture de biens intermédiaires et de biens d'équipement, contribuer à la conservation et à la transformation des produits agricoles.

La modernisation de l'agriculture a besoin d'intrants industriels tels que les engrais, les pesticides, le matériel et l'équipement agricoles. La construction de barrages hydro-électriques recquiert des centaines de tonnes de ciment, de fer de construction, des tuyauteries, des centrales hydro-électriques, etc. Si l'agriculture africaine n'est pas compétitive et si les infrastructures modernes de transport font défaut aux pays africains, c'est parce que les pays africains n'ont pas de base industrielle liée aux secteurs prioritaires. La structure industrielle de la quasi-totalité des pays africains se caractérise par l'absence d'industrie de base: industrie sidérurgique, industrie d'aluminium et du cuivre, industrie chimique, pétrochimique et pharmaceutique, d'industries de biens d'équipement: production de matériel de transport, équipement ferroviaire, véhicules de transport, matériels de travaux publics. La dégradation continuelle des termes de l'échange rend caduque le développement basé sur l'exportation des matières premières puisque le prix de vente tend à être inférieur au coût de production et que le prix des produits industriels importés des pays développés s'accroît continuellement. Les pays en développement accusent un déficit structurel. Ces pays doivent mettre un terme à l'importation des biens intermédiaires et des biens d'équipement pour se moderniser. La dislocation du vieil ordre économique international dicte à ces pays de s'engager résolument dans le processus d'industrialisation. L'industrialisation apparaît comme un objectif incontournable, un passage obligé pour le développement économique accéléré.

En Afrique, cette industrialisation doit être conçue au niveau sous-régional où l'échelle de production existe, car les pays africains ne disposent que de marchés exigüs et de capacités d'exécution trop faibles. L'intégration économique est un impératif pour l'Afrique, pour son industrialisation et partant son développement accéléré.

Les bailleurs de fonds des pays africains avancent que l'intégration africaine doit être ouverte sur l'extérieur, c'est-à-dire qu'il ne doit pas y avoir de tarif extérieur ou qu'il doit y avoir tout au plus de faibles tarifs entre les pays développés et les pays africains. Cela reviendrait à consacrer pour toujours le rôle des pays africains d'exportateurs de matières premières et à assigner aux pays industrialisés la responsabilité d'approvisionner les pays africains en produits industriels. En effet, sans une certaine protection, l'industrialisation du continent africain devient un objectif difficile à atteindre. Les forces sont inégales entre l'Europe fortement industrialisée, avec un environnement sain et l'Afrique sous-développée et handicapée par des coûts de production exorbitants. Pourtant l'Europe du marché commun a tenu à fabriquer l'Airbus alors que le Boeing était à même de satisfaire le marché mondial; de même l'Amérique tient à protéger son marché de l'automobile alors que le Japon et la Corée du Sud pourraient satisfaire le marché américain à des prix compétitifs. Il ne fait point de doute que pour se nourrir, s'équiper et offrir le niveau de vie auquel les populations africaines aspirent, l'immense continent africain doit s'industrialiser. Il importe donc d'étudier l'industrialisation et les mesures protectionnistes tout en s'interrogeant sur les moyens les plus rapides qui permettraient aux pays africains de s'intégrer à l'économie mondiale, c'est-à-dire d'atteindre le niveau de développement des pays industrialisés.

Nécessité du développement industriel de base en Afrique

A l'heure actuelle la plupart des pays africains sont bien intégrés à l'économie mondiale, mais dans le cadre de l'ordre économique désuet. Cette intégration de l'Afrique à l'économie mondiale se définit par les caractères suivants:

(1)   Fourniture aux pays industrialisés de produits primaires.

(2)   Achat massif des biens de consommation finale.

(3)   Achat limité de biens intermédiaires et de biens d'équipement pour un secteur moderne très restreint. Malgré des terres arables abondantes et fertiles, les pays

africains n'arrivent pas à réaliser l'autosuffisance alimentaire, certes à cause des sécheresses périodiques qui frappent le continent, mais aussi à cause de l'absence d'engrais, de pesticides et de machines agricoles bon marché.

La crise profonde et structurelle des économies africaines qui en est résultée s'explique par le fait que ces économies fonctionnent à perte car:

(1)   Il y a un déséquilibre entre la structure de production et la structure de consommation. Ces pays donnent encore la priorité à l'agriculture d'exportation et dépendent des importations alimentaires en provenance des pays développés. Les structures économiques nationales sont fortement extraverties.

(2)   Les structures de production désarticulées n'engendrent pas l'accumulation du capital interne, puisque ces économies fonctionnent à perte, à cause de la dégradation des termes de l'échange.

(3)   La structure industrielle est aussi désarticulée, à cause de l'absence d'une production locale de biens intermédiaires peu compétitive au plan international.

En conséquence, la majeure partie de l'économie africaine reste sous-développée, particulièrement l'agriculture de subsistance parce que les biens intermédiaires (engrais, fer long et fer plat, etc) importés sont chers. L'économie des pays africains se débat dans la stagnation. *La création d'une base industrielle dans les économies africaines est un impératif pour le développement et, partant, le redressement économique du continent.*

Le développement industriel doit viser la création d'une structure industrielle complémentaire et viable qui puisse répondre aux besoins des autres secteurs économiques et à ceux des populations africaines: des industries de base et de biens d'équipement qui soutiennent des industries de biens de consommation finale qui soient compétitives. Le problème n'est pas seulement de créer des industries, mais de promouvoir des industries compétitives dans ces trois sous-secteurs industriels et de faire en sorte qu'elles jouent leur rôle moteur: stimuler un développement accéléré en Afrique. Le problème crucial qui se pose est comment l'Afrique dans ce domaine de concurrence pourra-t-elle initier une industrialisation véritable et acquérir l'avantage compétitif dans un certain nombre de secteurs industriels. *Il importe par conséquent d'analyser les raisons qui expliquent pourquoi l'industrie africaine n'est pas compétitive et d'adopter une stratégie de développement qui donne à l'économie africaine et en particulier à l'industrie africaine l'avantage compétitif.*

Trois causes principales expliquent cette non-compétitivité:
(1)   Les causes liées aux facteurs de production:

>   (i)   Développement insuffisant des infrastructures; coût élevé des transports, de l'énergie; manque de communications;

>   (ii)   Pénurie de main-d'oeuvre spécialisée et manque d'innovation;

>   (iii)   Technologie inadaptée et très coûteuse parce que importée;

>   (iv)   Manque et cherté de ressources financières.

(2)   Les causes liées au mécanisme du marché. Manque de compétition: les sociétés transnationales imposent la loi du monopole.

(3)   Les causes liées à l'exiguïté du marché national. Le marché étant étroit et protégé, les consommateurs payent des prix de revient extrêmement élevés, comparables à ceux des produits importés.

En effet les industries de base et de biens d'équipement exigent une échelle de production élevée. Seul le marché sous-régional et quelquefois continental peut justifier l'implantation de ces industries.

En outre ces industries exigent l'existence d'une infrastructure solide: un système de transport lourd et de l'énergie à bon marché. Parce qu'elles emploient une main d'oeuvre très nombreuse, leur promotion et leur développement harmonieux doivent se faire en recherchant l'autosuffisance alimentaire, pour pallier l'élévation du coût de la vie et de la masse salariale. Leur développement doit être planifié, soit sur la base d'un tissu industriel déjà existant soit conjointement avec la promotion de leur filières. En somme, ces industries doivent être capables d'acquérir progressivement l'avantage comparatif.

Stratégie d'industrialisation

Nous estimons par conséquent que les pays africains devraient adopter une stratégie d'industrialisation en vue de créer un système productif viable qui puisse être compétitif. Ils devraient aussi poursuivre une politique d'intégration économique sous-régionale et continentale dont les grands axes seraient les suivants:
(1)   Réaliser l'intégration physique des espaces économiques des communautés économiques sous-régionales, par la mise en place d'une infrastructure sous-régionale de transport et de communication intégrée devant faciliter la circulation des personnes, des biens et services à des prix bas, grâce à:

>   (i)   des autoroutes inter-Etats;

(ii) des réseaux de chemins de fer communautaires;

(iii) des lignes d'interconnexion électriques communautaires;

(iv) des communications communautaires,

(2) Mettre en place un système productif sous-régional tirant avantage des complémentarités et de l'ouverture d'un marché plus vaste que rendrait possible la révolution agricole grâce à:

(i) la recherche agronomique au niveau communautaire;

(ii) la production des intrants agricoles et des machines agricoles;

(iii) la recherche d'une politique d'autosuffisance alimentaire au niveau sous-régional;

(iv) l'intégration des marchés, par la suppression des barrières douanières à l'intérieur des communautés sous-régionales et l'établissement d'un tarif extérieur commun.

L'industrialisation de base et la promotion d'industries de biens d'équipement devraient se faire à l'intérieur des communautés sous-régionales. Mais plusieurs de ces industries devraient profiter d'un tarif extérieur commun, soit au niveau de tout le continent c'est-à-dire, au niveau de la communauté économique africaine, soit naturellement au niveau sous-régional, dans le cadre des communautés économiques sous-régionales.

L'industrie africaine devrait développer son avantage compétitif:

(1) Grâce à la concurrence créée soit au niveau sous-régional, soit au niveau continental. La compétition doit être organisée progressivement, d'abord au niveau sous-régional, ensuite au niveau continental et finalement au niveau extérieur.

(2) En effet, si le tarif extérieur commun doit protéger cette industrialisation, il est nécessaire d'adopter des politiques visant à rendre les industries africaines rapidement compétitives sur le plan international.

Cette industrialisation doit être soutenue par la demande intérieure, celle des communautés économiques sous-régionales ou même du marché continental. Elle doit être renforcée par les flux des investissements sous-régionaux et régionaux, si possible extérieurs, par des innovations dont celle apportées par les investisseurs des pays industrialisés et soutenue surtout par la concurrence communautaire, pour permettre la conquête des avantages compétitifs internationaux.

Les mésures protectionistes permettant une intégration effective des pays africains à l'économie mondiale

L'intégration de l'Afrique à l'économie mondiale ne peut se faire que par le développement d'industries de base et de biens d'équipement, grâce à une protection régionale, quelquefois continentale.

La mise en place des sociétés d'économie mixte, avec la participation des pays développés dans ces domaines clefs, facilitant l'acquisition de la technologie et en apportant une solution au problème de la main-d'oeuvre spécialisée, du financement et parfois du marché pourrait hâter la suppression des mesures protectionnistes. En général, le développement industriel suivra deux étapes primordiales.

En une première étape, la suppression des barrières douanières à l'intérieur de la communauté et l'établissement d'un tarif extérieur commun devraient permettre de créer la concurrence entre les unités de production de la communauté et d'améliorer la compétitivité des entreprises communautaires, chaque pays développant ses avantages comparatifs.

En une deuxième étape, l'abaissement progressif du tarif extérieur commun devrait permettre d'exposer les entreprises communautaires à la concurrence extérieure, d'améliorer leurs résultats et de les préparer à conquérir des marchés extérieurs.

C'est là, à notre avis, la voie la plus rapide pour assurer l'intégration des économies africaines à l'économie mondiale. Il ne peut y avoir d'intégration spontanée sans risque de désinvestissement et de transformation des communautés économiques en simple marché d'écoulement des produits des pays industrialisés. L'industrialisation africaine se fera à ce prix. Certaines industries-clefs doivent bénéficier d'une protection non seulement sous-régionale, dans le cadre des communautés sous-régionales, mais d'une protection continentale, dans le cadre de la communauté économique africaine: les industries stratégiques, les industries de base et de biens d'équipement.

Les structures industrielles des Etats supportées par ces industries stratégiques pourront alors se renforcer. Pour la plupart des Etats, ce seront des industries agro-industrielles et des industries de transformation finale sur une échelle de production moyenne ou petite, utilisant les biens intermédiaires produits au niveau sous-régional.

En ce qui concerne ces industries, la suppression des barrières douanières doit avoir les buts suivants:

(1) permettre à chaque pays de créer sa base industrielle propre;

(2)   permettre une spécialisation sous-régionale pour éliminer les unités improductives;

(3)   hisser ces industries nationales au niveau sous-régional.

Conclusion

Si les pays industrialisés, particulièrement ceux de l'Europe souhaitent une intégration rapide de l'Afrique à l'économie mondiale, ils doivent accroître leur flux d'investissement en faveur de l'Afrique, sous forme d'investissement de participation à la mise en place des industries stratégiques—industries de base et de biens d'équipement. Le Japon a joué un rôle crucial dans le développement des nouveaux pays industrialisés du Sud-Est Asiatique. Si les pays européens, particulièrement la Communauté économique européenne souhaitent une libéralisation rapide des économies africaines, elle doit concerner en priorité le flux des investissements en vue du développement, moins les flux commerciaux qui risquent d'accentuer le développement inégal entre les pays industrialisés de l'Europe et l'Afrique.

Il est aberrant de prôner le concept d'intégration économique orientée vers l'extérieur. C'est ignorer le fait du sous-développement et surtout le processus de développement des pays en développement. Le secteur industriel et énergétique constituent les facteurs de transformation des structures nationales. L'industrialisation est un passage obligé pour les pays en développement. Les tenants du maintien de l'ordre économique international désuet causent un immense tort à l'humanité. Il est insensé de maintenir le continent africain si riche en potentialités économiques, dans le sous-développement et ensuite de parler de surpopulation, de problèmes d'environnement, de démocratie et de paix. L'Afrique développée et riche ne fera qu'accroître l'actif économique de notre planète et améliorer d'avantage les conditions de vie de l'humanité tout entière.

Annexes

Discours de Monsieur le Ministre des Universités

Monsieur le Secrétaire Général Adjoint de l'OUA, Messieurs les Ministres, Messieurs les membres du corps diplomatique, Monsieur le Responsable de l'Académie Africaine des Sciences, Honorables participants, Mesdames, Messieurs.

Permettez-moi tout d'abord de vous souhaiter la bienvenue et plein succès à vos travaux.

A partir d'aujourd'hui et pendant 4 jours, vous vous donnez comme objectif de passer en revue les expériences de coopération économique et d'integration régionale en Afrique, en vue d'en tirer les leçons, et de dégager les principes et les voies qui doivent rendre le processus de construction communautaire, à la fois bénéfique pour tous les partenaires et irréversible.

Le fait que votre réunion se tienne à Alger, en ce moment précis, témoigne de notre profonde conviction que sans coopération économique centré sur l'objectif d'integration régionale, l'elaboration et la mise en ouvre de politiques économiques de solution alternatives viables, en vue de résoudre la crise multiforme et complexe à laquelle fait face, sans exception aucune, chacun des pays du continent, risque d'être sans lendemain.

Les multiples problèmes auxquels nous sommes les uns et les autres confrontés, qu'il s'agisse de l'endettement toujours accru de nos Etats, de la déterioration de notre pouvoir d'achat et de notre capacité internationale de négociation, de la dégradation de l'environnement, des problèmes de santé et d'éducation, des problèmes démographiques et sociaux, multiples, appellent tous à la coopération comme voie de sortie.

Ils ne peuvent en effet trouver de solutions durables que dans le cadre d'une conjugaison des efforts, en premier lieu, entre les pays voisins, à commencer par ceux qui ont choisi la voie de l'intégration économique.

Cette démarche et cette problématique ne nous sont pas simplement imposées par le contexte international où il y a de moins en moins de place pour les Etats isolés et les petits pays. Elles le sont également par la faiblesse relative des moyens propres à chacun de nos Etats, pris isolément, face aux attentes et aux exigences de nos peuples, à leur volonté commune de vivre dans des sociétés démocratiques, fondés sur l'équité.

Le dépassement du dilemme posé par la relance de la croissance sur la base de politiques économiques fondées sur l'ajustement structurel, et la prise en charge simultanée des revendications sociales légitimes de nos peuples marginalisés par ces politiques ne peut se faire à l'échelle de chacun des pays pris isolément. Les ajustements sociaux sont toujours plus aisés à conduire dans le cadre des grands ensembles que dans celui des petits pays.

En fait, la relance de la croissance et l'exploitation optimale des synergies, à partir de tout investissement, commande la coopération économique et l'intégration régionale.

Cependant, une fois admis ce principe général, se pose la question des modalités concrètes de la construction communautaire et de l'intégration, surtout pour des pays et des régions qui ont adopté en la matière des cheminements différents et qui se sont engagés solennellement, à travers un Traité, en l'occurence le Traité d'Abuja, d'oeuvrer ensemble pour asseoir rapidement l'avènement d'une seule communauté économique, réunissant dans le même espace Alger à Harare, voire demain dans une Afrique du Sud libérée de l'Apartheid, d'Alger au Cap.

C'est ici que réside pour nous l'intérêt de vos travaux. En comparant les expériences passées et en cours, en examinant l'impact de l'environnement économique international sur la coopération régionale et internationale, vous allez probablement tirer des leçons et éclairer les décideurs que nous sommes.

Cependant, sans vouloir anticiper sur le contenu de vos travaux, ou sur les réponses aux questions que vous allez étudier, je voudrais vous livrer mon point de vue sur le lien qui me semble être très fort entre développement, démocratie et coopération économique.

S'il existe aujourd'hui un large consensus pour insister sur le fait qu'il ne peut y avoir développement sans construction démocratique, c'est-à-dire sans la participation de tous ou du moins de la majorité à l'action, il y a lieu de rappeler que la construction démocratique présuppose la stabilité et la croissance économique, c'est-à-dire l'existence d'une valeur ajoutée à répartir.

Or la croissance économique passe aujourd'hui plus qu'hier par une révision des rapports Nord-Sud, dans le sens d'une inversion des flux financiers, d'un rétablissement des termes de l'échange en faveur des pays du Sud, d'un desserrement de la contrainte financière sur nos Etats. Malheureusement force est de constater que telles qu'elles se déroulent, les négociations internationles, notamment dans le cadre de l'Uruguay Round sont loin de s'inscrire dans une telle orientation.

Peut-être dès lors faut-il chercher d'autres voies complémentaires voire alternatives pour la relance de la croissance.

C'est ici que la coopération Sud-Sud en général, la coopération africaine et régionale en particulier nous paraît l'une des voies les plus appropriées. Il y a lieu de les identifier et de les valoriser, en vue d'épargner nos faibles ressources financières par un recours moindre aux marchés internationaux et en vue de relancer certaines filières ou certains secteurs condamnés autrement à une mort certaine, du fait de leur mode d'insertion dans le marché mondial. D'autres formes de complémentarité existent également et mériteraient d'être expolitées dans l'intérêt bien compris de tous les partenaires.

Mesdames, Messieurs, ainsi apparaît le caractère stratégique de la construction communautaire, de la coopération et de l'intégration économique. De là notre intérêt à vos travaux et vos analyses.

C'est pour cette raison que nous resterons attentifs à vos travaux et à leurs conclusions.

La conjoncture actuelle exige la conjugaison de tous les efforts, pour l'élaboration de solutions alternatives, à la mesure des espoirs nés et nourris par les mouvements de libération nationale du continent, espoirs qui continuent d'animer nos peuples, tant au Nord, qu'à l'Ouest, au Sud et à l'Est de notre continent.

Je voudrais saisir cette occasion pour vous réaffirmer notre souhait et notre disponibilité, pleine et entière, de voir se renouveler et s'intensifier ce type de rencontres entre les décideurs politiques, les hommes d'affaires, les experts et les universitaires que vous êtes; car c'est là l'unique voie dans la promotion d'un développement fondé sur la concertation et la réflexion communes.

Permettez-moi avant de me retirer de souhaiter plein succès à vos travaux et de remercier encore une fois l'AAS pour le choix de l'Université Algérienne comme partenaire dans l'organisation de cette réflexion.

Opening Statement
by
Ambassador Ahmed Haggag
Assistant Secretary-General
Organization of African Unity

Honourable Professor D . Liabes,
Minister of Higher Education and Scientific Research,
Distinguished Representatives of the Government of Algeria,
Distinguished Participants,

Allow me, before addressing this important subject before us, to thank the Government of Algeria for the hospitality and the facilities which they have made available to all participants. Honourable Minister, H.E. Dr. Salim Ahmed Salim, Secretary General of the OAU asked me to convey his appreciation and thanks to the Government of Algeria for hosting this very important conference on Regional Integration and Economic Cooperation in Africa. This is an extremely important subject to which the OAU has always attached great importance and especially now. However, because of other urgent matters and particularly because of the preparation of the Fifty-Sixth Ordinary Session of the OAU Council of Ministers and the Twenty-Eighth Session of the Assembly of Heads of States and Government next month, he could not attend this conference personally. He has therefore asked me also to thank the African Academy of Sciences and Professor Thomas Odhiambo, in particular, for organizing this Conference.

To the participants, the Secretary-General of the OAU requests you to address the topics under discussion as comprehensively as possible and to bear in mind the fundamental fact: That Africa's survival will depend on its resolve, commitment and implementation of the Treaty establishing the African Economic Community.

Honourable Minister, Distinguished Participants,
I find the papers presented to this conference particularly useful. They are comprehensive in coverage and well researched. Permit me therefore to thank the authors of these papers. I do believe that the time they put in to prepare these papers is not for the sake of academic or intellectual satisfaction alone. It is rather, a clear pointer to the interest you all have in the search for the best ways Africa can move forward through economic integration and cooperation.

I will be shortly speaking about OAU's history in the area of regional economic integration and economic cooperation. But before doing so, I would like to share with you some thinking about the concepts of "economic integration" as opposed to, or as a process within the wider context of "economic cooperation". A clear understanding of these two concepts which constitute the theme of this conference will enable us to come up with clear, concrete and actionable recommendations.

I would like to emphasize this point because we, in the OAU have embarked on the promotion of economic integration and cooperation. Your views on these concepts and the recommendations that you will make will be extremely valuable to us. I would like to assure you that we shall take your recommendations with the seriousness they deserve.

Mr Chairman,
My view is that economic integration and economic cooperation go together. Whilst they are mutually supportive, economic integration is, and it constitutes the most critical component in the process of economic cooperation . Economic integration presupposes the abolition of market imperfections. The removal or reduction of barriers during the process of economic integration is an important prerequisite. It will free the movement of factors and services so as to enable the proper functioning of market forces, facilitate the expansion of the economies of scale and increase efficiency in resource allocation.

On the other hand, economic cooperation must be seen in a wider context which involves deliberate policy instruments by cooperating countries in order to enhance the process of economic integration within the broader concept of economic cooperation. These policy instruments sometimes go counter the principles of the functioning of market forces . They are nonetheless extremely important instruments which will enhance both processes of economic integration and economic cooperation. Thus, the introduction of a common external tariff for instance, preferential treatment and favourable clauses or even protectionist measures which are common in many Treaties of most economic groupings are instruments used in economic cooperation arrangements even if they contradict the principles of the functioning of market forces in the context of regional integration.

Economic cooperation, therefore, is broader and it goes beyond simple economic integration. I will not expand on these concepts as I am well aware that there are many scholars here who may not agree with my understanding of these two concepts. In any case, I will be satisfied if we do not agree, because, it will give us an opportunity to rethink why we did not agree. That way, more thoughts will generate a common ground for agreeing.

Mr Chairman, Distinguished Participants
Apart from the above conceptual aspects, regional integration and economic cooperation have been the major objectives of the OAU since its inception. The principle drive behind being the fact that when African countries emerged from the colonial yoke, the need for closer political and economic cooperation and integration during the formative stages of the OAU is understandable. The major pre-occupation of the OAU was that for assisting those other African countries which were still under colonial domination to gain their independence.

In spite of the fact that the OAU was involved in the decolonization of the Continent during the sixties and seventies, the Organization never lost sight of the need to launch economic cooperation and integration in Africa. Beginning from 1986 here in Algiers and throughout the 1970s for instance, the OAU took major decisions which called on African countries to work together in order to promote economic cooperation . Thus, besides the adoption of an OAU resolution which called for the setting up of the African Development Bank (ADB) in 1973, the adoption of the "African Declaration on Cooperation, Development and Economic Independence" which was adopted during the tenth Anniversary of the Organization in 1973; the Kinshasa subregional and regional economic integration and cooperation among African countries during the 1980s and the establishment of the African Economic Community in the 1990s.

Mr Chairman,
Let me give a short background of activities which have preoccupied the OAU during the 1970s up to now. For a period of 6 years (1984-1990) the OAU Secretariat conducted a number of studies, seminars and symposia on the question of the African Economic Community. The OAU Permanent Steering examined these studies and the draft Treaty with all the seriousness that was required. Negotiations of the Treaty establishing the African Economic Community were serious and difficult. But it would not have been easy to finalize the Treaty without going through this process. This Treaty was signed by 49 OAU member states on the 3rd of June in Abuja, Nigeria. Exactly a year ago. Todate, 50 OAU Member States have signed the Treaty and 8 countries have already ratified it. I am pleased to say here that there can be no less demonstration of Member States' political will than these positive developments in Africa.

We are now in the process of the preparations and negotiations of draft protocols which are already in the pipeline including those on the relationship between the African

Economic Community and the regional economic communities, the free movement of persons, the rights of resistance and establishment, trade and customs cooperation, transport and communications and the Pan African Parliament.

We do believe that both the Treaty and the protocols are very important instruments for enhancing closer economic cooperation in Africa.

Mr Chairman,

I started by saying that the theme of this conference is an extremely important one. I did point out that Africa's survival in the decades ahead will deepen the process of economic integration and cooperation. In this regard, I do notice that the subjects you will be addressing during this conference are specially relevant. They are an important contribution to the ongoing process and thinking on how to enhance closer economic cooperation. Your discussions on how we can strengthen cooperation within the framework of the African Economic Community will be very helpful.

Mr Chairman,

We are all aware of the fundamental changes which are unfolding in the World. Today, we are witnessing significant developments in the globalization of the World economy. We are witnessing the re-ordering of the geopolitical and economic space in which Africa needs to stand united more than ever before in order to avoid marginalizing ourselves. Nobody can marginalize Africa. We can and shall marginalize ourselves if we do not act swiftly and consolidate the process of economic cooperation which we have stated. The African Economic Community must be supported by all of us so that we may tackle together not only integration activities, but also, some of the adverse external factors such as the heavy debt burden, commodity problems, protectionism or the management of the macro-economic policies.

Mr Chairman, Distinguished Delegates

I would be amiss if I do not mention one of the major concerns of the OAU. The divisive usage of the term "sub-Sahara Africa". You will have noticed that this usage is increasingly gaining ground. Recent publications, seminars and symposia or even conferences are being organized on this divisive approach. The OAU is one and it is not divided into Africa South of the Sahara or North of the Kalahari. The Treaty establishing the African Economic Community is all inclusive of African countries in the South, Central, Eastern and Northern countries. We want to strengthen this continental institution and unity and not to weaken it by sub-dividing the continent.

Communiqué Final

Le symposium sur la Coopération Economique et l'Intégration Régionale en Afrique organisé à l'initiative du Ministère des Universités et de la Recherche Scientifique et de l'Académie Africaine des Sciences à Alger au 03 du 06 juin 1992 a été l'occasion de se pencher sur un certain nombre de questions liées à la promotion de la coopération économique et de l'intégration intra et inter-régionale en Afrique comme moyen de développement.

Cette rencontre a permis de passer en revue les problèmes que pose la construction communautaire en Afrique, au regard des contraintes internes et internationales.

Les principaux thèmes et questions soulevés ont été les suivants:

Thème 1: Développement National, Construction Communautaire et Environnement Economique International
(1)   Les limites au développement national autonome.

(2)   Les types de construction communautaire viables dans le contexte géo-économique et stratégique actuel.

(3)   Les incidences de l'évolution économique internationale sur les accords de coopération entre certaines communautés du Nord, principalement la C.E.E et les pays Africains (convention de LOME/Politique Méditerranéenne Rénovée …)

Thème 2: Construction Communautaire et Contraintes Structurelles Internes
(1)   Niveau d'adéquation entre le mode d'organisation et de fonctionnement des institutions et des organisations inter-gouvernementales, la réalité socio-économique et politique des pays concernés, les objectifs fixés et les moyens mis en place (ressources financières, encadrement humain, etc …)

(2)   Degré de compatibilité entre les politiques économiques nationales et les choix stratégiques communautaires.

(3)   Organisations inter-gouvernementales et participation des partenaires économiques et des forces sociales locales aux projects communautaires.

(4)   Niveau d'adéquation entre les objectifs assignés aux organisations inter-gouvernementales et les moyens mis à leur disposition.

Thème 3: Développement Economique Régional et Stratégies Industrielles

(1)   Logiques de comportement des firmes transnationales et objectifs d'intégration régionale.

(2)   Rôle des Etats dans l'élaboration et la mise en oeuvre des stratégies industrielles.

(3)   Promotion de la coopération régionale dans la perspective du co-développement entre les pays de la Communauté.

(4)   Développement de l'engineering comme outil principal de la promotion industrielle en Afrique.

Thème 4: Intégration Economique Régionale et Coopération Monétaire et Financière

(1)   Contenu de l'intégration monétaire.

(2)   Mécanismes de la coopération monétaire et financière.

(3)   Intégration économique et devenir des zones monétaires.

Thème 5: Les Pré-requis de la Coopération Régionale

(1)   Position et rôle de l'Afrique dans le nouveau contexte géo-stratégique.

(2)   Rôle des acteurs sociaux dans la dynamique de l'intégration régionale.

(3)   Mécanismes de coopération économique à mettre en place, dans le cadre de la mise en oeuvre du Traité d'Abuja.

Des questions soulevées et des discussions auxquelles elles ont donné lieu, il se dégage les conclusions générales suivantes:

(1)   L'intégration économique doit être conçue comme un moyen dans la renégociation du mode d'insertion des différentes économies dans la division internationale du travail.

(2)   L'intégration économique doit permettre la création progressive d'un espace économique et institutionnel viable, cohérent et performnt à l'échelle du

continent, par l'organisation des complémentarités et la promotion des interdépendances dynamiques. Ce nouvel espace économique est seul capable de permettre à l'Afrique de se repositionner favorablement dans les rapports économiques mondiaux.

(3)   L'intégration économique doit être placée dans le contexte d'un développement collectif auto entretenu.

(4)   Cela suppose la réorientation des politiques nationales, par la prise en compte des contraintes technologiques et financières extérieures.

(5)   Cela implique un développement des capacités africaines, à même de permettre aux pays du continent de tirer avantage des opportunités offertes par une amélioration de la coopération internationale.

(6)   Cela devrait se traduire par la promotion d'un partenariat adapté avec les centres de décisions et les opérateurs économiques internationaux.

La mise en oeuvre de cette forme de partenariat doit tenir compte du fait que la tendance est à l'établissement d'un ordre international "Uni-Multipolaire". Dans celui-ci, l'influence et la marge de manoeuvre de l'Afrique se trouveront réduites. Dans ce cadre du fait même des liens qui se tissent entre les principaux blocs économiques et les résultats des négociatons au sein du GATT, les accords particuliers de coopération entre les pays africains et leurs partenaires traditionnels (convention de LOME) pourraient ne plus être renouvelés dans des conditions aussi favorables.

Pour être opérationnel ce partenariat suppose l'existence de grands ensembles économiques fondés sur l'harmonisation des politiques économiques et sociales nationales.

Cela suppose le renforcement des centres de décisions communautaires, le transfert d'un certain nombre de prérogatives de souveraineté nationale aux organes communautaires, la réadaptation des structures et des moyens propres aux organes communautaires (notamment les moyens humains).

Le renforcement des communautés passe également par la mise en place de relais structurels nationaux. Ils auront à veiller sur le respect des cohérences entre les décisions et les actions nationales et communautaires.

La promotion de l'industrie, conçue comme vecteur essentiel dans la création d'espaces économiques intégrés suppose le renforcement des liens entre les différents noyaux industriels nationaux, la promotion des relations de sous-traitance entre les pôles industriels structurants et les petites et moyennes entreprises à l'échelle régionale.

Bien plus que par le passé, la réalisation de ces objectifs implique:

- La maîtrise de l'engineering en général et de l'engineering industriel en particulier.

- La formation du personnel technique nécessaire. Cela suppose en particulier le développement de centres d'excellences technologiques (engineering industriel, gestionnaire, commercial, financier etc.).

- La redéfinition du rôle de l'Etat. Il ne doit plus être un acteur intervenant directement dans la production et la gestion. Il doit être l'initiateur des politiques de développement et un régulateur des flux monétaires et des équilibres macro-économiques.

- La réduction des barrières tarifaires et non-tarifaires communautaires et leur harmonisation.

S'agissant des aspects financiers et monétaires de l'intégration économique il y a lieu:

(1)   D'affiner les processus sequentiels de mise en oeuvre des politiques d'intégration.

(2)   De mettre en harmonie les modes d'intégration monétaires avec les objectifs poursuivis.

(3)   De favoriser les politiques visant la stabilisation des taux de change, la suppression des restrictions aux mouvements de capitaux, la recherche de garanties extérieures pour la convertibilité, le développement efficient des marchés monétaires et financiers nationaux et enfin la surveillance des flux monétaires.

(4)   D'approfondir la réflexion et l'analyse sur les incidences éventuelles des zones CFA et Rand sur les processus d'intégration monétaire et financière intra-régionaux.

(5)   De promouvoir la création d'institutions bancaires, à même de faciliter les échanges commerciaux et la réalisation des projects communs, au niveau inter-régional.

(6)   De renforcer le rôle des chambres de compensation par l'élargissement des listes des produits éligibles, et l'adoption de monnaie de compte "clearing".

(7)   De promouvoir la multiplication des accords de paiement pour permettre le développement des échanges sur une base élargie.

(8)   De poursuivre la réflexion sur l'impact du processus d'unification monétaire et financière sur la réalisation des objectifs d'intégration économique.

Les participants au symposium d'Alger appellent les acteurs des différents pays africains concernés et des organisations ayant en charge la gestion et la promotion des politiques de coopération économique et d'intégration régionale à:

(1)   Intensifier les réunions de concertation sur les problémes d'intégration africaine.

(2)   Poursuivre l' approfondissement de la réflexion sur chacun des avis et thèmes abordés lors du présent symposium.

(3)   Faire participer l'ensemble des opérateurs économiques et sociaux concernés, notamment la communauté intellectuelle, à l'effet de favoriser la plus large interpénétration possible des opinions, des décisions et des programmes.

(4)   Assurer la médiatisation la plus large et la plus efficace de l'ensemble des textes régissant le processus d'intégration africaine, dans le but d'en populariser le contenu.

(5)   Créer un groupe africain de réflexion et d'animation sur la coopération économique et l'intégration régionale.

(6)   Créer des réseaux panafricains de banques de données économiques spécialisées, accessibles à l'ensemble des opérateurs, notamment aux universités et aux centres de recherche.

(7)   Développer l'enseignement et la recherche sur les groupements économiques, les expériences de coopération et d'intégration régionale, ainsi que sur le Traité d'Abuja et ses implications.

(8)   Préserver, développer et assurer l'utilisation des capacités de création disponibles, au service du renforcement des économies africaines, en tirant les leçons des expériences africaines en la matiére.

Final Communiqué

The Symposium on Economic Cooperation and Regional Integration in Africa organized in Algiers from 3 to 6 June 1992, at the initiative of the Ministry of Universities and Scientific Research of the Government of Algeria and the African Academy of Sciences, provided an occasion for reflection on several questions relating to the promotion of economic cooperation and intra-regional and inter-regional integration in Africa as an instrument of development.

The meeting also provided an opportunity to review the internal and external constraints to the establishment of economic communities in Africa.

The main themes and issues considered were as follows:

Theme 1: National Development, Economic Communities and the International Economic Environment

(1)   The constraints to self-sustaining national development;

(2)   The types of viable economic communities in the present geo-economic and strategic context;

(3)   The impact of international economic developments on existing cooperation agreements between certain communities of the North, principally the EEC and African countries (Lome Convention/New Mediterranean Policy)

Theme 2: Economic Communities and Internal Structural Constraints

(1)   Balance between the method of the organization and the functioning of intergovernmental organizations and institutions, the socio-economic and political reality of the countries concerned, the objectives set and the available financial and human resources.

(2)   The degree of compatibility between national economic policies and community strategic options.

(3)   Inter-governmental organizations and participation of economic partners and local social forces in community projects.

(4)   Balance between the objectives assigned to intergovernmental organizations and the resources at their disposal.

Theme 3: Regional Economic Development and Industrial Strategies

(1)   The logic of behaviour of transnational corporations and objectives of regional integration.

(2)   The role of States in the formulation and implementation of industrial strategies.

(3)   Promotion of regional cooperation to ensure cooperative development among countries of the Community.

(4)   Development of engineering as the principal means of promoting industrial development in Africa.

Theme 4: Regional Economic Integration and Monetary and Financial Cooperation

(1)   The scope of monetary integration

(2)   Monetary and financial cooperation mechanisms

(3)   Economic integration and future of monetary zones

Theme 5: The Prerequisites of Regional Cooperation

(1)   The position and role of Africa in the new geo-strategic context.

(2)   The role of social actors in the dynamics of regional integration.

(3)   Mechanisms of economic cooperation required for the implementation of the Abuja Treaty.

Below are the general conclusions arrived at following the consideration of the issues raised:

(1)   Economic integration should be conceived as a means of re-ordering the position of different economies in the new international division of labour

(2)   Economic integration should enable gradual establishment of viable, coherent and performing institutional space at continental level, through the organization of complementarities and promotion of dynamic interdependence. It is

only such a new economic space that will help Africa to play a positive role in world economic relations.

(3)   Economic integration should be placed within the context of a collective self-sustaining development.

(4)   This presupposes the reorientation of national policies taking into account technological and external finance constraints.

(5)   This implies development of the capacities of African countries, which will enable them take advantage of the opportunities resulting from improvement in international cooperation.

(6)   This should be translated into the promotion of an appropriate partnership with decision-making centres and the international economic operators

The implementation of this form of partnership should take into account the present trend towards the establishment of a uni-multipolar economic order. In such a situation, Africa will have less influence and less room to manoeuvre. In fact, within this framework, even the growing links developing the major economic blocs and the results of the GATT negotiations, the special cooperation agreements among the African countries and their traditional partners (Lome Convention), could no longer be renewed under very favourable conditions.

For it to be operational, this partnership presupposes the existence of large economic groupings to ensure the harmonization of national economic and social policies.

This requires the strengthening of community decision-making centres, the transfer of certain areas of national sovereignty to community organs, and the readaptation of structures and resources (notably human resources) in favour of community organs.

The strengthening of existing communities also depends on the establishment of national focal points. These will ensure consistency between actions and decisions at national and community levels.

The promotion of industry, conceived as an essential vehicle for the establishment of 211 integrated economic space, presupposes the strengthening of the links among various national industrial units, the promotion, at the regional level of sub-contracting relations between the major industrial poles and small and medium scale enterprises.

More than ever before, the realization of these objectives implies the following:
- The mastery of engineering in general and of industrial engineering in particular.

- The training of the necessary technical personnel. This presupposes especially the development of technological centres of excellence (industrial engineering, as well as managerial, commercial and financial training).

- The redefinition of the role of the State. The State should no longer be seen to be involved directly in industrial production and management. It should initiate development policies and regulate monetary flows and macro-economic equilibrium.

- Reduction in tariff and non-tariff barriers and their harmonization.

As regards financial and monetary aspects of economic integration, it is necessary to:
(1)   enhance the sequential processes for implementing integration policies.

(2)   harmonize monetary integration systems with the objectives to be pursued.

(3)   promote policies aimed at stabilizing exchange rates, removing restrictions to capital flows, securing external guarantee for convertibility, developing efficient national money and financial markets, and, finally, maintaining surveillance over monetary flows.

(4)   reflect thoroughly on, and analyze the possible impact of the CFA and Rand monetary zones on the processes of intra-regional monetary and financial integration.

(5)   promote the establishment of banking institutions, to facilitate trade and implementation of joint projects at inter-regional level.

(6)   strengthen the role of clearing houses by expanding the list of eligible products and adopting a clearing unit of account.

(7)   encourage increase in payment agreements in order to facilitate the development of trade on a wider scale.

(8)   undertake further study on the impact of monetary and financial unification on the attainment of economic integration objectives.

Participants at the Algiers symposium called on the actors in the different African countries, as well as organizations responsible for the administration and promotion of regional economic cooperation and integration policies to:

(1)   Increase their consultations on African integration problems.

(2)   Continue to reflect deeply on issues addressed by the symposium.

(3)   Ensure the participation of all relevant economic and social operators, notably the intellectual community, with a view to promoting the widest possible involvement of opinions, decisions and programmes.

(4)   Ensure the widest and most effective publicity of all the texts governing the African integration process with the aim of popularizing their contents.

(5)   Create an African group for reflection and action on African economic integration.

(6)   Create pan-African networks of specialized economic data banks, accessible to all operators, notably, universities and research centres.

(7)   Develop training and research on economic groupings, regional cooperation and integration experiences, as well as the Abuja Treaty and its implications.

(8)   Preserve, develop and ensure the utilization of existing creative capacities, for strengthening African economies, by drawing lessons from relevant African experiences.

Subject Index

Abuja Treaty 19, 20, 24, 196, 197, 201-204, 205, 210-212
Affinity areas 27, 28
Africa-Re 209
ACP countries 23, 24, 39, 57, 115-121
AAF-SAP 134
ACBI 131
African Center for Monetary Studies 24
ADB 25, 126, 131, 206, 209
AEC 20, 24, 106, 113, 114, 122-135, 196
AEA 129
Algeria 17, 18, 21, 64, 98, 99, 236, 238
Angola 71, 72, 75, 79, 80, 91
Angolan conflict 79, 80, 81
Armed struggle 76, 77, 78
Arrangement Multi-Fibres 215, 216, 223-225
Asia 39, 45, 64, 100
Assemblee Reprentative 96
ABCA 196
ASEAN 39, 42, 43
Australia 56, 71, 85, 126
Austria 138, 223
Banque Centrale Africaine 196, 204
BEAC 190, 199, 200
Bantustan 78
Basutoland 71
BCEAC 156, 167, 168, 169, 170, 175
Bechuanaland 71
Beira 71
Belgium 56, 138, 219, 223
Bénin 62, 144
BENLUX 56, 58, 60
Bilateral cooperation 17
Black majority rule 81, 83, 85

Botha 73
Botswana 71, 75, 78, 79, 80, 82, 91, 138
Brazil 35, 224
Bretton Woods 68, 190, 202
British Commonwealth 57, 73
British Protectorates 71
Bulgaria 138
Burkina Faso 22, 61-68, 138, 144
Burundi 78
CFA 25, 67
Cabora Bassa Hydro-electric Project 78
Cameroon 57, 138
Canada 56, 71, 85, 126, 223
Capital 24, 48, 56, 126, 140, 172
The Caribbean 39
CARICOM 60
Casablanca 98
Cavour 55
Central African Republic 78, 138
CACM 43, 177
CAEM 196
Charlemagne 55
CCAO 197, 198, 207
Chambers of commerce 27
China 39, 221, 223, 224
Chidzanga, Richard 77
Chipeto, Herbert 80
Chona, Mark 77
CILSS 68
Clearing houses 176-177
Cocoa 62
Code of conduct 28
Coffee 62
Cold War 17